THE CRIMEAN WAR

From Our Own Correspondent
JOHN MAXWELL HAMILTON, SERIES EDITOR

Illuminating the development of foreign news gathering at a time when it has never been more important, "From Our Own Correspondent" is a series of books that features forgotten works and unpublished memoirs by pioneering foreign correspondents. Series editor John Maxwell Hamilton, once a foreign correspondent himself, is dean of the Manship School of Mass Communication at Louisiana State University.

PREVIOUS BOOKS IN THE SERIES

Evelyn Waugh, *Waugh in Abyssinia*

Edward Price Bell, *Journalism of the Highest Realm:
The Memoir of Edward Price Bell, Pioneering Foreign
Correspondent for the "Chicago Daily News,"* edited
by Jaci Cole and John Maxwell Hamilton

THE CRIMEAN WAR

AS SEEN BY THOSE WHO REPORTED IT

• • •

WILLIAM HOWARD RUSSELL
AND OTHERS

EDITED BY ANGELA MICHELLI FLEMING
AND JOHN MAXWELL HAMILTON

Originally published as
The Complete History of the Russian War

LOUISIANA STATE UNIVERSITY PRESS
BATON ROUGE

Originally published as *The Complete History of the Russian War* by John G. Wells,
Publishing Agent, 1856
Introduction © 2009 by Louisiana State University Press

DESIGNER: Michelle A. Neustrom
TYPEFACE: Century Schoolbook BT
PRINTER AND BINDER: Thomson-Shore, Inc.

LIBRARY OF CONGRESS CATALOGING-IN-PUBLICATION DATA

Russell, William Howard, Sir, 1820–1907.
The Crimean War : as seen by those who reported it / William Howard Russell and others ; edited by Angela Michelli Fleming and John Maxwell Hamilton.
   p. cm. — (From our own correspondent)
   Originally published: New York : J.G. Wells, 1856, under title The complete history of the Russian War, from its commencement to its close.
   ISBN 978-0-8071-3445-0 (cloth : alk. paper) 1. Crimean War, 1853–1856—Campaigns. 2. Crimean War, 1853–1856—Personal narratives, British. 3. Crimean War, 1853–1856—Press coverage. 4. Russell, William Howard, Sir, 1820–1907.
5. Crimean War, 1853–1856—Journalists. 6. War correspondents—Great Britain—Biography. 7. War correspondents—Ukraine—Crimea—History—19th century.
I. Fleming, Angela Michelli, 1961– II. Hamilton, John Maxwell. III. Russell, William Howard, Sir, 1820–1907. Complete history of the Russian War, from its commencement to its close. IV. Title.
   DK214.R95 2009
   947'.0738—dc22
                                              2008048711

The paper in this book meets the guidelines for permanence and durability
of the Committee on Production Guidelines for Book Longevity
of the Council on Library Resources. ∞

CONTENTS

——◆◆◆——

INTRODUCTION

Angela Michelli Fleming and John Maxwell Hamilton

———◆◆◆———

On March 28, 1854, Great Britain and France declared war on Russia. By coincidence, that date also marked the thirty-fourth birthday of William Howard Russell. The young *Times* of London reporter had come to Malta on a supposedly brief trip with British Guards, whose deployment was intended to prevent Russian aggression against the Turkish Sultan. "You will be back by Easter," John T. Delane, Russell's editor, assured him before his departure in February.[1] It was nearly two years before the Irish-born correspondent saw London again.

The Crimean War, as the conflict came to be called, established little politically. But it marked important firsts, one of them being the emergence of professional war correspondents. Russell is considered the father of these colorful reporters as a result of his evocative, independent reporting, which was a relatively new thing in journalism. Russell's reporting significantly shaped attitudes at home about the conduct of the war. Although reviled by many people in government as well as senior officers in the field, he returned to London a celebrity who could command a good seat at the theater.[2] A book publisher courted him for an account of the war. In Paris, on his way back to the Crimea, he made a deceptively self-deprecating entry in his leather-bound diary: "I find that I am unpleasantly well known principally by my portrait."[3]

The authors are thankful for the assistance of Eamon Dyas, archivist of News International, where the Russell and Delane Papers are housed.

This book is a ground-eye view of the war by Russell and others who witnessed it. It draws from dispatches by professional journalists and military men who acted as part-time reporters for British newspapers as well as others at the front who wrote letters that were published in newspapers back home. Rapidly pulled together by American publisher John G. Wells, the volume is a fascinating historical artifact akin to the modern phenomenon of quickie books to sum up dramatic international events.

This introduction provides context, much of which Wells and his audience would have assumed from their vantage point in time.

I

The Crimean War began as a religious dispute between Russia and France over custody of holy places in Jerusalem. As the wrangling continued, the czar claimed the right to protect Orthodox Christians in the Ottoman Empire, a step that pressed the hot button of Great Power relations known as the Eastern Question: Who would control this strategically important area now that Turkish power was ebbing? The resulting war, memorable for its mismanagement on both sides, was fought in the Baltic region and southern Russia as well as the Crimea, a peninsula jutting into the Black Sea. After the fall of Sebastopol and with Austria threatening to enter the war on the side of the Allies, Russia accepted defeat in early 1856.

The treaty signed in Paris did not resolve the geopolitical Eastern Question. In other ways, though, the war had lasting significance.[4] This was the first Great Power war in which steamships and railroads were used. Florence Nightingale improved sanitation and lowered death rates at the British base hospital at Scutari, near Istanbul, and inspired subsequent changes in military and civilian hospitals. By establishing modern nursing, Nightingale also provided women with a path to advanced education and careers. On the British side, the war brought a new medal for valor, the Victoria Cross, along with inglorious soul searching as to what had gone wrong with the military in the field. British inquiries into the bungling in the Crimea, which brought down the Aberdeen government, led to reforms that, among other things, improved the selection and training of officers.

To this were added advances in public information. The first war photography was done in the Crimea, although largely under the auspices of the British government, which was intent on showing that conditions in the field were not so bad as newspapers were saying.[5] The chief cause of this bad press was the trend of professionalization among newspapers. The press was becoming a highly profitable commercial enterprise based on advertisers, not political patronage. To attract readers newspapers began to emphasize independent, reliable reporting that was also colorful. William Howard Russell and his colleagues showed how this could be done through organized reporting on the battlefield.[6] Another new technology, the telegraph, figured into the new reportorial equation. Priority was given to military reports, usage charges were high, and for a time the British army blocked Russell from using the lines. But with a message able to reach London from Balaclava in a few hours instead of two weeks, correspondents could begin to think seriously about speed in news delivery.[7]

In considering Russell's significance, qualifications are in order. This was not the first war covered by bona fide civilian correspondents. George Wilkins Kendall of the *Daily Picayune* and other reporters working for newspapers in New Orleans distinguished themselves covering the Mexican War in the previous decade, although Kendall also offered advice to commanders, carried dispatches, and fought alongside the regular troops. (Two generals cited him for gallantry.)[8] Even earlier Henry Crabbe Robinson of the *Times* covered the Napoleonic War and Charles Lewis Gruneisen of London's *Morning Post,* the Carlist War, although their roles were comparatively minor. Gruneisen was the only one of the two to witness fighting, and he is best remembered as a music critic.[9] Russell himself had covered a previous conflict, the Danish Schleswig–Holstein War of 1850, a task he did with little verve. A few others could have made a claim on their being the first war correspondent.

Although Russell's name overshadows all others when the coverage of the Crimean War is discussed, he was far from alone at the front. In addition to stringers, some recruited in the traditional fashion from the ranks of the military, the *Times* had Thomas Chenery and Frederick Harman, among others. Other newspapers fielded correspondents, to name just a few: George Alfred Henty for London's *Morning Post,* Nicholas A. Wood for the *Morning Herald,* also in London, William Simpson for the *Illustrated London News,* and another Irishman, Edwin L. Godkin, for the *London Daily News.*[10] What made Russell outstanding was the power of his descriptive reporting and the forcefulness of his newspaper and its editor, Delane.

This latter point is often lost in assessing the work of foreign correspondents. While enterprise and courage are essential in outstanding war reporting, the most intrepid reporter is impotent without the added ingredient of an editor who sends the reporter in to the field, takes care to ensure the reporting is solid (Delane made a short visit to the front in late 1854), and then backs him up. When Russell worried how far he should go, Delane responded, "Continue as you have done, to tell the truth, and as much of it as you can, and leave such comment as may be dangerous to us, who are out of danger."[11] It also mattered that the *Times* cut a wide swath. By 1853 the newspaper sold 50,000 copies a day, more than all of its competitors combined.[12] As the *Times*'s "circulation is enormous and its influence abroad very great," observed Lord Clarendon, who served as foreign secretary during the war, "a Government must take its support on the terms it chooses to put it."[13] It was said the czar learned of the impending declaration of war from the *Times,* which obtained an advance copy under the table, and that the paper's editorial policy contributed to the British government's decision to besiege Sebastopol.[14]

Russell was a dogged reporter. His descriptions of the fighting were detailed and gripping. Lines from his dispatches were devoured by Londoners; Alfred, Lord Tennyson, drew from Russell's description of the fighting at Balaclava for his famous poem *The Charge of the Light Brigade.* But it was not the quality of Russell's prose alone that distinguished his work. It was how he brought it to bear on the problems that arose in the field. The British leadership in the field was weak. Some officers initially approached their deployment as if on a fox hunt, and the poorly organized logistics made the rigor of the war much harder on the troops. (The French forces, in contrast, were well organized, although French journalists were not. The new news agency Havas did not cover the war. The government newspaper *Le Moniteur* had a correspondent in the field, but his job was to forward official reports. The Russian press was equally official in orientation, and a Turkish press scarcely existed.)[15]

"Meat is bad and dear," Russell reported in an April 21, 1854, dispatch. "The beef being very like coarse mahogany; the mutton is rather better, but very lean. Milk is an article of the highest luxury and only seen on the tables of the great; and the only attempt at butter is rancid lard packed in strong-smelling camel's-hair bags."[16] During the siege of Sebastopol, trench soldiers standing in icy slush did not have sufficient waterproof gear or enough blankets when they slept at night. Their tents were ripped and sometimes full of water.

Russell was an affable, cigar-smoking, brandy-drinking, story-telling Irishman who made friends easily, a talent that helped him get information.[17] These same qualities led him—as it did Ernie Pyle in World War II and many other embedded reporters—to identify with the frontline soldiers, and this came through in his dispatches. "These are hard truths," he wrote in a dispatch published in the *Times* on December 18, 1854 (and appearing in this book on page 103),

> but the people of England must hear them. They must know that the wretched beggar who wanders about the streets of London in the rain, leads the life of a prince compared with the British soldiers who are fighting out here for their country, and who, we are complacently assured by the home authorities, are the best-appointed army in Europe.

In his dispatches Russell criticized Lord Raglan, the commander, among other things questioning his tactics. But some of his harshest comments came in private letters to Delane. These did not find their way into the newspaper, lest the *Times* seem unpatriotic. But the editor circulated the letters to government cabinet ministers.[18]

So powerful was Russell's reporting that he has been credited with accomplishments that were not his at all. It is often claimed that Russell was the author of the dispatch that stirred the public with a description of the horrible hospital conditions at Scutari. In fact, the dispatches of Thomas Chenery, the *Times* Constantinople correspondent, had the greater effect, as when he wrote,

> It is with feelings of surprise and anger that the public will learn that no sufficient medical preparations have been made for the proper care of the wounded. Not only are there not sufficient surgeons—that, it might be urged unavoidable—not only are there no dressers and nurses—that might be a defect of a system for which no one is to blame—but what will be said when it is known that there is not even linen to make bandages for the wounded?[19]

While such a mix-up between Russell and Chenery may seem curious in our times, in those days bylines were not used on stories. Russell's reports in the *Times* were typically identified as "FROM OUR SPECIAL CORRESPONDENT."

War reporting is among the most difficult. The reporter is on one side of the lines literally and figuratively. This creates a practical dilemma of having to choose where to position oneself. Being close to the action gives eyewitness detail, but the range of vision is limited to a small piece of terrain. Being at headquarters makes one subject to the official view of what is happening. Russell's lack of perspective showed up in his tendentious criticism of Lord Raglan. The commander was hobbled by his advanced age (he died in the field before the war was over) and lack of command experience, but other factors deserved attention as well. He was surrounded by inept subordinate officers and was trapped in a dysfunctional, antiquated military system. Forced to deal with the bureaucracy, he became imprisoned at his desk, answering inquiries that never should have been asked in the first place. Not realizing the strain he was under, Russell criticized him for staying in his quarters and neglecting his men.[20]

As to the figurative problem of being on one side of the line, Russell was guilty of the very common correspondent's sin of glorification. Whatever criticism he might level, he was, after all, for his side. He never questioned the value of the enterprise, only tactics. Although Russell made it clear that the Charge of the Light Brigade and other errant military actions that same day were ill-advised, the average reader could easily be swept away by the glory he heaped on the men who made the cavalry charge. The dispatch began this way:

> If the exhibition of the most brilliant valour, of the excess of courage, and of a daring which would have reflected lustre on the best days of chivalry can afford full consolation for the disaster of to-day, we can have no reason to regret the melancholy loss which we sustained in a contest with a savage and barbarian enemy.[21]

The British command, not knowing what to do with Russell and his press colleagues when they arrived on the scene, decided the best course was to show them little courtesy. Raglan never spoke a word to Russell. "I have a good chance of starving if the army takes the field,"[22] Russell wrote to Delane, explaining his treatment by the British military brass. "I am living in a pigsty— a mud wallow room without chair, table, stool, or window-glass. . . . I live on eggs and brown bread." Senior officers who did talk to Russell often used the occasion to suggest that he leave.

Attitudes did not improve when Russell reported facts that might have been news to the enemy. This prompted Delane to

restrict him to reporting "past events," although Delane did not
tone down editorial criticism of the military.[23] "All the battalion
officers are delighted," Russell wrote to his boss of the impact of
the *Times*'s continuing editorial comment, "and believe without
exception, but the staffs & generals are furious & I doubt if I can
again take up my quarters near them."[24] By the time that the
military came up with the idea of censorship to fence back organized news coverage it was too late—at least for that war.

In the future, generals saw themselves fighting on two battle
fronts. One with the enemy, the other, in the words of General
Garnet Wolseley, who served in the war as a junior officer, with
"Those newly invented curses to the armies—I mean newspaper
correspondents."[25] In the soon-to-erupt American Civil War,
Northern general William Tecumseh Sherman court-martialed a
reporter for writing that Sherman would have won the battle of
Vicksburg if he had "acted as earnestly and persistently against
the enemy as against the press."[26] Upon hearing three reporters
might have been killed, Sherman said, "That's good! We'll have
dispatches now from hell before breakfast." By the time of World
War I, censorship of the press was becoming a science.

In this way modern warfare and modern foreign reporting
evolved hand in hand. Many of the British correspondents, who
did more than those of any other nation to advance foreign reporting at the time, had distinguished careers ahead of them.
Chenery replaced Delane as editor of the *Times*. Godkin immi-
grated to the United States and founded *The Nation* magazine
and edited the *New York Evening Post*.

Russell, who garnered the most acclaim in the war, went on
to cover the Indian Mutiny, the American Civil War, the Austro-
Prussian War, the Franco-Prussian War, the Zulu War, and others. He dripped with medals, among them the Chevalier of the
Order of Franz Josef of Austria, the Indian War Medal, and Officer of the Legion of Honour. His alma mater, Trinity College
in Dublin, conferred an honorary LL.D., so henceforth he was
called Dr. Russell, rather exalted for a journalist. After the death
of his first wife, he married a countess. Although Queen Victoria's husband, Prince Albert, called him that "miserable scrib-
bler," he became a personal secretary to the Prince of Wales, the
future King Edward VII.[27] After Sir William Howard Russell died
in 1907, a memorial was erected to him in St. Paul's Cathedral.
The inscription below his bust reads, "first and greatest of war
correspondents."[28]

II

The war inspired a slew of books. Many were written during the conflict or immediately afterward. Officers and their men wrote memoirs and published their letters and diaries, some quite compelling. "It was a catharsis which was to have no equal until the First World War," observed historian Trevor Royle.[29] Russell produced two books on the heels of his reporting from the Crimean War: *The War: From the Landing at Gallipoli to the Death of Lord Raglan,* published in 1855, and *The War: From the Death of Lord Raglan to the Evacuation of the Crimea,* published the next year. Both of these are made up of his dispatches, as is a third book, *The British Expedition to the Crimea,* which was published in 1858 and showed the market value his reporting continued to have.

Enthusiasm for the full story of the war was not limited to Europe. While the United States was neutral in the Crimean War, its people were not uninterested. The excited attention that Americans gave to the war prompted the editor of *Harper's* to observe: "When we hear the elaborate discussions that arise . . . concerning the great war in the East, we often find ourselves asking our friends whether, after all the enthusiasm with which they enter into politics of other nations, they have any left for those of their own."[30]

Many Americans picked sides the way they do today when following European soccer tournaments. The choice was purely subjective, with the Russians seeming to have the most friends. This was curious, considering that most of the news came from the Allied point of view. But the Russians appealed to those who instinctively sided with the underdogs. In addition, the Russians were Christians while the Turks were Muslim; Irish immigrants lost no love on the British; and slave-owning Southerners felt a common bond with the Russian aristocracy, whose domination of the serfs seemed to reaffirm their own view of the natural order.

Elements of the public, especially national leaders, perceived that concrete national interests were at stake, although again personal predilections came into play. Franklin Pierce, president at the time, was expansion minded in the wake of the U.S. victory in the Mexican War. There was talk of annexing Cuba and enlarging influence in Central America. This brought the country into diplomatic confrontation with France and Great Britain, which had their own interests in the Americas and, besides, were not eager to see the United States join the ranks of the Great Powers. Thus arose what we might call the Latin American Question: Would a victory in the Near East embolden the Allies to assert themselves south of the United States? Both the United States and Russia, wrote an Ohio minister, "stand confronted by the Anglo-French Alliance—the one in the Baltic and at Sebastopol, the other in the Gulf of Mexico, in the Sandwich Islands, and in Central America, ready to say 'No' to our progress when 'Russia is settled.'"[31] Opponents of the Pierce administration, meanwhile, foresaw great danger in a victorious Russia that would hold sway over Europe and in the process repudiate Western values.

Although no American reporters covered the fighting, American newspapers reprinted stories from British and French newspapers, particularly Russell's. Similarly, books written by citizens of Allied nations dominated in American book stores. British and French authors wrote the five books on the war that were published in the United States in 1854.[32] The book you hold in your hands right now came to market in 1856, just months after the war ended. As the inside title page shows, it was originally published as the *Complete History of the Russian War, From Its Commencement to Its Close.*

This book's pedigree is a testament not only to Americans' interest in the war but also to the loose ways of publishing in the country at midcentury. Like modern developing nations that pirate movies and make knockoff versions of Rolex watches, American printers often saw it to their advantage to publish foreign books without paying for the privilege. Not that Americans did not try to cloak this propensity in altruistic terms. As a group of Philadelphia publishers said in 1872, "Thought, when given to the world, is, as light, free to all."[33]

The most obvious way to spread this light was simply to reprint a book. But a publisher could just as well lift bits and pieces from others' work. This had an analogue in the common practice of newspapers since the Colonial period of borrowing stories from other papers. The first American foreign news was acquired by printers who greeted incoming ships and afterwards hurried back to their shops with British newspapers that could be plundered for news.[34]

The latter approach was at play in the creation of the *History of the Russian War.* The book is often attributed to William Howard Russell. It is recorded as such, for example, in the Oxford University Bodleian Library catalog. This may result from the same celebrity factor that accounts for Russell's being credited with inspiring the British to aid its wounded soldiers in the Crimea, his overwhelming fame. It may also be recognition that the book contains much of Russell's work. But Russell cannot be said to be *the* author. It is really a pastiche of the work of different authors, including John G. Wells, an obviously entrepreneurial New England publisher who assembled the book.

Wells's motivation seems clear enough. A passage on page 43, which he probably wrote himself, points to his appreciation of the commercial opportunities for a book such as this: "There is a terrible romance in War. We may deprecate it as the worst of evils, but there is an indescribable fascination in its bloody records."

We know some things about Wells (1821–80). Like many printers, Wells had an inky finger in many pots. The American Antiquarian Society lists him as a New York author, publisher, and bookseller. In the fashion of the time, he used a pen name, Gracchus Americanus, for his book *The Grange: A Study in the Science of Society.* (Gracchus was a Roman tribune who promoted land reform.) The books that Wells published often had a timely side to them, for instance an 1872 book on the great Chicago fire. His shop sold foreign newspapers, which may have helped in piecing together this book, and specialized in illustrations and maps. The original, hand-colored maps in this book, which can be found at http://lsu.edu/lsupress/crimeanwarmaps, are elegant and highly useful to the reader. This kind of printing is out of fashion today because of the great expense involved. On the other hand, the book is full of broken type (that is, letters of type that did not print clearly); and Wells was, to say the least, a careless proofreader. We have not corrected most of this, as it conveys a sense of what his readers received. For the same reason, this book retains the promotional material found at the back of the original version, which lists Wells's other merchandise. The sketches, now located at the center of the book, were originally scattered throughout.

The first section of the book, roughly pages 13 to 42, summarizes the run-up to the war, which seems to be mostly Wells's work. A great deal of the material after that comes from reports from the field, woven together by the enterprising printer. Much of this material can be traced to Russell's dispatches, which in turn were printed in Russell's first two books of dispatches, but the work of other professional and part-time correspondents is included. So are letters published in newspapers as well as military reports, two practices that were typical for previous wars and continued to be used during this period of transition to modern professional journalism.

On page 80, for instance, Wells acknowledges that he is using reports both from the *Times* of London and the *Morning Herald;* the work of "a correspondent of the Austrian *Military Zeitung*" appears on page 118. On page 88, Wells refers to the "emphatic testimony" of an "English officer who participated in and was severely wounded in the battle." On page 152, he reprints a lengthy after-action report written by a Russian commander, Prince Michael Gortschakoff (today usually spelled Gorchakov), after the Allies took Sebastopol. A letter by a soldier informing a mother of her son's death in battle on page 55 in this book appeared in the *Times* of London on October 17, 1854.

Unconstrained by rules, other than those he chose to make up, Wells in other instances did not bother to attribute the material to anyone, even when he used quotation marks. Not that Wells was faithful about indicating when he was quoting and when he wasn't. The printer behaved as though his shop had run low on typefaces bearing quotation marks. In his freehanded editing, he sometimes left in the word "I" without ever saying who "I" was. Tenses were often confused as he jumped from one pirated quote to another. He freely rewrote reports by others, dropping sentences and adding his own. A paragraph beginning on page 48—after the subhead "THE BATTLE OF THE ALMA"—is taken verbatim from Russell, except for the first sentence in the paragraph, which may have been written by Wells, and the inexplicable deletion of one sentence in the middle of the original dispatch. Nowhere in the passage does Wells use quotation marks or indicate whence the passage came.* Long excerpts of Russell's "thin red streak" dispatch on the Charge of the Light Brigade appear on pages 65 to 75 with no attribution at all.

And he not only plundered from the *Times*. Wells similarly picked up an emotional squib in the *Morning Herald* on October 16, 1854. This was a postscript added by someone to a letter

---

*The dropped sentence reads: "If the reader will place himself on the top of Richmond-hill, dwarf the Thames in imagination to the size of a Hampshire rivulet, and imagine the lovely hill itself to be deprived of all vegetation and protracted for about four miles along the stream, he may form some notion of the position occupied by the Russians, while the plains on the north or left bank of the Thames will bear no inapt similitude to the land over which the British and French armies advanced, barring only the verdure and freshness. " The full passage can be found in Russell's book, *The War: From the Landing at Gallipoli to the Death of Lord Raglan* (London: George Routledge, 1855), 178.

written by a French soldier who died in action before his missive could be sent home. It appears on page 55 of this book without any mention of its original publication in the *Morning Herald.*

Wells was obliquely frank about his scissors-and-paste technique. "It is time," he writes in the preface, "to weed this literary wilderness; to preserve only what is valuable; to put even that in its right place; and to supply a compendious, lucid, and reliable narrative of a conflict which might be said to have been long impending, and yet which virtually took Europe by surprise."

American publishers have become much more constrained in our own time. They now honor international law, for reasons of self-interest. As the United States has become a source of much valuable literature, publishers want to do anything they can to discourage plunder by others. But the quickie war book is as much a viable commodity now as it was in Wells's day. Not infrequently, such books are made up of (and acknowledged as coming from) correspondents' reports.

III

The Crimean War is to be looked back upon as a golden age for war reporting.

There were shortcomings, to be sure, in terms of balance, accuracy, and fairness. Some of Russell's reporting is weighed down with too much minutia for anyone but a specialist. Also the war saw age-old problems for correspondents.[35] Russell, for all his brilliance, was insecure and needed constant stroking from Delane. His expense accounts, considered somewhat extravagant, were a mess. The *Times* management finally threw up its hands; it told Russell that it would pay him what he asked and then start the accounting all over again.[36]

But correspondents were in the exhilarating process of inventing the idea of an active, responsible press that served as a flywheel against powerful government. It was far better to have independent, if flawed, news media than simply official versions of what happened. And once the military became more adept at controlling journalists, the correspondents openly regretted the loss of the good old days when they were harassed but left largely alone. In 1892, one of the great British war correspondents, Archibald Forbes of the *Morning Advertiser,* another London newspaper, observed that censorship had turned the role of war correspondents into "a mere transmitter, by strictly specified channels, of carefully revised intelligence. . . . That new order of things has taken war correspondence out of the category of the fine arts."[37]

"The real beginning of newspaper correspondence was the arrival of 'Billy' Russell with the English army in the Crimea," fellow correspondent E. L. Godkin reflected half a century after the war:

> In his hands correspondence from the field really became a power before which generals began to quail . . . I therefore cannot help thinking that the appearance of the special correspondent in the Crimea, to whatever evils and abuses it may afterward have led, was a troubling of the waters which was a good thing both for the British army and people. It led to a real awakening of the official mind. It brought home to the War Office the fact that the public has something to say about the conduct of wars.[38]

That is worth keeping in mind while reading this volume, which offers considerable insight into how the war looked at the time. As such, the *Complete History of the Russian War* remains useful as well as illuminating history.

NOTES

1. John B. Atkins, *The Life of Sir William Howard Russell: The First Special Correspondent*, vol. 1 (London: John Murray, 1911), 124. The date of Russell's birth is sometimes listed as 1821, but Atkins, relying on Russell, puts it at 1820, which would make him thirty-four when the war was declared.

2. Ibid., 244–45.

3. William Howard Russell, diary, February 25, 1856, William Howard Russell Papers, News International Archives, London.

4. Trevor Royle, *Crimea: The Great Crimean War, 1854–1856* (New York: St. Martin's Press, 2000), 502–14; J. M. Roberts, *A History of Europe* (New York: Allen Lane, 1997), 357; Winston S. Churchill, *A History of the English-Speaking People*, vol. 4 (London: Cassell, 1959), 62–63; Kellow Chesney, *Crimean War Reader* (London: Frederick Muller, 1960), 41.

5. A discussion of photography in the Crimean War can be found in *The Camera Goes to War: Photographs from the Crimean War, 1854–56* (Edinburgh: Scottish Arts Council, n.d.).

6. Philip Knightley, *The First Casualty: The War Correspondent as Hero and Myth-Maker from the Crimea to Kosovo* (Baltimore: Johns Hopkins University Press, 2000), 2. Knightley does a good job of summing up Russell's career.

7. Robert W. Desmond, *The Information Process: World News Reporting to the Twentieth Century* (Iowa City: University of Iowa Press, 1978), 181–82.

8. Background on Kendall is found in Fayette Copeland, *Kendall of the Picayune* (Norman: University of Oklahoma Press, 1943).

9. F. Lauriston Bullard, *Famous War Correspondents* (Boston: Little, Brown, 1914), 5–9.

10. A listing of correspondents is found in Desmond, *The Information Process*, 179–81.

11. John T. Delane to W. H. Russell, January 4, 1855, John T. Delane Papers, News International Archives, London; Knightley, *The First Casualty*, 11.

12. Royle, *Crimea*, 46.

13. Ibid.

14. Arthur Irwin Dasent, *John Delane, 1817–1879*, vol. 1, 169; Nicholas Bentley, ed., *Russell's Despatches from the Crimea, 1854–1856* (London: Andre Deutsch Limited, 1966), 49.

15. Desmond, *The Information Process*, 181, 186.

16. William Howard Russell, *The War: From the Landing at Gallipoli to the Death of Lord Raglan* (London: George Routledge, 1855), 38.

17. Rupert Furneaux, *The First War Correspondent: William Howard Russell of "The Times"* (London: Cassell, 1945), 27.

18. Knightley, *The First Casualty*, 6.

19. Ibid., 12.

20. Atkins, *The Life of Sir William Howard Russell*, vol. 1, 181.

21. *Times* of London, November 14, 1854.

22. William Howard Russell to John T. Delane, April 8, 1854, Delane Papers.

23. Knightley, *The First Casualty*, 11.

24. William Howard Russell to John T. Delane, January 21, 1855, Delane Papers.

25. Bullard, *Famous War Correspondents*, 1.

26. James M. Perry, *A Bohemian Brigade: The Civil War Correspondents* (New York: John Wiley and Sons, 2000), 144, 159.

27. Furneaux, *The First War Correspondent*, 78.

28. Knightley, *The First Casualty*, 1–2.

29. Royle, *Crimea*, 508.

30. Quoted in Alan Dowty, *The Limits of American Isolation; The United States and the Crimean War* (New York: New York University Press, 1971), 85. Information in this section on American public opinion draws heavily from Dowty's book.

31. Quoted in Dowty, *The Limits of American Isolation*, 99.

32. Ibid., 87.

33. Hellmut Lehmann-Haupt, *The Book in America: A History of the Making and Selling of Books in the United States* (New York: R. R. Bowker, 1952), 204.

34. Charles E. Clark and Charles Wetherell, "The Measure of Maturity: The *Pennsylvania Gazette*, 1728–1765," *William and Mary Quarterly* 46 (April 1989): 295.

35. Knightley, *The First Casualty*, 3.

36. Atkins, *The Life of Sir William Howard Russell*, 246.

37. Archibald Forbes, "War Correspondence as a Fine Art," *The Century*, December 1892, 290.

38. Rollo Ogden, ed., *Life and Letters of Edwin Lawrence Godkin* (New York: Macmillan, 1907), 101–2.

By the end of his career, William Howard Russell had as many medals on his chest as the greatest generals and was a hero in his profession.

Frontispiece, F. Lauriston Bullard, *Famous War Correspondents*, 1914

Behind every great foreign correspondent is a great editor.
John Delane, the editor of the *Times* of London, was one of the outstanding
editors of the 19th century and, as much as anyone, accounted
for his paper's coverage of the Crimean War.

William Howard Russell in camp, not always a happy experience
for him as the senior British officers did not welcome the presence
of a correspondent who reported bad news as well as victories.

Photograph by Roger Fenton, Library of Congress

THE

COMPLETE HISTORY

OF THE

RUSSIAN WAR.

COMPLETE HISTORY

OF THE

RUSSIAN WAR,

FROM ITS COMMENCEMENT TO ITS CLOSE:

GIVING A

GRAPHIC PICTURE

OF THE

GREAT DRAMA OF WAR,

BY RUSSELL,
CORRESPONDENT OF THE LONDON 'TIMES.

EMBRACING A SUPERB

MAP OF THE SEAT OF WAR,

AND A MAGNIFICENT ENGRAVING OF THE

Bombardment and Fall of Sebastopol,

SHOWING THE ATTACK AND CAPTURE OF THE MALAKOFF, ASSAULT ON THE REDAN, AND FALL OF SEBASTOPOL, DRAWN BY AN ARTIST WHO WAS EIGHT MONTHS IN THE CRIMEA.

TOGETHER WITH

Sixteen Full-Page Engravings,

Illustrative of the Stirring Scenes in the Crimea.

NEW YORK:
JOHN G. WELLS, PUBLISHING AGENT,
11 BEEKMAN STREET, CORNER NASSAU.
1856.

PREFACE.

IF the most intelligent man moving in common society were asked to give a brief, clear, and connected account of all the transactions of the Russian War, from the beginning to its termination, he would first perhaps be surprised that any body should need such information. But he would immediately be still more surprised to find how difficult it was for him to furnish it; that instead of being able to state off-hand, in their real order and due arrangement, the facts required, he would be obliged to ask time for reflection ; and then even, time to make references. He would discover that his impressions, though very vivid respecting the principal particulars, were, after all, a mass of anachronous entanglement and historical confusion.

Perhaps, indeed, the very facilities which now exist for publishing diurnally every premature version which may arrive of affairs interesting to the public, have contributed to heap upon the progressive reports of this great war a burden of crude messages and announcements which confuse the true chronicle of facts ; and, in short, we have not so much to *learn the story* as to recall it succinctly and to *unlearn the many successive misstatements of it.* Already the newspaper records of a single year—stimulating, and, to our generation, novel and portentous intelligence—with second versions, and third versions, and corrections, and alterations—exceed in bulk the immense history in which Gibbon chronicles the stupendous revolutions, the many memorable conflicts, and the countless European vicissitudes of *fifteen centuries.*

It is time to weed this literary wilderness; to preserve only what is valuable; to put even that in its right place; and to supply a compendious, lucid, and reliable narrative of a con-flict which might be said to have been long impending, and yet which virtually took Europe by surprise.

COMPLETE HISTORY

OF

THE RUSSIAN WAR,

FROM

ITS COMMENCEMENT TO ITS CLOSE.

THE ORIGIN OF THE WAR.

So lengthy have been the official documents from which the alleged causes of the war were to be obtained, and so confused their details, that the mass of Americans have found it a discouraging task to study them. Hence we have heard, on all sides, inquiries as to the "grounds of the dispute," the "pretexts for the invasion," etc., indicating the necessity of the present publication, affording a clear, however brief, statement of the historical facts, so far as accessible to us. These will show that religious bigotry has had much to do with the matter, as has been the truth of too many of the conflicts that have desolated the earth. The various churches of Jerusalem, and "the region round about Jordan" generally, have been always objects of veneration to the Roman Catholics as well as to the members of the Greek Church. The guardianship of their holy shrines had been shared between them, the Greek Christians claiming under the protection of the Sultan, and the Roman Catholic Christians under France. The claim of this religious protectorate by the French was based on a treaty made in 1740. A number of conventions had been "concluded" by the interested parties, to use the language of diplomacy ; but this, as is too often the result of treaties, proved only a technical "conclusion" of the difficulty. None of the conventional arrangements had defined the rights of the churches with sufficient clearness to prevent contentions. Consequently these were constantly springing up. The Sublime Porte issued his *firmans*, defining the religious privileges of his Grecian subjects, while France as pertinaciously insisted upon the rights for the Catholics. The dispute finally assumed a temper which showed it to be religious only in name, and became a foolishly stubborn contest between hierarchies, urged forward and stimulated by political intrigue. The Revolutionary Government of the First Republic was as warm in the contest as the Catholic House of Orleans, and the Protestant Guizot as either; and Louis Napoleon, when President of the Republic, showed an active desire to conciliate the clergy by vigorously asserting the privileges of the Catholic Church. Violent disputes having arisen as to the abstraction of a large silver star, placed above the Shrine of the Nativity, and the question as to which Church was bound to repair the cupola of the Holy Sepulchre, which was fast falling into decay, in 1850, General Aupich, the French Ambassador at Constantinople, received orders to institute an inquiry into the matter; and obtained the appointment of a mixed commission to consider the dispute. The Latins claimed the exclusive possession of twelve " Holy Places," of which the four principal were the great cupola of the Holy Sepulchre, the Tomb of the Virgin, the great church at Bethlehem, and part of the garden of Gethsemane. This claim the Greeks disputed; but the commission considered the right as firmly established, the places having been specially named in firmans granted to the Latins. The Emperor of Russia now interfered, and, in an autograph letter to the Sultan, claimed for the Greeks the preservation of all their ancient privileges in Jerusalem, and condemned the Turkish ministry for countenancing the pretensions of the Latins. Unwilling to offend so powerful a neighbor, the Sultan dismissed the " mixed" commission, and appointed a new one, composed exclusively of Ottoman functionaries. While this new commission was engaged in reïnvestigating the dispute, Nicholas proposed to the French President that they should themselves settle the question, leaving to Turkey simply the office of carrying out their wishes. To this suggestion Louis Napoleon returned a decided negative, and shortly afterwards the commission presented their report. They proposed that the great cupola of the Holy Sepulchre should be common property, that the Latins should have access to the Tomb of the Virgin, and a key of the church of Bethlehem. This arrangement was communicated to France in a somewhat apologetic manner, and was accepted under a protest by France, reserving the discussion of the rights of the Latins should the question be reöpened. The Emperor of Russia now demanded, and the Porte conceded, the publication of a firman throughout the Sultan's dominion, announcing the new arrangement. This step greatly offended the French Government, and M. Lavalette was dispatched to Constantinople to demand the recall of the firman. The Russian Ambassador, mixing in the dispute, insisted that the key granted to the Latins should be the key of a side-gate only ; but the Porte adhered to its decision that they should have access to the principal entrance, thus placing the contending sects on an equality. At length the French Government conceded the issuing of the firman, on condition that it should be promulgated with as little publicity as possible. But here was a new difficulty. Afif Bey, the officer charged with the commission, upon arriving at Jerusalem, was met by a clamorous demand from the Greeks for a public read· ing of the document, with all the usual parade and ceremony. Afif Bey wrote home for instructions, and the Russian Ambassador supported the claims of the Greeks, and the Porte sent new orders to Jerusalem for the public reading of the firman. The delivery of the promised key now became the subject of renewed discord and much anxious consultation. Again was the whole question discussed at Constantinople, and finally the previous decision was confirmed, and the key of the great portal of the Church of the Holy Sepulchre handed to the Latin monks. Nicholas was but little disposed to brook this resistance to his wishes ; and it was at length announced that a special ambassador was to be dispatched from St. Petersburg to Constantinople, with specific demands and extraordinary powers. Prince Menchikoff was intrusted with this mission ; and thus, from the dispute of the "Holy Places," became developed the germ of an European war. Prince Menchikoff entered Constantinople on March 1st, 1853, and, on the following day obtained an interview with the Sultan. His first step was characterized by an act of insolence, which marked his whole proceedings. According to diplomatic etiquette, an ambassador is bound to visit the Foreign Minister ; this Men· chikoff omitted to do, and Fuad Effendi, who then held that office, a high-spirited man, strongly opposed to Russian influence, immediately resigned. A ministerial crisis was the result, and so alarming did matters become, that Colonel Rose, then the only British representative at the Porte, wrote to the Admiral of the Mediterranean fleet, requesting his presence in the Turkish waters. Admiral Dundas, however, did not deem it prudent to comply with the request ; and, in a few weeks, Lord Stratford de Redcliffe resumed his position as ambassador at Constantinople.

There was now a new aspect of affairs   On the 5th of May

Prince Menchikoff presented an ultimatum, demanding the acknowledgment of a Russian protectorate over all the Greek subjects of the Ottoman empire, equivalent to the sovereignty over nearly four fifths of the entire population. The squabble between a few monks of rival churches had now grown into the dimensions of an European difficulty. England, France, Austria, and Prussia felt it incumbent to interfere. Six days had been first allowed for the consideration of the Russian ultimatum, and the Prince had conceded six more. The Turkish ministry resigned, and the new Minister of Foreign Affairs, Reschid Pacha, addressed a note to the four great Powers, announcing that Turkey had refused to accede to the Russian demands, and felt it incumbent to make preparations for defense against any offensive measures which Russia might adopt. The Czar, anxious apparently to gain time for military preparations, transmitted another ultimatum, or "ultimatissimum," as it was called, for the consideration of which eight days were allowed. This was also rejected, and the Turkish population enthusiastically clamored for war. The rejection of this last Russian demand reached St. Petersburg on the 26th of June; and on the same day, the Emperor Nicholas issued a manifesto announcing his intention of occupying the Danubian Principalities, Moldavia and Wallachia, as "material guarantees." On the 2d of July, a Russian army corps, under General Dannenberg, crossed the Pruth, near Jassy, and entered Moldavia. The Western Powers now earnestly endeavored, in conjunction with Austria and Prussia, to avert the threatened storm. A conference of the representatives of the four powers was held at Vienna, and several ineffectual attempts made to frame a treaty which should be agreeable to the contending parties. The Porte was firm in its determination to concede nothing, and on the 5th of October the Sultan signed a declaration of war, giving the Russians fifteen days to evacuate the Principalities. Omar Pasha, the most renowned of the Ottoman generals, with a force of 120,000 men, established his headquarters at Shumla, a strongly-fortified town near the Danube, and awaited the expiration of the guaranteed time, to oppose himself to the large army which now occupied the Principalities.

On the 27th March, 1854, Queen Victoria, in a message to both Houses of Parliament, announced that she "felt bound to afford active assistance to her ally the Sultan, against unprovoked aggression," and on the succeeding day the *Gazette* contained the official declaration of war. The Emperor Napoleon about the same time made a similar announcement. In anticipation of the war, which had long been seen to be inevi table, the English Mediterranean fleet had anchored in Besika Bay, just outside the entrance of the Dardanelles, where they were soon afterwards joined by the French fleet; and the most powerful flotilla which ever left the shores of England, under the command of Admiral Sir Charles Napier, had passed the Sound, and awaited but the intelligence of the declaration of hostilities, to threaten the immense fortresses of the Baltic and the Gulf of Finland; thus not only blocking the great commercial ports of the north of Russia, but, by causing a diversion, preventing a concentration of the Russian power on the Danube. In the mean while, both countries were preparing large expeditionary armies to proceed immediately to the seat of war.

Public feeling had been greatly exasperated in England by the publication of the celebrated "Secret Correspondence," in which Nicholas proposed to the British Government the partition of Turkey, and the division of the empire between the two countries; and this exasperation was certainly not diminished when it was discovered that precisely similar overtures had been made to France, in which England was carefully left out of the bargain. For the first time, England and France— for so many years such deadly foes—stood side by side in arms. The old hereditary animosity was seemingly extinguished, and both nations hailed with hearty acclamations the new era.

The Allies had thrown away the scabbard, and the sword was brandished for the fight.

FIRST PERIOD, INVASION OF MOLDO-WALLACHIA, AND STATE
OF RUSSIAN TROOPS.

It was towards the end of August, 1853, that the first Vienna note was declined by the Porte, and not very long afterward that the second was peremptorily rejected by the Czar; but nearly three months earlier, orders had been dispatched from St. Petersburg to carry the Russian Divisions forcibly across the Pruth into the Turkish territory, thus making war but not declaring it. On the 3d of July the order was executed. Those rich corn countries were seized; taxes for the maintenance of eighty thousand troops were imposed by the Czar upon four millions of the subjects of Abdul-Medjid-Khan, and contracts for nine months were based on these new imposts; the Danube, the greatest inland highway of commerce of Europe, was brought under the invader's immediate and stringent control; the Hospodars were deposed; a Provisional Administration, at the head of which Prince Michael Gortchakoff was nominated to represent with su-

2

preme powers the undefinable Protectorate of Nicholas, was established; and, in short, the Czar carried into effect the very claims concerning the admissibility of which he was at the same time holding an illusory discussion with all Europe. The movement was made suddenly and rapidly. In the very first instance fifty thousand troops—of which, perhaps, a third was cavalry, and which were attended with proportionate parks of artillery (seventy-two guns, in fact, of large calibre) —were pushed into Moldavia; and these troops were virtually but the advance-guard of the intended army of occupation. Two immense lines of march—one from the centre of European Russia, and another, equally long, from the very confines of Asia, were all alive with armed men, succeeding each other, and pressing forward to a common destination. From Kherson and Kief moved those who were to replace the garrison of Bessarabia; and the vacant and remoter cantonments were, in their turn, supplied by the advancing columns of Taurida and the Don Cossacks of Pultowa and the Ukraine. Osten-Sacken's corps was in movement behind, when Gortchakoff and Lüders were entering the Turkish territory.

The Czar had long succeeded in raising a party in his favor in Moldo-Wallachia; but, be it observed, it was only a party; it was not the people, it was such a party as he has in Prussia, or in Baden. That such a party existed in the Principalities, is proved by the fact that, *before* the Russians had sent one soldier across the Pruth, the Divan of Moldavia assembled on the 14th of June, at Jassy, and there voted an address of sympathy and homage to the Emperor Nicholas. Under the circumstances of the crisis, sympathy and homage amounted to an invitation, which he scarcely needed.

Five days after Prince Gortchakoff had passed the frontier stream, (more fatal than the Rubicon,) he assisted at a "Te Deum," which was intoned with solemnity at St. Spiridion, the great Greek Church of Jassy.

A week later—that is, on the 15th of July—instead of the seventy-two guns with which the Russians had entered the country, they possessed in Jassy alone 144 heavy pieces of artillery; and this great park and 40,000 men were instantly directed to advance upon the Danube. In another fortnight, having put this formidable column upon the march, Prince Gortchakoff was 160 miles away, at Bucharest, exchanging compliments with the bishops, who had there assembled to give him welcome. Thus he was solemnly received in the respective chief cities of the two provinces. Between his stay in the first of these capitals and his arrival in the other Ghike, the Hospodar, had sent to the Sultan a memorial of so equivocal a nature that it was considered a renunciation of the Ottoman allegiance. Under this impression, which was perhaps just, Abdul-Medjid deprived him at once of the title to that office, from the exercise of which he had already been practically excluded. First the Russians robbed him of the possession, and then the Divan deposed him from the dignity. The invaders, with whom he temporised, terminated his jurisdiction *de facto;* and the Suzerain, whom he betrayed, abrogated it *de jure.* Ghika shortly afterwards explained his conduct, and was readmitted into partial confidence at Constantinople.

The Czar felt that he had now taken steps from which he could not recede without incurring humiliations abroad which might impair his authority at home, and perchance imperil his dynasty. The armaments of Russia, therefore, proceeded with such activity, that they were apparent to the most casual observation; and, not content with the resources in his hands, the Autocrat decreed, on the 23d of July, a new conscription of seven in the thousand. Meanwhile, a concentric dispatch of troops was continued from all the southern provinces of the empire upon Bessarabia. They arrived diseased, ill-provisioned, exhausted, after a desolating march of sometimes thousands of miles, over roadless countries.

MEASURES TAKEN BY THE DIVAN; AND FIRST PROCEEDINGS OF THE CZAR.

On the other side, the Sultan was not inattentive to events, nor unequal to his dangerous and difficult position. He had to provide against attacks in Asia, as well as to guard the European seat of his government. So early as the 23d June, Selim Pacha was nominated Seraskier in Anatolia, and a large army was placed under his command. The first object was to provide against the advance of the Russians from Georgia along the southern shores of the Black Sea — an advance which, unopposed, would place Constantinople in a worse position than if the invaders, having forced the Balkans, lay encamped in the European province of Roumelia, which corresponds to the home-counties of London. In this other position, the capital might still rescue the empire; and, with the Allied fleets in the Bosphorus, and off the Golden Horn, might await events with tranquil defiance. More than this, a Russian army in Roumelia might be said to have crossed the Balkans only to perish. A victory near Adrianople, over a fresh and vigor-

ous Anglo-French army, would, to those wearied troops, (a
moral impossibility; while retreat over the mountains would
offer the alternative of certain annihilation.   But if a large
force from the Transcaucasian provinces could succeed in pushing through Erzeroum and Trebizond, and occupying Anatolia,
then both the Channel of Constantinople and the Straits of the
Dardanelles would be effectually commanded by the enemy;
the key of the entrance of the Black Sea would be in his
hands; and he could imprison in those waters, or exclude from
them, the maritime defenders of the Porte.   A favorable moment would then allow the Russian legions to be thrown across
into the very metropolis.

This Asiatic danger being averted, Omer Pacha was appointed
the Turkish Generalissimo in Europe; and so soon as the news
of Prince Gortchakoff's invasion had reached the Divan,
Omer was ordered to break down all the bridges over the
Danube, and immediately to adopt what strategic measures he
deemed advisable for the defense of the State.

On the 1st of September, the Sultan ordered an immediate
additional levy of 80,000 men, which was answered on the
24th by a ukase of the Czar, calling out a new conscription.

Four days after the Sultan's Hatti Sheriff, Prince Gortchakoff, who was at Bucharest, about twenty-five miles from the
great river which he had orders to pass, issued a proclamation,
concluding with these extraordinary words: " Russia is called
to annihilate Paganism, and those who would oppose her in
that sacred mission shall be annihilated with the Pagans!
Long life to the Czar!   Long life to the Deity of the Russians!"

The last fruitless diplomatic effort before Turkey declared
war—an effort on the one side to come to an understanding,
and on the other to overreach Europe—was the conference at
Olmütz, where the Czar tried his personal influence over the
young Emperor Francis Joseph.   Nicholas arrived at Warsaw
on the 20th of September, and thence reached Olmütz on the
23d.   Seven days later, he was again at Warsaw, disappointed
and baffled, as it was commonly imagined, in all the objects of
his late visit—a visit which had not been undertaken until
envoy after envoy (each of higher reputation than his pre-
decessor) had failed at Vienna.   The subsequent conduct of
Austria, is, perhaps, the best light by which we can guide our
conjectures; and, whatever praise may be due to Francis
Joseph, this reflection will occur to every body, that he might
have earned a still higher praise, *for he might have prevented the
European conflict altogether.*

SECOND PERIOD: HOSTILITIES AFTER TURKEY, BUT BEFORE ENGLAND AND FRANCE HAD DECLARED WAR.

It was not before the beginning of October that the Sultan, who could wait no longer for the Allies, and, indeed, no longer restrain the eagerness of his own people, formally declared war against Russia, and decreed that 150,000 fresh troops should be raised and organized at once, for the defense of Islam. The Czar, when this heroic act of the Sultan was announced to him, declared that, " from that moment forth, *he retracted all his concessions.*"

The declaration of war could not have been further delayed. Even before it was possible for the news to have reached the Danube, about 1300 Redifs suddenly passed the river, and made a foray on the Russian side. They met part of Lüders' division, fought their way successfully back to the water's edge, and re-crossed in safety with their spoils.

Omer Pacha had been diligently employed in organizing his wild troops since the early part of July ; and, with the aid of some European officers, chiefly French, belonging to the artillery, engineers, and other military classes and denominations, he soon saw himself at the head of an army in which he could place confidence, and which proved itself equal to all the exigencies of the war. The Turks are patient and hardy in the field ; their courage is proverbial, and has been proverbial for more than four hundred years.

Omer Pacha, having duly received notification that war was declared, granted yet three weeks to all neutral flags to pass to and fro on the Danube, and proclaimed that this license would terminate on the 25th of the month then current, (October.) All Russian subjects resident in Turkey were placed under Austrian protection.

The Russians were diligently using the Black Sea as a highway for the movement of troops, the rearrangement of strategic posts, and the transit of provisions, arms, and ammunition. For example, 5000 Russian soldiers, whom the fleets might have intercepted, were landed in October at Redout Kaleh, to succor the army of the Caucasus, and to attack Batoum.

On the 1st of November, M. de la Cour was recalled, and General (now Marshal) Baraguay d'Hilliers appointed ambassador at Constantinople on the part of the French Emperor.

BATTLE OF OLTENITZA.

On November 2d, Omer Pacha began to cross the Danube. He had been ordered by the Turkish government to break

down all the bridges. Establishing securely his communications with the sea through Varna, and rendering Shumla, at
the distance of thirty miles inland, impregnable, he collected
such a force of infantry and artillery around and within easy
reach of that powerful basis, that by always refusing, as military men say, the right wing of his position, and throwing the
left forward, which it will be seen he did throughout, he was
sure, *at the very least*, of fulfilling his trust, and of defending
the remainder of Turkey effectually.

Having taken these defensive precautions, and having collected a disposable body sufficient for his purpose, he determined to divert the Russians from passing the Danube, by
passing it himself. His sudden presence would compel the
enemy to much marching and counter-marching, perhaps even
to a great concentration of troops; operations not performed
without serious fatigue, or without disturbing the combinations, and arresting the more general designs of the hostile
commander. Besides all this, he might inflict some direct and
severe loss on the enemy. But the great object was, by a bold
movement, to animate and cheer his own troops, and to dispel
the delusion of Russian superiority.

On the 2d of November, and on the 3d and 4th, Omer
Pacha forced his passage fifteen miles lower down from Turtukai to Oltenitza, with 13,000 men. The Russians were numerically much stronger; but they had been, in part, per-
plexed respecting the designs, and even respecting the presence
of the Turkish generalissimo ; in part, they were out-maneuvered
during the actual operations, and in part they were beaten fairly
on the field. The Turks forced the passage with artillery, held
it manfully by the bayonet, and then secured it with spade and
axe. The conflict lasted, omitting the intervals which interrupted it, for about three hours ; and will ever be memorable under the name of the "Battle of Oltenitza."

The combat deserves a special description. The Turks had
entrenched themselves by ten o'clock in the morning of November 2. At eleven o'clock, a cloud of Cossack skirmishers
attacked them, and were followed by four columns of infantry
and twenty cannon. Large masses of cavalry immediately
afterwards appeared against the right of the Turks, the only
part of the field where horse could maneuver. The Russians
could on that day collect but 8000 men, and these were with
ease repulsed ; for, though the occupants of the entrenchments
were but 3000, that number was sufficient, with the advantage
of their field-works ; and there was the protection of the river
batteries besides. Next day the Russians were in greater number, but the Turks had also been reïnforced incessantly, and,

moreover, the entrenchments were stronger. Omer Pacha
gained a second victory, precisely like the first. On the 4th
of November, the third and greatest attack was made. The
Russians were now 30,000 strong, while Omer had flung into
this venturesome and forward outpost all the men he could
spare, amounting to 18,000.

A very protracted and desperate engagement ensued. The
Turkish left was impregnable, and as it was both very uninvit-
ing, and had in front of it covered ground and brushwood,
where the enemy lay, the carnage was here not great. But on
the Turkish right, which was assailed over an open and level
space, a fearful slaughter ensued. The Russian infantry tried
to storm this side. When first advancing, they were mowed
down in whole companies by the Turkish artillery from the
south bank; on their nearer approach, the fire of the Turkish
musketry, and even pistol-shots, discharged from behind a
cover, which forbade any effective retaliation, continued to
shake their array and thin their ranks. But "they would not
be refused." They reached (in some disorder, it is true, and
much weakened, but still they reached) the foot of the earth-
works. At this time the Osmanlis had hardly lost a man since
morning. A sudden shout arose among them, they leaped over
their own entrenchments, and charged the astonished, decimated,
and already half-broken assailants with the bayonet, routing
them completely. The movement could not extend far on account of the Russian cavalry, which prohibited all pursuit. In
many respects, it was a very peculiar contest; and we can not
account for the smallness of the number slain on the side of
the Turks. It is stated to have been under twenty. The Russians lost a thousand men. Omer Pahca, all this time, showed
the temperament of a Turk, instead of that of a German, which
he is. He is an Austrian, of the name of Lattas, a soldier of
fortune, who has become a great general, and has secured to
himself, already, a considerable place in history. During the
engagement he remained on his own side of the river. He
had taken every measure in his power. He had done what he
could do to insure victory; and he now watched the varying
phases of the action while smoking his pipe. He was quietly
seated on the high ground with a celebrated stranger, who was
present through motives of professional curiosity — General
Prim, the Spaniard. They gazed on the scene through tele-
scopes, seated, with their feet comfortably stretched towards a
large wood-fire. They saw the test-fight of an army hitherto
untried, and they saw its victory.

After this event, the Turkish position seemed to be, for some
time, that of assailants, much more than of men acting on the

defensive. They occupied both sides of the Danube in the most important places. These Turks were but part of the same division which held Rustchuk and Giurgevo, and were led by Omer in person. Sistova, Nicopolis, and Rahova were also in their hands. They had, under the command of Ismail Pacha, crossed the river at Widdin, and not only had seized Kalafat, but had entered Kalarasch with 4000 men. They had placed two thousand men on an island, as though they would hold both the banks, and likewise what lay between.

Nine days elapsed before the Russians ventured again to attack the Turkish redoubt between Oltenitza and the river. They were waiting for reïnforcements. The season was now growing late; but as rapidly as its rigors would allow, large reïnforcements were poured from Bessarabia into the Principalities. On the 11th, they again attacked the stubborn entrenchments. General Engelhardt had arrived with the reserves. They were repulsed with loss. They then endeavored to mask the position; and, by getting possession of the island for even an hour, to force this out-garrison, on their own bank, to lay down its arms. All these attempts were unsuccessful; and, on the 14th of November, they were even forced to look more to defense and less to attack; for, on that day, the Turks had the spirit and strength to make an outburst; and having fallen upon Oltenitza itself, and ravaged its suburbs, retired without loss. On the 26th, Omer Pacha established a bridge between the south shore and the island of Mokan or Mokannon, higher up the Danube, not far from Giurgevo; and about the same time he withdrew the troops which were in position on the further bank, in front of Turtukai, and under Oltenitza; and though retaining also the island of Ramadan, he was obliged to concentrate his soldiers rather more, in the face of the ever-increasing numbers of the enemy.

MASSACRE AT SINOPE.

Selim Pacha was reported to have stormed Saffa, and to have won a battle at Gumri or Alexandropol, on the 13th. Five days later, Ali Pacha was beaten at Akhalrick by General Andronikoff. The terrible 30th of November arrived; six Russian ships of the line, with several smaller vessels of war, suddenly filled the aperture of the harbor of Sinope. There were in port thirteen Turkish sail, unprepared for action, and not expecting it. But had they even received warning, their whole fleet was no match for the six Russian first-rates, without counting the powerful frigates, and other craft, by which they were supported.

Admiral Nachimoff commanded the Russian fleet at Sinope, and Osman Pacha the Turkish naval detachment. This last was in a short time burnt and destroyed. Seven frigates, one steam-frigate, two schooners, and three transports were, all except two, reduced to a shapeless heap of floating timbers, blackened with gunpowder, stained with blood, and covered with mutilated human limbs, and the corpses of 5000 brave and unfortunate Turks, who, taken at fatal disadvantage, had fought to the last with unshaken heroism. In a few minutes after the action began, the outer vessels of the Turkish detachment were blown " into one long port-hole." The feeble battery of Sinope, over-head, brought no succor. When its untimely guns were at length fired, some of their shot fell among the friends whom they were destined to protect. Admiral Nachimoff's squadron sustained comparatively little injury, though some of the vessels showed how strenuous had been the unavailing resistance. A few Turks swam to land, and, clambering over the heights, escaped. Osman Pacha, before he could set fire to his own flag-ship, was taken prisoner, desperately wounded. The chief prizes which the Russians thought it still possible to remove, foundered while towed behind them in the Black Sea. Osman Pacha, whom they carried half-dead to Sebastopol, expired there within six weeks from his arrival. The news of this event electrified all Europe. When it was known at St. Petersburg, the Czar distributed naval decorations, ordered a solemn *Te Deum* in his churches, and published an exulting manifesto.

BATTLE AT CITATE.

Of the three Russian corps who were ordered to execute a simultaneous advance, the western was that which was ready to enter first into action. " The Pagans," stationed at Kalafat, were those whom it was the special business of this column " to annihilate." It was commanded by General Fishback, under whom acted Generals Engelhardt and Bellegarde ; while Prince Vassilitchkoff led the cavalry. Their whole corps consisted of but 22,000 men, of whom 7000 moved more slowly to act as a reserve, loitering near Karaul, on the left of the line of march. There was a neighboring column, only a few miles to the left, as strong as their own. Not being joined by the column on his left, nor by any of the idle garrisons to the rear of his right, and having disposed of seven thousand of his own men as a reserve, he found, when he arrived at Citate, that he had with him only fifteen thousand. Now, the Turks at Kalafat, whom he was going to attack, were entrenched ; and no soldiers defend entrenchments better. Moreover, their force was numerically equal to his own; and they were in immediate communication with Widdin, across the Danube, and probably from Widdin would be largely supported. He began to doubt whether he was strong enough for his undertaking; accordingly, he suddenly halted at Citate, and began to throw up entrenchments. In this deliberate manner he was occupied on the 4th and 5th of January, and the assault upon Kalafat was postponed to the 13th. Large reïnforcements were demanded; the inactive columns on his right were summoned to join him from Radowa, Orsova, and the Transylvanian frontier; and then a grand combined onslaught would drive the Turks into the Danube or, at the worst, compel them to cross it, and seek refuge in Widdin.

The Pachas, Achmet and Ismail, who commanded at Kalafat, were informed of all General Fishback's movements, and well knew that the intended attack of the 13th of January would be very serious. Resolute leaders of resolute troops, they yet looked forward with anxiety to an encounter with forty-five thousand Russians, exactly three times the number of their own force. They determined not to await the leisure of the Russians, or the ultimate danger of such an assault, but to sally forth at once, and to fight General Fishback at Citate on more equal terms. At day-break, therefore, on the 6th of January, (Christmas-day in Russia,) they marched from Kalafat. They had fifteen field-guns, ten thousand regular infantry, whom Ismail and Achmet Pachas themselves led in person; four thousand cavalry, commanded by Mustapha Bey; and a thousand Bashi-bozouks, under the colonelcy of the gallant and adventurous Skender-Beg, of historic name. The road to Citate led through Roman, Galantza, Funtina, and Moglovitz. To prevent any surprise of Kalafat in their absence, Ismail had ordered over 3000 of the garrison of Widdin, as a temporary guard. He took the further precaution of leaving about an equal number of troops at Moglovitz, on the road, in order to maintain his communications, and at need, protect his retreat, if he was beaten. By their help he would, at the worst, rally his force at Moglovitz. It was nine o'clock as the assailants entered Citate, in the streets of which were posted 3000 Russians and four guns. By a cross-street the Turks brought some of their own pieces to play upon the defenders, and then Achmet charged them in front with his infantry. After the first onset, the Turks disdained the restraints of rank and file—restraints not suited to street-fighting. The battle resembled a meeting of innumerable pairs of duelists; and for this species of close and personal action, the Turks had the advantage in

arms, in bodily vigor, and in courage. The Russian soldier
possessed now no weapon but his bayonet, and was cumbrously
accoutred. The agile Turk had the bayonet also, and if, in the
crush, or the turns of the dense and wild struggle, a blade and
its shorter thrust, or its cut, were more desirable, he instantly
had the ready and national weapon in his hands. From house
to house, storming every place out of the window of which a
shot had been fired, from crossing to crossing, in-doors and out
of doors, the assailants pressed back the Russians; and, in three
hours, had driven them into their entrenchments. Against
these the Turks forthwith brought up their field-pieces, which,
we believe, were as many as fifteen; and here they suffered
their principal loss that day. The cannonade was briskly sustained on both sides, and several bold assaults upon the works
were repulsed. In the midst of this conflict, the Russian reïnforcements from Karaul appeared. Had they arrived while
the Turks were entering the village, they would, perhaps, have
finished the action almost as soon as it had been begun. But
now the position taken by those who were beleaguering the
Russian trenches, and a part of whom faced about to meet the
new enemy, must be reached through some suburban orchards
and gardens; and as the reserves ventured upon these, they
were used as a natural entrenchment by the Turks; with this
difference, that the defenders were prompt to sally from them.
It was a curious position; the Turks were, at the same moment,
assailants in front, and on their defense in the rear; and, while
their original attack was repulsed, they were victorious over the
attack against themselves. The hedges, the walls, every tree,
every bush, served them as so many fortresses. Meantime
Ismail Pacha, when he had driven the Russians out of the
streets of Citate, had re-collected the force he had left at Moglovitz, and bethought him with what object. His circumstances were now altered. He no longer contended for safety;
he contended for victory; and he wanted to make victory as
complete as possible; he, therefore, sent for these reserves.
They arrived just as the Russian column from Karaul had
been entirely repulsed, with the loss of 250 men, and were dis-
persing in a disorderly flight, pursued by a sufficient body of
horse to prevent them from rallying. The Turkish ranks were
now re-formed; and, with new vigor and augmented numbers,
they returned to the assault of the entrenchments, out of which
the Russians had never been able successfully to sally. This
last effort was triumphant. The Turks burst through the defenses, and routed the disheartened troops behind them. About
2400 Russians were slain in the village, among the gardens, and
in the field-works. A proportionate number were wounded,

and, among these, two generals, who are stated to have been
Aurep and Tuinont. We believe that the Turks took not a
dozen prisoners, so ferocious was the engagement. They, on
their side, had 200 men killed, and 700 wounded. They captured four guns, and all the ammunition and stores in the entrenchments; besides, of course, obtaining the arms of the
slain. The village of Citate remained in their hands; and on
the next day, and the next again, they held it by force against
the vehement efforts of the enemy to retake it. They ranged
about the neighborhood as masters for a few days longer, and,
by several brilliant raids and forays, drove the Russians all the
way back to Krajova. This division of the invading army
now established its head-quarters at Slatina, a more distant and
more modest situation than they had recently intended to
select; and Europe thenceforward heard no more of the great
deed appointed for the 13th of January, namely, the storming
of Kalafat. All the Russian combinations were, in fact, ar-
rested and dislocated by this prompt, this brilliant rush·of the
Turks upon Citate—a dictate of genius. They saved their
post, in the only way in which it could have been saved, by
assailing that of the enemy. Such was the remarkable combat
of Citate; an action which proves that the Turks know how
to attack and to storm entrenchments, as well as how to defend
them.

After a short time, the Turks retired to their entrenchments
at Kalafat, where they had by this time mounted 250 heavy
guns. There, and at Widdin, immediately behind it, on the
other side of the Danube, they had increased their force to
25,000 men.

SUBSEQUENT OPERATIONS; AND THE PROCEEDINGS OF THE
EUROPEAN POWERS.

On the day before the battle of Citate, (the 5th,) Omer Pacha
had again alarmed the Russians at Giurgevo, where there was
a sharp skirmish, in which the Turks had rather the advantage.
They then re-crossed the river.

The Russians were incessantly reïnforced. Their siege-trains
had begun to arrive, and they had parked a hundred and twenty
large guns at Galatz, opposite the Bessarabian frontier, and a
hundred at Giurgevo.

In the Crimea, the Czar, prescient of coming dangers, had
ordered the erection of coast-batteries, which were now rising
in every favorable spot upon the cliffs. At such a time, and
after such occurrences, the order reached the English fleet *to
salute* the Russian ships. At Constantinople, news arrived that

Kars was taken; and that, on the other hand, all Abasia had pronounced for Schamyl, and that a great attack upon Shef-ketil had been repulsed. The Allied squadrons patrolled the Euxine; there was no danger of another Sinope; and Turkish reïnforcements, therefore, were dispatched by sea to Armenia. In the following March, the Sultan, it was announced, would join the army of Bulgaria. Less depressing intelligence was brought from Asia; the Turks were again the assailants, and were operating at Akhaltzik, and against Gumri.

On the 19th of January, Lieutenant-General Schilders, who, in 1829, had taken Silistria, and who was at the head of the engineering department in the Russian army, left Warsaw, in pursuance of a command of the Emperor Nicholas; and, on the 26th, reached Krajova, to assume the supreme direction of the siege operations of the ensuing campaign.

General Schilders made his first report before the end of January. It was not the loose and cursory conjecture of a hostile witness, but the official return of an experienced Rus-sian general to his sovereign, respecting the losses of a Russian army. He states that, in January, 1853, *thirty-five thousand Russian soldiers* had already perished in the Principalities. And yet, at that date, there had been only two months, or, at most, ten weeks of actual fighting. Nor was it, in truth, chiefly by the sword that this stupendous loss had been inflicted. Fatigue, hunger, want, cold, the marsh-fever, and the cholera, had swept away five sixths of these wretched victims to mili-tary ambition.

For about a month, dating from the battle of Citate, both armies on the Danube were occupied chiefly in preparations for fighting; and it is fortunate that the illness of Omer Pacha, which lasted three weeks, occurred after such exploits as secured his troops for a while from the chance of any serious molestation. But, further, he had made already his principal arrangements, and his part now was to wait.

It was on the 8th of February that, at length, Baron Brun-now, the ambassador of the Emperor Nicholas at the Court of St. James, took his reluctant and memorable departure from London. M. Kisselef, at the same moment, said the same sig-nificant farewell at Paris, to Napoleon the Third. Thus Eng-land and France, confederates for the first time in a great mili-tary struggle, were left face to face with the most important war which had occurred for many centuries, and, beyond com-parison, the most awful (in the means of destruction) ever known since the foundation of the world. Count Orloff's mis-sion having failed to preserve peace, war became the only road to its restoration; and in the hope that that war might be short,

all good men wished it should be vigorous. Still the Allies
were unwilling to make the rupture irrevocable. They framed
a statement of the terms on which they could yet treat with
Russia; and, having obtained the assent of Austria to the
principles of their proposal, sent it to St. Petersburg. They
then redoubled their preparations for the conflict. The Baltic
fleet was fitted out, and Sir Charles Napier selected for its
command. The French contributed their contingent to this
fleet; but, while in the Black Sea, they maintained a magnifi
cent naval force, and even a greater number of first-class ships
than the English, their proportion of the Baltic fleet was considerably smaller. Therefore, Admiral Parseval Deschênes
here gave precedence to Admiral Napier, just as Lord Raglan,
in the united army in the East, yielded the highest post to
the Maréchal de St. Arnaud, who brought a larger force into
the field. It was agreed that the expedition of the Western
Powers to Turkey should, in the first instance, consist of about
seventy-five thousand men, of whom the French should furnish
about fifty or forty-five thousand, and the English rather more
than half that number. But the Emperor Napoleon openly
announced, that, in case of necessity, he could spare, and would
send, a hundred thousand troops to that particular scene of
conflict; that he would maintain, in addition, a great army in
camp and ready for the march, on the northern frontier of
France; and that this host he would, if compelled, lead in person to a part of Europe where no operations were originally
contemplated, and where, he hoped, there would be no occasion
finally to act—a part of Europe where he should regret to
renew the memorable lessons of 1806 and 1807. Nor was this
all. Besides the splendid army which he would at once dispatch to Turkey; besides the mighty fleet which would act in
the East; besides the camp at Toulon, in the south of France,
and the military centres to be formed at Brest and Lorient, in
the north; besides the vast, effective, and independent army
which would be soon collected in the Pas de Calais; besides
the second, and necessarily smaller, fleet of twenty-five ships
of war, which were to support and share the Baltic expedition;
he determined further to send—what would be very much
needed in the latter seas, but what England could not sufficiently soon supply, or, indeed, well spare at all—a strong
body of land troops to operate in connection with the naval
force. On the 22d of the month, the first British detachment,
destined for the East, the Coldstream and Grenadier Guards,
left London by railway, for Southampton, and there embarked,
amidst the acclamations of an immense multitude, who had
flocked from neighboring and even from distant counties, to

bid good speed to their defenders. After this date regiment followed regiment in quick succession. The cavalry went last. All this time the French were also in full activity. Great forces of cavalry and infantry and field-guns were directed toward the south; and, passing through Lyons and Grenoble, reached the sea-ports of the Mediterranean There a sufficient fleet was fast assembling for their transport; and they were rapidly embarked at Marseilles and Toulon. The heavier artillery required for siege operations was not so soon prepared.

DESULTORY CONFLICT ON THE DANUBE.

Such were the occurrences in the West, while the long suffering world awaited the answer of Nicholas to the last offers of the Western powers, sent through the hands of Austria. It was wisely agreed to prepare for war, though it was modestly determined to defer declaring it until the superb autocrat should, by his next message, in whatever sense, deliver the nations from further uncertainty. The news that the Russian envoys had quitted London and Paris reached Constantinople in about twelve days, (that is, on the 20th of February, 1854,) and excited the wildest joy. The delight of the Osmanlis overcame their habitual gravity. The ancient capital of the East broke into a frenzy of exultation. Intelligence of the great event was dispatched to the army of the Danube; but, before the messengers arrived, that army already knew it from the wild Syrian recruits and the Bashi-bozouks of Asia, who tried the mettle of their Arabian coursers in a race against the government couriers, which should be the first to report the awful and final rupture between the Giaours of the East and the Giaours of the West. Hostilities had been actively resumed. After their late repulses and humiliations at Matchin, at Giurgevo, and at Citate, the Russians, as though retreat were their next business, began to fortify Fokshani, a place far to the rear, seated at the foot of the Carpathians, and about half-way between Bucharest, the chief town of Wallachia, and Jassy, the distant capital of Moldavia. In Fokshani, they laid up large military stores; and then, finding that there was no advance of the Turks, and that their own reinforcements were constantly, if slowly, arriving, they resumed the offensive. About the 13th of February, they collected a considerable strength against Giurgevo, and attacked it, with much loss indeed; but in this sense, with such success, that the Turks, after two or three days' resistance, evacuated the place in per fect order, and took boat to Rustchuk. This was on the 19th of February. The enemy immediately seized the town. Guns were then directed against Rustchuk. Day and night the Russians sought, by force and by guile, to cross at that point. The resistance was desperate. On the 24th of February, the Russians were still on their defense, and rather timidly commanded, in front of Kalafat, a town which, according to their own plans, ought to have been stormed on the 13th of the previous month.

March opened with a change. The Russians had completed their dilatory preparations; and they now had, for attack, all the means which they were likely to have. Still, on the very eve of their grand and irresistible advance into Bulgaria, Wallachia was the scene of another warning blow. The Turkish column at Rahova crossed the Danube on the 4th of March, and drove back the Russian outposts of Kalarasch with perfect success, and no small slaughter. Then, while the whole force of the enemy was assembling to punish this inroad, the Turks returned in safety to Rahova. On the 5th of March, martial law was proclaimed through all the Russias, and in Poland; and orders came to the Russian generals in the Principalities to press the war more vigorously. On the 11th of the same month, there was a violent struggle around Kalafat; but the Turks remained masters of the place. It was their last stronghold on the northern bank of the Danube. But they continued to keep the south bank, as well as some islands in the stream. Prince Gortchakoff attacked it on the 15th of March, and lost 2000 men in the attack; at the same time, he failed to take the island. It would have been a victory of very uncertain value; but it was a bloody defeat instead. About this time, between the 12th and 16th, two frigates, one English and one French, were dispatched from Beicos Bay to open by force the Sulineh Mouth (which is the middle mouth) of the Danube.

MEASURES TAKEN BY ENGLAND AND FRANCE.

On the 12th of March, 1854, the Emperor Nicholas vouchsafed to the terms proposed by the Western powers, this memorable reply: *"That those terms required not five minutes' consideration."* He, in fact, rejected them with contempt; and announced to his own ministers and great officers that, before he submitted to such conditions, he would sacrifice his last soldier, and spend his last rouble. While this haughty decision, the general purport of which the electric-wires sent flashing at once through all Europe, was borne to London and Paris by the over-land couriers, the French and English troops began, though very gradually, to muster in force at Gallipoli. It was no considerable time before they had assembled on the little peninsula to the west of the Dardanelles about 14,000 French and about 7000 English troops. The French had a shorter voyage to make ; but then they had more soldiers, more materials of war, and more provisions to transport. They arrived the first.

It was on the 11th of March that the Baltic fleet, under Sir Charles Napier, sailed from Spithead ; a noble fleet of sixteen war-steamers, of which eight were line-of-battle, two being three-deckers, and three carrying admiral's flags. Another great division was preparing to follow.

On the 27th of March, the formal rupture between Turkey and Greece occurred. The Greek envoy, General Metaxes, receiving, on that day, his passports at Constantinople. The Sultan had sent whatever troops he could spare to the frontier of Thessaly, under Achmet Pacha, to oppose the inroads of the Greeks, who were endeavoring to organize a general insurrection of their co-religionists all over the Turkish Empire ; the *foreign* Greeks thus abetting against the Divan its Greek *subjects*, to the profit of Russia.

FINANCIAL CONDITION OF RUSSIA.

Russia had been for a considerable time husbanding her resources and preparing her means for some unusual exertion. In 1853, she had freed herself from the annual interest of certain old loans, by paying up the principal. She then withdrew the sums placed in the public stock of France and England ; issued treasury bills to meet the current expenses ; and prohibited the export of the precious metals from her own territory. The ordinary revenue of Russia would, perhaps, be £32,000,000 ; but, allowing for the inevitable abatement caused by war in the proceeds of the customs and excise, it can scarcely amount to £24,000,000 at present; while the expenditure is enormously and concurrently increased. No doubt the sums obtained just after the Hungarian war, under the plea of finishing the Moscow railway, were not yet exhausted when this vast conflict commenced. But the stress of it is evident, from the financial expedients to which the Czar presently resorted. He appropriated at once five millions sterling of the bullion which forms the basis of the paper money ; and, at the same time, he issued four millions sterling of treasury bills. He also invited loans and *accepted gifts* (praising the patriotism of the latter) from various public funds, from the clergy, and from the charitable trusts of the empire ; and when "the Dutch loan" failed, he levied a forced loan, amounting to eight millions sterling, from his own subjects indiscriminately, and called it a voluntary contribution. By these means he realized, in a year and a half, nearly thirty millions sterling.

ACTIVE ENTRANCE OF ENGLAND AND FRANCE INTO THE WAR.

The English and French expeditionary forces having landed in Turkey, and as it were set themselves down within reach of the enemy, with the exception of one vigorous blow struck by the fleet, had little to do with the war that was waging between Turkey and Russia, until the battles of the Crimea. In short, although dispatched in spring, they were not destined to engage the foe till autumn.

BOMBARDMENT OF ODESSA.

Before any thing was attempted against Odessa, some shots from the batteries had been aimed at an English flag of truce, (borne by the Fury.) Next day, the 23d, twelve war-steamers of both nations were detached from the fleet, and sent within range of shot; the order being to spare the town, if possible, but to destroy the batteries, the magazines, and the vessels in the harbor. The order was scrupulously obeyed in the first particular, and executed with brilliant effect in the second. The detachment of steamers approached, accompanied by rocket-boats; these ventured further in, being a smaller mark for the land artillery, which dared not besides waste its fire *short* of the covering frigates and steamers. The boats having taken their station, the attacking detachment began a most singular and beautiful movement in file, tracking one the other's wake with exquisite precision, along an ever-repeated circle; and as each vessel touched those points of her orbit which were nearest to the Russian batteries, she delivered her broadside, passing onwards, and made way for her successors in the revolving chain, until her own turn should come again. The ever-returning evolution of these graceful ministers of a memorable act of vengeance seemed, in the distance, to be performing a sort of wild waltz together, as they laid low the fortifications of the proud Russian seaport. In the midst of the action, one of the French steamers, struck by a red-hot shot through the hull, caught fire, and returned for a brief space to the fleet, to have assistance in extinguishing the flames. This was very soon effected; and the wounded falcon hastened to take again her destructive place in what may be said to have resembled also the wheeling flight of some beautiful birds of prey, swooping at intervals, each in its turn, upon the quarry. The defence from the she y was at first very spirited, and the Russians are described as having stood well to their guns; but in range these were inferior to the artillery of the ships, and, by sensible degrees, the fire of the garrison became slower. At length two great powder-magazines of the Russians blew up in quick succession, while most of the batteries were dismounted, the forts knocked to pieces, and the ruins strewn with the bodies of the artillerymen. When the defenses were shattered into a shapeless ruin, and the resistance of the Russians had evidently ceased in despair, and when thirteen of the enemy's ships, laden with munitions of war, had been captured, the Allied detachment drew slowly off, and rejoined the fleets. Their comrades who had, from the yards of the distant men-of-war, witnessed the action, descended now and welcomed them with shouts that might have been heard on shore. The officers engaged have estimated the number of the enemy killed at about eight hundred or a thousand soldiers. The Allies had ten sailors wounded and five killed. Such was the bombardment of Odessa, on the 23d of March.

Shortly afterwards, the loss of the Tiger (16 guns) occurred. She grounded at the Campagna Costazzi, near Odessa, in such a position that she could not use her batteries against the field artillery on shore. After a short fight she surrendered, and her crew (250) were all made prisoners, and carried to Odessa, where they were well treated.

PASSAGE OF THE DANUBE BY LUDERS AND GORTCHAKOFF.

It was about this epoch that Prince Dolgorouki, sent to Teheran to involve Persia in the Czar's quarrel, struck the Seds Azim, or Prince Minister of the Shah, with a cane, to punish his reluctance. The most imperative instructions had now come from St. Petersburg to the Russian generals in the Principalities, to effect some great exploit, at *whatever cost.*

Lüders had crossed the Danube at Galutz. He was in force, having 24½ battalions, 8 squadrons, 6 sotnias, and 64 guns. Gortchakoff, learning the fact of the passage so far down the river to the rear of his own left, determined to abandon for the present his disheartening operation against Turtukai and Rustchuk, and to fly to the support of Lüders; thus imparting, he hoped, a decisive character to the advance of that enterprising general. By a retrograde circuit, he passed even beyond the rear of Lüders' left flank, and threw himself across the river a little above Tultscha, with 14 battalions, 16 squadrons, 6 sotnias, and 44 guns. He brought with him more cavalry than Lüders, though a smaller general force ; and their united columns amounted to nearly 50,000 men. The reader is aware

that Omer Pacha had decided not to dispute possession of the
Upper Dobrudscha; and it is, therefore, nearly incomprehen
sible, though stated in all the contemporary accounts of these
operations, that Prince Gortchakoff should have there taken
eleven guns and 150 prisoners. This event took place about
the 23d of March, the day of the bombardment of Odessa.

On the same 23d of March, the Danube was forced by the
Commander-in-Chief of the Russian army of occupation ; the
fortifications of Odessa were laid in ashes, and the Governments of England and France agreed that they would at last
publish in all form their acceptance of the Russian challenge.

The divisions which had crossed the Danube continued their
advance, taking Babadagh on the sea, and Hirsova on the
river. All the Upper Dobrudscha, except Tultscha, was now
occupied by the invaders ; and by April the 3d their Cossacks
patrolled as far as Kustendjeh, which the Turks kept, and
which was their grasp upon the sea, at the east of Trajan's
Wall. On the north shore of the Danube, the Turks retained
nothing except Kalafat, two hundred miles to the west.

The Russians, having seized Hirsova, spent some time in
preparing for a great attempt to pass Trajan's Wall; but,
though their Cossacks scoured the country down to the very
ramparts of Kustendjeh, they found that they had selected a
most difficult part of the Turkish line to force ; and at Czerna
voda, on the 25th of April, more than five weeks after General
Lüders crossed the Danube, at Galatz, and nearly a month
after the second Russian column had followed near Tultscha
to his support, their united divisions were taught a severe
lesson. The Turks, at that place—which is some five miles to
the south of Trajan's Wall—once more checked the Russian
advance ; and, in a sharp action, repulsed the enemy with
considerable loss. The avenues by which the Russians endeavored to penetrate from the Dobrudscha were defended for
about seven weeks; during which time, the invaders—being
locked up amid the marshes of the worst district of the whole
Turkish territory in Europe—suffered incomparably more
from ague, fever, cholera, and privations, than they suffered in
the field. It must not be supposed that this advance along
the coast against Omer Pacha's right wing was an isolated
movement. On the contrary, it was part of a very large combination, which Marshal Paskiewitch, Prince of Erivan, was,
on the 8th of April, summoned from Poland to superintend in
person, and in which the famous General of Engineers, Schilders, was to take an eminent part. General Lüders' instructions
were to press forward at whatever cost, *and to interpose between
Varna and Silistria.*

SIEGE OF SILISTRIA.

So early as the 14th, great batteries had been erected on the
north bank of the Danube, opposite Silistria; and the town was
bombarded from morning till night; and the Russians now began to show themselves in force on both banks of the Danube,
near and around that fatal fortress. On the 28th of April, the
Russians, being completely established on the south bank, attacked the outworks of Silistria. On the same day, one hundred miles to the west, at Nicopolis, Sali Pacha had a battle with
the Russians, who had neglected all the country lying to their
right, because they were endeavoring to envelop Silistria in
every direction, and they thought they had excluded the western or left wing of the Turkish army from the real business
then in hand. Sali Pacha defeated the enemy, killing nearly
2000 of them. In conformity with their usual strategy, straggling and indecisive, the Russians, at the same time they were
thus endeavoring to force the Danube from Turna, tried also to
exhibit themselves in apparent strength at Radowan, nearly
sixty miles to the right. Suleiman Bey, whose rank was that
of a colonel, stormed Radowan, and had the glory of beating
the invaders with almost as much slaughter in this place as
Sali Pacha had inflicted on them at Nicopolis and Turna. But
these reverses of the Russian right might have been expected,
when they were weakening it in order to strengthen the divisions destined by them to take Silistria. The assault on the
outworks was so hotly received, that full three weeks elapsed
before General Schilders had completed the investment. On
the adverse shore he piled up batteries of heavy guns, which
maintained a continual bombardment; and with those guns he
left his portable hospitals (or ambulances) and his reserves.
The forces which he transported over the Danube to form the
actual leaguer, were not less than 53,000 men, while the garrison mustered 8000 only. His artillery, which was numerous
and heavy, has been variously computed. Probably the most
effective batteries were those which he directed against the
south-west fronts; and here, indeed, the fire was severe and
terrible. On this side the ground rises in a series of platforms,
which could not be surrendered to the enemy with safety to the
town. They were occupied, therefore, by outworks which were
all-important· for, on the day when they were taken, Silistria
was virtually taken. The outworks were called respectively Arab
Tabia and Illanli. They were of earth. The Turkish artillery
protecting them was repeatedly silenced; the walls behind them
were repeatedly breached; but, burrowing in the cavities of that
redoubt, the indomitable defenders waited only till the thunder

of the guns had ceased, and till the tramp of the storming
columns made the ground about to tremble, when they appeared
swarming out of the bowels of the earth, and—dagger in hand,
rather than sword in hand—flung themselves upon the assailants. The Russians, in these great assaults—which, as the siege
progressed, were conducted in larger and larger force, committed one of the most incredible military blunders on record.
They advanced in heavy costume, and even with their knapsacks
on their shoulders. They met those, therefore, who soon neutralized and reversed the effects of General Schilder's artillery.
The slaughter on these occasions, (and from May the 11th to
June the 29th they were numerous,) is hardly to be believed.
Always bearing in mind this species of inter-act, we may
describe in one sentence nearly a month's operations before
Silistria: to wit, it was alternately bombarded and assaulted.
Armed only with their temperance and their fanaticism, the small
Turkish garrison flinched not for a moment. As the earth-
works were damaged, it was necessary to repair them; and as
the Russians mined, (a last resource,) it was indispensable to
countermine. Enormous hardships and evident risks were
to be encountered in these duties. For the most part, the
patient Osmandi displayed the spirit of a true soldier. As he
smoked, or rather sucked, a pipe in which there was no longer
any tobacco, (the facts have been witnessed,) he lay at the bottom of a trench watching with envy, the better-supplied comrade whose tarbooch rose above the level of the margin—
because that comrade worked with the spade, and was therefore on his legs. A cannon-ball sweeps away the red cap and
the head within it. The incumbent spectator arises, saying
that "Allah is great!" He takes the spade from the yet warm
hand, disengages the nargilly from the clenched teeth, and fills
the brief vacancy—his own tarbooch now surmounting the
clay embankment. Soon, the place is again vacant, and a suc-
cessor equally intrepid and equally serene, continues the excavation; and in ten minutes, it has thus taken, as it were, three
generations of valiant Osmanlis to fortify one soldier's post in
a bombarded intrenchment, and, while doing so, to smoke one
pipeful of Latakia tobacco.

On the 11th of May, Silistria itself was assaulted, the assailants were beaten and lost more than 2000 men. Meanwhile
the works were incessantly advanced. On the 21st of May,
another general assault was repulsed. On the 26th of May,
the left wing, being now an isolated division of Omer Pacha's
force, felt its way eastward to Turna, Semnitra, and Giurgevo,
in all which places it found and severely defeated the enemy
On the 29th of May, a very fatal day to choose for a contest

with the Mussulmans, (it being the anniversary of the Turkish conquest of Constantinople,) Prince Gortchakoff and General Schilders ordered a combined assault upon the south and west of Silistria. Thirty thousand were used in the attack, and the loss was near five thousand. Two days after the assault, the outflanking left wing of the Ottoman army had pushed to Slatina, and there had won another victory; and, indeed, on the previous day, the day immediately following the great assault upon Silistria, they had fought a battle at Karakal, had taken six field-pieces and had slain three thousand Russians. On the 4th of June, Omer Pacha put 30,000 men in action, and ordered them to do something for Silistria. On that same day he commanded his garrison at Rustchuk to try their fortune against the Russian works on the Island of Mokan; and the works were completely destroyed. A detachment of the column dispatched to the relief of Silistria, entered it on the 5th, partly stealing, partly breaking through the Russian lines. Mehemet Pacha led this reïnforcement. Some of the succoring force were repulsed and shut out; but they remained near, watching for the next sally. It took place exactly three days afterward, on the 8th of June. It was by night; and then, over a thousand Russian corpses, about a thousand more of the Turkish troops entered Silistria. On the 13th, a still more tremendous sortie was effected. Three Russian mines were sprung during the conflict, all their works were destroyed, and the carnage was enormous. At last an end was put to this desolating enterprise. A grand assault was ordered for the 28th of June. The Russian soldiers had now been eleven months in the provinces of Turkey, and had never yet seen a Turk's back. They had known nothing but disaster, unvaried even by an episode of success; and when ordered on the 28th to the breaches, stood doggedly in their ranks. Prince Gortschakoff, in alarm, adjourned the attack until the next day. Next day came. Silistria "must be taken." Repulsed twice from the defense, they hesitated to obey when once more ordered to advance. Upon this, Count Orloff, General Schilders, General Gortchakoff, and General Lüders placed themselves at the head of the men, crying to these to follow, while Prince Paskiewitch rode up to the spot and addressed them partly with reproaches and partly with encouragements. The assault was unsuccessfully renewed, and a murderous carnage took place. General Schilders, not again destined to take a fortress, the capture of which twenty-five years before had been the commencement of his reputation, was struck by a cannon-ball, which carried off his thighs. General Lüders had his jaw struck away; Count Orloff was killed; General Gortchakoff was severely, and Prince Paskiewitch desperately, wounded. The Turks had not only repelled the assault, but had pursued the assailants up to their very batteries. Some of the relieving column outside had meanwhile alarmed and disordered the Russians in the rear. This practically terminated the siege; for the garrison was again succored during the confusion of the engagement, and the Russian works were so damaged, that they would have all to be recommenced. Mussa Pacha, struck by a spent ball, died of the hurt in a few hours. Such was this memorable siege of Silistria, which might be compared with that of Saragossa for the bravery of the defense. It was estimated that, from first to last, the Russians lost, under or near the walls of Silistria, 30,000 men.

They now re-crossed the river, so thoroughly demoralized, that, had there been a sufficient force to pursue them, they must have either laid down their arms or been annihilated. They retreated from every point towards Fokshani and Birlat, evacuating not only Lesser but Greater Wallachia. Skender Beg, and some of the other Turkish chiefs who commanded in the south-west of the Principalities, pursued the enemy at leisure beyond the Aluta. It was only in the Upper Dobrudscha that the Czar now held any portion of the further bank of the Danube.

The Allies had meantime assembled, to the number of about 50,000, in Varna and the neighboring camps; and, as the campaign was finished upon the Danube, they began to meditate some other expedition; and, after many councils of war, it was secretly decided to invade the Crimea, and to attack Sebastopol. Siege-trains were ordered from England and France, transports were prepared, and every thing gradually provided. But the cholera attacked both the armies and the fleets, which for two months lay prostrate under this dreadful scourge. It cost the English at least 700 men; the French, including those who perished in the fatal excursion through the marshes of the Dobrudscha, must have lost *more than* 4000. It was in July that the greatest mortality occurred; and the corps which suffered most was that of Generals Canrobert and Espinasse, at the bivouac of Kavarlik, near Kustendjeh—the Zouaves being more than decimated. When Khan Mirza, on the 23d July, allowed himself to be surprised at Karassu, by the retiring Russians, General Youssouf took his fine corps forward; and in that one long march 1500 dropped down and died, without counting the regular daily losses. The Austrians, who had seemed constantly on the point of joining the Allies, but without ever really joining them, and who were expected to aid the Turks, but never did, now began to muster in large numbers along the confines of Transylvania. During the next month the discomfited columns of the Czar were all behind the Sereth, and Prince Gortchakoff had been borne in litters to Jassy. General Dannenberg assumed the chief command of the routed forces. Numerous vacancies had rendered his promotion rapid; and Prince Dolgorouki, who had returned from Persia, was dispatched by Nicholas from St. Petersburg to investigate the cause of so many and such huge calamities. On the 22d of August, Omer Pacha, seated in an open carriage, with Can-tacuzene, (a name recalling old Byzantine recollections,) made his triumphal entry into Bucharest. He published a concilia-tory proclamation, and the Sultan decreed an amnesty for all treasons committed during a time of terror and military coërcion. In the beginning of the following month, the Rus-sian head-quarters were removed from Jassy, and withdrawn behind the Pruth. The expulsion of the invaders was com-plete, the campaign was finished, and then, and not till then, Count Coronini and his Austrians entered the Principalities, "*to protect,*" they said, a territory which had been effectually protected by its own lawful owners, and which these obliging strangers had, in no one particular, assisted in defending.

Such was the glorious Danubian campaign, from its com-mencement to its close.

OPERATIONS IN THE BALTIC.

Meantime, tne Allied fleets had been active in the Baltic, the French division having passed through the Channel to join Admiral Napier so early as the 23d of April. It consisted of twenty-five sail, nine being ships of the line, and, with the English squadrons, made the whole a fleet of about sixty-seven vessels of war. The navigation of the northern waters was not universally practicable till the middle or end of May; and, even when it was, not much was effected, beyond the blockade of the Russian navy, which shrank behind granite fortresses; and the reconnoissance and study of the various maritime strongholds of the Czar along those seas. On the 20th, a gallant exploit was performed at Hango, two Russian ships being cut out from under the very guns. On the 30th, Brahestadt was bombarded; and the next day Uleaborg was destroyed. Prizes of not much importance continued to be sent home. But on the 20th of next month a check was sustained in attempting to land at Gamba Karleby, where the Allies were repulsed, with the loss of fifty-four men, killed or miss-ing. Shortly afterward the greater part of the fleet—fifty-one sail, in fact- —were assembled in Baro Sound; and the French and English Admirals pressed their respect ve governments to send them a military force. This was made ready with great energy by the Emperor Napoleon; and 25,000 French troops, under the command of Baraguay d'Hilliers, sailed in the beginning of August, on board English ships, for the Isles of Aland, which lie across the mouth of the Gulf of Bothnia, half-way between Stockholm and Wirmo, in Finland. The soldiers were landed in company with a body of our marines, and under the protection of the united fleets. The nature of the soil obliged them to use earth-bags for their batteries; and in one battery alone there were 15,000 such bags. The conoidal rifle-balls of the French sharp-shooters soon drove the Russian artillerymen from their casemates, while the walls were breached both by sea and land. The Leopard threw one hundred and twenty-pound shot from a distance of 2500 yards; and it was afterward ascertained that thirty-pound or forty-pound shot will, at a distance of 500 yards, breach granite works. The roof of the principal fort was of iron, and underneath the roof there were six feet deep of sand, then granite. This roof was torn to pieces in a few hours. On the 15th of August, General Bodisco, having lost his two subsidiary forts, surrendered, with two thousand prisoners, who were sent at once to England and to France. The forts were then destroyed; and such was the new and sudden mistrust which the Russians conceived of their boasted defenses, that they themselves blew up, a few days afterward, the fortifications of Hango.

BATTLES OF THE CRIMEA.

THERE is a terrible romance in War. We may deprecate it as the worst of evils, but there is an indescribable fascination in its bloody records. Of this we have striking evidence in the eagerness with which every account of the progress of the war now raging in the Crimea, between the Allies on one side and Russia on the other, is sought after and read. The details of the crimson fields of the ALMA, BALAKLAVA, and last and bloodiest of all, INKERMANN, are pored over with the most absorbing interest. To satisfy this natural curiosity, we present a condensed and graphic history of those fiercely contested battles, with as many of their wild, romantic, and thrilling incidents as can be obtained from the best sources of information, all of the accounts being from eye-witnesses of, and participators in, the terrible scenes described.

INVASION OF THE CRIMEA.

BRIEF HISTORY OF THE CRIMEA.

THE Crimea is a large peninsula lying in the northern portion of the Black Sea, the larger portion being north of the parallel of 45°, and connected with continental Russia by a narrow neck of land only a few miles in width. It is the southernmost province of Russia, about the size of the State of Massachusetts, and its population, though considerable in the aggregate, sparsely scattered over the country. Its valleys are rich and fruitful; its climate favorable for a great variety of products; and under a good system of cultivation and a good government would be one of the finest countries in the world.

The Crimea was invaded and conquered by the Tartars in 1226, except some important points on the southern coast which were held by the Genoese, who had founded several towns and carried on an extensive commerce. In 1473, the Turks drove the Genoese out of the Crimea, and the Tartars became the vassals of the Porte. In 1771, Russia, which had long coveted this beautiful country, interfered with a large army, to place a Tartar prince on the throne, drove out the Turks, and in 1783 the Russian dominion was fully established.

CONCENTRATION OF THE ALLIED TROOPS.

The troops of the Allies, about 50,000 in all, which had been lying in a state of inactivity, near Constantinople, during the summer, were concentrated at Varna, a port of Bulgaria, on the eastern shore of the Black Sea, in the latter part of August. They had suffered severely from disease, and the cholera was especially fatal. Great joy was therefore diffused throughout the combined army when it was announced that the expedition to the Crimea had been determined upon. Any thing was preferable to remaining where they were; and in their imagination every fresh battle-field was to be the theatre of new victories. To invade the Crimea was a holiday pastime; to take Sebastopol, the work of a single daring, heart-stirring assault.

THE EMBARKATION AND VOYAGE.

On the 4th of September, the British transports, in tow of steamers, set sail from Varna to join the French and Turkish fleets at Baltsckik Bay, the place of general rendezvous, whence the whole armada, numbering more than a hundred vessels, exclusive of the regular war-ships, proceeded northeast to the coast of the Crimea. The French numbered 25,000, the English the same, and there was a picked corps of about 8000 Turks, exclusive of sailors and marines, thousands of whom participated in the siege of Sebastopol. Though the distance is not much above a hundred miles, the combined fleet did not reach Eupatoria, the landing point determined upon, until the 14th. Eupatoria is a town of 8000 inhabitants, situated on a low promontory, about forty miles from Sebastopol, with a low, flat country in the distance. Towards noon the ships of the expedition closed in with the shore, and a grander sight, says an eye-witness, was never seen at sea. A line of lights extended along the whole coast, and when, as signal, the Banshee lighted a blue-light, the effect was magnificent. The bulwarks of Old England, surrounded by the imposing number of transports, rose faintly in the distance ; whilst, in our immediate vicinity, a formidable row of line-of-battle ships, including the flag-ship Britanuia, stood out boldly, in the majesty of their proportions, the largest spar and the tiniest rope emerging from the darkness of night. The blue-light once extinguished, and all sank into the shade; and who would have guessed, amidst the surrounding tranquillity, that here was assembled the most imposing armada that ever cleft the seas, bearing the strength, the pride, and the hopes of three empires?

A flag of truce was sent off from the Allied generals and the garrison invited to lay down their arms. The head of the place, a sort of civil governor or mayor, replied that there was no garrison and consequently no arms to lay down, but that the Allies would be allowed to occupy the place without molestation from the inhabitants, who trusted in turn to receive good treatment. The governor then delivered up his official sword with a low and formal bow, the officer returned with the trophy, and preparations were made to occupy the place.

THE LANDING.

On the 14th, the English and French infantry were landed, and so admirable had been the arrangements, that the work was accomplished with great expedition and without serious accident of any kind. A boat-load of sixteen Frenchmen were the first to land, who immediately planted a flag-staff, surmounted with the tri-color, on a neighboring eminence, and saluted it with a discharge of fire-arms. Early on the following day preparations were made to land the cavalry and artillery. The process of disembarkation was effected in barges in tow of man-of-war boats, which, on approaching the shore, dropped anchor and allowed themselves to be washed forward by the surf. The anchor's rope was but very gradually let out, in order for the barge to approach stern forward. At the moment she was about to strike, a dozen sailors—chiefly, if not all, crews of merchantmen—dashed into the water, and seizing her ropes, dragged her high up on the beach, with all the strange cries and noisy energy peculiar to sailors on shore. A flap hanging on to the stern then formed a platform, over which the cannon landed, and where the horses were coaxed to pass. To land the latter was rather a difficult task; for the poor animals, notwithstanding their long imprisonment on board ship, one and all declined to walk the plank, although *terra firma* was the reward. By dint of pushing and pulling, the sailors managed to land the horses, and this part of the programme seemed to afford them immense delight. It certainly enabled them to display that equestrian science and profound knowledge

of horse-flesh which, as every body knows, is characteristic of
the naval profession.   If now and then a horse would roll
off the plank over into the water, it was unfortunate; but this
certainly did not occur more than three times out of six.   The
only result was a ducking for man and horse, which did neither
any harm.   The horse would have a comfortable roll on the
dry sand, and join his place in the rank.   But if, as sometimes
would occur, a stiff artilleryman, with a straggling moustache,
missed his footing, and fell plump into the water, then matters
became tragic.   The surrounding sailors and his very comrades
would burst out into that delicate and pleasant laugh peculiar
to Englishmen ; whilst the sympathizing crowd on the beach,
composed of English, French, and native Tartars, would re-
echo the jeer, and welcome the poor wight to Russian ground.
If the sea presented a lively scene, it was certainly surpassed
by the land.   Here the small breadth of space was crowded
by a busy throng.   Artillerymen collecting their horses, officers
cantering up and down, inspecting the landing, foot soldiers
going to fetch water—all were mixed up with a miscellaneous
crowd of lookers-on.   Now a troop of horses would pass to
collect forage, or a body of native Algerians return from a
successful *razzia* of cattle and odd-looking country cars.   The
beach was lined with bathers, mixed up in a delicious equality,
the dashing hussar breasting the same wave as the mild looking
man of the line, or a small drummer-boy.   Then on shore were
groups of French soldiers calmly looking at the scene, and
ejaculating a good-humored *sacré* when jostled by a too energetic sailor.   Some of the soldiers were endeavoring to open a
conversation with the natives, whom this unexpected invasion
had surprised.   Although the conversations in themselves
were limited, they were successful in making both parties
laugh and shake hands.   The native Tartar—of course, not
one Russian, the dominant race, dare show himself—has much
resemblance with the Turk.   His religion, language, and
mental development are the same ; his costume alone is different.   The Russians have done their utmost to transform him
into a Russian peasant.   The turban and flowing garment have
been proscribed in favor of the brimless lamb-skin hat and
shapeless gown, but through this disguise the Tartar face is
recognizable.   The arrival of the Allies has given them much
satisfaction, which they openly express.   One man came from his
village to say that two Russian families of great wealth were
preparing to leave, and demanded a few soldiers to be sent to
arrest them.   The soldiers and sailors were on the best of terms
with them, as I have already observed.   Probably from igno-
rance of their family names, and fearful that this trifling cir-

cumstance might interrupt their cordiality, the inhabitants have been indiscriminately christened by the soldiers by the name of Joey. Consequently, if a slow, native Tartar lies in danger of being run over by a hasty dragoon, he is requested to " Look out for your eye, Joey ;" and should another hesitate to take British coin in payment for an unripe melon, he meets the reproach of " You are an ass, Joey." Joey Tartar has therefore become as historical a character as Jonny Frenchman or John Turk.

For two days after the landing the rain fell incessantly, and as neither officers nor troops were yet provided with tents or other means of shelter, their state of discomfort may be imagined. Many who had been accustomed only to the genteelest lodging were thankful for a blanket, and found themselves in a puddle of water on awaking in the morning. Sir George Brown slept the first night under a bullock-wagon, which, under the circumstances, might be considered a rather aristocratic bed-chamber.

MARCH TO THE ALMA.

Early on the morning of the 19th September, 30,000 sleepers were woke to life by the beating of the reveille, and made hasty preparation to obey the order for the march for the Alma. The French occupied the right, the English the left, and 7000 Turkish infantry marched along the sea-side. The combined forces extended seven or eight miles. The right wing they covered by the fleet, which moved in magnificent order, darkening the air with dense columns of smoke, and within range of the Russians for two miles inland.

The troops presented a splendid appearance. The effect of these grand masses of soldiery, descending the ridges of the hills rank after rank, with the sun playing over forests of glittering steel, can never be forgotten by those who witnessed it. Onward the torrent of war swept ; wave after wave, huge stately billows of armed men, while the rumble of artillery and tramp of cavalry accompanied their progress. At last, the smoke of burning villages and farm-houses announced that the enemy in front were aware of our march. It was a sad sight to see the white walls of the houses blackened with smoke, the flames ascending through the roofs of peaceful homesteads, and the ruined outlines of deserted hamlets. Many sick men fell out, and were carried to the rear. It was a painful sight; a sad contrast to the magnificent appearance of the army in front, to behold litter after litter borne past to the rear, with the poor sufferers who had dropped from illness and fatigue.

Presently, from the top of a hill, a wide plain was visible, beyond which rose a ridge, darkened here and there by masses, which the practised eye recognized as cavalry. It was the first sight of the enemy. On the left of the plain, up in a recess formed by the inward sweep of the two ridges, lay a large village in flames; right before the advancing army was a neat white house unburned, though the out-houses and farm-yard were burning. This was the imperial post-house of Bouljanak, just twenty miles from Sebastopol.

The Cossacks hovered on the outskirts of the Allies, and the skirmishers were often compelled to face about to repel their attacks. Meantime, they had advanced within range of the enemy's guns, whose shots ploughed up the English cavalry. After receiving some thirty rounds, the English returned the fire of the Russians, who were soon compelled to disperse in broken lines. The French, meantime, surprised a body of Russian cavalry with a round from a battery of nine-pounders, and scattered them in all directions. Four men and six horses were lost on the side of the Allies in these skirmishes. Night was approaching, and the combined armies bivouacked on the left bank of the Bouljanak, a small stream not far from the Alma, the lines of the Allies extending for several miles. On the heights of the Alma slumbered the main body of the Russians, numbering some 45,000 men. Did the opposing hosts dream of the fierce combat of the morrow?

THE BATTLE OF THE ALMA.

Prince Menchikoff had well chosen his position. A remarkable ridge of mountain, varying in height from 500 to 700 feet, runs along the course of the Alma on the left or south side, with the course of the stream, and assuming the form of cliffs when close to the sea. This ridge is marked all along its course by deep gullies, which run toward the river at various angles, and serve no doubt to carry off the floods produced by the rains and the melting of the winter-snows on the hills and table-lands above. At the top of the ridges, between the gullies, the Russians had erected earth-work batteries, mounted with thirty-two and twenty-four pound brass guns, supported by numerous field-pieces and howitzers. These guns enfiladed the tops of the ravines parallel to them, or swept them to the base, while the whole of the sides up which an enemy, unable to endure the direct fire of the batteries, would be forced to ascend, were filled with masses of skirmishers armed with an excellent two-groove rifle, throwing a large solid conical ball, with force, at 700 and 800 yards, as the French learnt to their cost. The principal battery consisted of an earth-work of the form of two sides of a triangle, with the apex pointed toward the bridge, and the sides covering both sides of the stream, corresponding with the bend in the river below it, at the distance of 1000 yards, while, with a fair elevation, the thirty-two-pounders threw beyond the houses of the village to the distance of 1400 and 1500 yards. This was constructed on the brow of a hill, about 600 feet above the river, but the hill rose behind it for another 50 feet before it dipped away toward the road. The ascent of the hill was enfiladed by the fire of three batteries of earth-work on the right, and by another on the left, and these batteries were equally capable of covering the village, the stream, and the slopes which led up the hill to their position.

Against the face of these heights, thus defended, was the attack of the Allies to be made. Early in the morning the troops were ordered to get in readiness, and at half-past six o'clock they were in motion. It was a lovely day; the heat of the sun was tempered by a sea-breeze. The fleet was visible at a distance of four miles, covering the ocean as it was seen between the hills, and the steamers on the right as close to the shore as possible.

The Generals St. Arnaud, Bosquet, and Forey, attended by their staff, rode along in front of the lines, with Lord Raglan and his generals, at second halt, and were received with tremendous cheering.

The whole line of the Allies extended five or six miles. The action became general at 1.45 on the part of the French and Turks, who carried the heights on the right. Meantime, the French steamers in shore commenced throwing shells on the height occupied by the Russians in front. The shell could be seen falling over the batteries of the Russians, and bursting right into them; and then the black masses inside the works broke into little specks, which flew about in all directions, and when the smoke cleared away, there were some to be seen strewed over the ground. The Russians answered the ships from the heights, but without effect. A powder-tumbril was blown up by a French shell; another shell fell by accident into an ambuscade which the Russians had prepared for the advancing French, and at last they drew off from the sea-side, and confined their efforts to the defense of the gullies and heights, beyond the fire of the heavy guns of the steamers.

At one o'clock the French columns were seen struggling up the hills, covered by a cloud of skirmishers, whose fire seemed most deadly. Once, at sight of a threatening mass of Russian

3

infantry, in a commanding position above them, who fired
rapid vollies among them, the French paused, but it was only
to collect their skirmishers; for as soon as they had formed, they
ran up the hill at the *pas de charge*, and broke the Russians at
once, who fled in disorder, with loss, up the hill.   Men could
be seen dropping on both sides, and the wounded rolling down
the steep.   At 1.50, the English line of skirmishers got within
range of the battery on the hill, and immediately the Russians
opened fire at 1200 yards with effect, the shot ploughing through
the open lines of the riflemen, and falling into the advancing
columns behind.

Shortly ere this time, dense volumes of smoke rose from the
river, and drifted along to the eastward, rather interfering with
the view of the enemy on the left of the English position.
The Russians had set the village on fire. It was a fair exercise
of military skill—was well executed—took place at the right
time, and succeeded in occasioning a good deal of annoyance.
The English troops halted when they neared this village, their
left extending beyond it by the verge of the stream; their
right beyond the burning cottages, and within range of the
batteries.   The Russians opened a furious fire on the whole of
the English line, but the French had not yet made progress
enough to justify them in advancing. The round shot whizzed
in every direction, dashing up the dirt and sand into the faces
of the staff of Lord Raglan, who were also shelled severely,
and attracted much of the enemy's fire.   Still Lord Raglan
waited patiently for the development of the French attack.
At length an aide-de-camp came to him, and reported that the
French had crossed the Alma, but they had not established
themselves sufficiently to justify an attack. The infantry were,
therefore, ordered to lie down, and the army, for a short time,
was quite passive, only that the artillery poured forth an unceasing fire of shell, rockets, and round shot, which ploughed
through the Russians, and caused them great loss.   They did
not waver, however, and replied to the English artillery manfully, their shot falling among the men as they lay, and carrying off legs and arms at every round. Lord Raglan at last gave
orders for the whole line to advance. Up rose these serried
masses, and passing through a fearful shower of round, case
shot and shell, they dashed into the Alma, and "floundered"
through the waters, which were literally torn into foam by the
deadly hail.   At the other side of the river, were a number of
vineyards, which were occupied by Russian riflemen.   Three
of the staff were here shot down; but led by Lord Raglan, in
person, cheering on the men, they advanced.

And now came the turning point of the battle. Lord Rag

tan dashed over the bridge, followed by his staff. From the
road over it, under the Russian guns, he saw the state of the
action. The British line, which he had ordered to advance,
was struggling through the river and up the heights in
masses, firm indeed, but mowed down by the murderous fire
of the batteries, and by grape, round shot, shell, canister, case
shot, and musketry, from some of the guns of the central battery, and from an immense and compact mass of Russian infantry.

Then commenced one of the most bloody and determined
struggles in the annals of war. The 2d Division, led by Sir
D. Evans, in the most dashing manner, crossed the stream on
the right. The 7th Fusileers, led by Colonel Yea, were swept
down by fifties. The 55th, 30th, and 95th, led by Brigadier
Pennefather, who was in the thickest of the fight, cheering on
his men, again and again were checked indeed, but never drew
back in their onward progress, which was marked by a fierce
roll of Minié musketry; and Brigadier Adams, with the 41st,
47th, and 49th, bravely charged up the hill, and aided them in
the battle. Sir George Brown, conspicuous on a gray horse,
rode in front of his Light Division, urging them with voice
and gesture. Gallant fellows, they were worthy of such a
gallant chief. The 7th, diminished by one half, fell back to
re-form their columns lost for the time; the 23d, with eight
officers dead and four wounded, were still rushing to the front,
aided by the 88th, 33d, 78th, and 15th. Down went Sir George
in a cloud of dust in front of the battery. He was soon up, and
shouted, "Twenty-third, I'm all right. Be sure I'll remember
this day," and led them on again; but in the shock produced
by the fall of their chief, the gallant regiment suffered terribly, while paralyzed for a moment. Meantime the guards
on the right of the Light Division, and the Brigade of
Highlanders, were storming the heights on the left. Their line
was almost as regular as though they were in Hyde Park.
Suddenly a tornado of round and grape rushed through from
the terrible battery, and a roar of musketry from behind thinned
their front ranks by dozens. It was evident that they were
just able to contend against the Russians, favored as they were
by a great position.

At this very time an immense mass of Russian infantry were
seen moving down toward the battery. They halted. It was
the crisis of the day. Sharp, angular, and solid, they looked
as if they were cut out of the solid rock. It was beyond all
doubt, that if our infantry, harassed and thinned as they were,
got into the battery, they would have to encounter again a
formidable fire, which they were but ill calculated to bear

Lord Raglan saw the difficulties of the situation. He asked if it would be possible to get a couple of guns to bear on these masses. The reply was "Yes," and an artillery officer brought up two guns to fire on the Russian squares. The first shot missed, but the next, and the next, and the next cut through the ranks so cleanly, and so keenly, that a clear lane could be seen for a moment through the square. After a few rounds the columns of the square became broken, wavered to and fro, broke, and fled over the brow of the hill, leaving behind them six or seven distinct lines of dead, lying as close as possible to each other, marking the passage of the fatal messengers. This relieved the infantry of a deadly incubus, and they continued their magnificent and fearful progress up the hill. The Duke of Cambridge encouraged his men by voice and example. "Highlanders," said Sir C. Campbell, ere they came to the charge, "I am going to ask a favor of you ; it is, that you will act so as to justify me in asking permission of the Queen for you to wear a bonnet ! Don't pull a trigger till you're within a yard of the Russians !" They charged, and well they obeyed their chieftain's wish ; Sir Colin had his horse shot under him ; but his men took the battery at a bound. The Russians rushed out, and left multitudes of dead behind them. The Guards had stormed the right of the battery ere the Highlanders got into the left, and it is said the Scots Fusileer Guards were the first to enter. The Second and Light Division crowned the heights. The French turned the guns on the hill against the flying masses, which the cavalry in vain tried to cover.

A few faint struggles from the scattered infantry, a few rounds of cannon and musketry, and the Russians fled to the south-east, leaving three generals, drums, three guns, 700 prisoners, and 4000 wounded behind them. The battle of Alma was won, but it was won with a loss of nearly 3000 killed and wounded on the side of the Allies, and three or four times that number on the part of the Russians.

The Russians fled with precipitation towards Sebastopol, though in such order as to be able to carry off all but three of their guns, and the Allies remained masters of the field. The want of cavalry prevented pursuit by the victors, and changing the order of retreat into a complete rout. As it was, Prince Menchikoff left his carriage on the field.

THE HORRORS OF THE BATTLE-FIELD.

It would be impossible to describe the frightful scene presented in the square mile occupied by the Russian infantry after the action. The greater part of the English killed and wounded were here, and there were at least five Russians to every Englishman. One could not walk for the bodies. The most frightful mutilations the human body can suffer—the groans of the wounded—the packs, helmets, arms, clothes, scattered over the ground—all formed a scene that one could never forget. There, writhing in their gore—racked with the agony of every imaginable wound—famishing with thirst—chilled with the cold night air—the combatants lay indiscriminately, no attempt being made to relieve their sufferings until the next day.

On the morning of the 23d, as the Allied army was leaving the ground, a picture was presented which must for ever impress itself on the memory of those who beheld it. What is that gray mass on the plain, which seems settled down upon it almost without life or motion? Now and then, indeed, an arm may be seen waved aloft, or a man raises himself for a moment, looks around, and then lies down again. Alas! that plain is covered with the wounded Russians still. Nearly sixty long hours have they passed in agony on the ground; and now, with but little hope of help or succor more, we must leave them as they lie. All this nameless, inconceivable misery —this cureless pain—to be caused by the caprice of one man! Seven hundred and fifty wounded men are still upon the ground, and we can do nothing for them. Their wounds have been bound and dressed—we have done all we can for them— and now, unable as we are to take them along with us or to send them away, we must depart. Ere our troops marched, however, General Estcourt, by order of Lord Raglan, sent into the Tartar village up the valley, into which the inhabitants were just returning, and having procured the attendance of the head men, he proceeded to explain to them that the wounded Russians would be confided to their charge, and that they were to feed and maintain them, and when they were all well they were to let them go their ways. In order to look after their wounds an English surgeon was left behind with these 750 men. This most painful and desolate duty devolved on Dr. Thomson, of the 44th Regiment. He was told his mission would be his protection in case the Cossacks came, and that he was to hoist a flag of truce should the enemy appear in sight; and then, provided with some rum, buscuit, and salt meat, he was left alone with his charge, with the exception of his soldier servant. Ere the army went, however, one of the Russian officers addressed the wounded and explained the position in which they were placed, and they promised to obey Dr. Thomson's orders, to protect him as far as they could, and to ac quaint any Russsian force which might arrive with the peculiar circumstances under which he was among them.

Dr. Thomson and his servant deserve to be honored as heroes. For four or five days they, and they alone, had to wait upon and support this enormous mass of severely wounded men. The task was in many respects a most dangerous one. The patients themselves were not to be trusted. The Cossacks might also at any time make prisoners of them on the retreat of the Allied armies. The dead were festering in heaps around the sick and dying. These two men frequently had to bury a horrible mass of carcases and fragments before they could get at some poor wounded wretches. In this way they must, with their own hands, have dragged out and buried some two hundred. There was no food of any kind for the sick, so the soldier managed to drive in a stray bullock, and with the aid of some Russian convalescents, he killed it and made some soup for them. At the end of this time, 340 of the wounded were placed on board the ship Avon and carried to Odessa. Dr. Thomson, we regret to say, subsequently died of cholera, in the English camp before Sebastopol.

INCIDENTS OF THE BATTLE OF THE ALMA.

Here is a letter which gives a life-like glimpse of the battle scene :

" I felt (writes a corporal of the 42d) what I never felt but once in my life before, and that was when a boy at school, and fighting with another—I felt possessed of a nerve and resolution which I never believed was in me, though I winced a little when I saw a cannon-ball or shell coming direct in my way, and seeing some of my comrades cut in two by it. The bullets were so thick, it would make you think you were in a shower of hailstones. After we had taken the heights, (mind 'the Forty-twa' were the first to crown it,) we sort of half fell out and were half-permitted. As I was looking at the awful carnage, I came across a poor Pole: he was shot in the belly, and was in great agony. I went down on my knees, the tear stood in my eye, and I cried like a child. I clapped him, and gave him a drink of water, which was all I could do for him. At that time the Duke himself came up, the same as if he was one of our chums; and at the same time up comes a colonel on horseback. 'I have to thank your royal highness for saving us to-day.' 'Oh!' says the Duke, 'you must not thank me, for these are the gentlemen that won the day, and saved you.' The colonel replied, 'And Sir Colin too.' 'Ah!' says the Duke, 'Sir Colin is a brick.' 'Aye,' says a serjeant of ours, 'and you are a brick yourself!' and so we gave them three times three. Sir Colin told us that he had been granted the favor from the Commander-in-chief to wear a 42d bonnet in future."

An officer of the 95th describes his narrow escape from decapitation:

" While in line, and standing up, we could plainly see the shot, nine, twelve, and twenty-four pounders bounding along the ground towards us, and over our heads; one of the latter—I judge from its size—I saw almost when it left the gun; it came apparently very slow, right for me, so slow that one would imagine it could be stopped by the hand, and about a few feet horizontally from the ground. I made sure that my last moment was at hand, when, by instinct, I bent myself double, and, at that moment, whiz, I heard the shot pass, and felt the wind of it on my head. On rising I turned round, and I saw the shot strike against a small elevation of the ground three hundred or few hundred yards in the rear, throwing up a cloud of dust; it then bounded in the air, and fell, spent, half-a-mile further on. Had I remained in the erect position, my head must have been struck off. A short prayer of thanks to Him who had thus so miraculously preserved me, burst from my lips."

The following touching letters are records of domestic calamity which might be multiplied by thousands:

"MY DEAR DELME: I shall wring your heart, indeed, and poor Mrs. Radcliffe's, by the sad intelligence I have, alas! to communicate. Your poor dear boy fell yesterday at the head of the company he commanded, (No. 1,) while gallantly leading them to the attack of a Russian entrenched battery, heavily armed, and most strongly occupied. Never was a more noble feat of arms done than the capture of this battery; and in that capture the poor dear old Welsh were foremost. Their loss has been frightful. Chester, Wynn, Evans, Connelly, my poor sister's boy, Harry Anstruther, Butler, Radcliffe, and Young, were all killed dead at the same moment, and within a space of one hundred square yards. Applethwaite, (it is feared mortally,) Campbell, Sayer, Bathurst, and Stopton wounded. Only six officers remain untouched, and nearly two hundred men are *hors du combat.* The exploit was noble indeed; but what a sacrifice! * * * I am heart-sick at the loss of so many dear and valued friends, and at the thought of my poor sister's anguish. God alone can comfort us in these overwhelming calamities, and to His almighty will let us humbly bow. Your dear boy died instantly, without pain, and lies buried in a deep grave along with his brave comrades, close to the spot where he so nobly died. * * *   ARTHUR W. TORRENS.

" P. S.—Harry Torrens and Bulwer buried him. His wound was in the centre of his breast. He lay on his back, and his body had been untouched and respected. God bless and save him. His face was calm, with almost a smile on it.   A. W. T."

A letter was found upon Lieut. Poitevin, the French officer mentioned in the dispatch of Marshal St. Arnaud as having been shot while planting the French flag on the telegraph tower. It was addressed to his sister, and gave an account of the landing in the Crimea, and the events prior to the battle. "I will write again," he concluded, "from Sebastopol or from the entrenchment." At the bottom of the letter, which is now a relic for the family of the writer, in the blank which he had left to add further details, is written this simple and affecting postscript:

" MADEMOISELLE: It is with the deepest grief that I write these few lines, which are to announce to you the loss of the brother who, three days ago, wrote to you the above letter. This worthy friend was taken from us in the battle of the 20th, while filling the glorious functions of *porte-drapear.* If the regrets which he leaves among all the officers and soldiers of the 30th can alleviate any part of the grief which that death will cause to his family, I am happy to have a good part in it.— A friend who loved him."

Among the many daring exploits of the intrepid men by whose energy and unshaken courage the Allied arms have been

carried to the heights of the Alma, we have not heard of an
instance which surpasses in cool daring the conduct of Lieutenants Lindsey and Thistlethwaite, of the Scots Fusileer Guards,
the Queen's color being carried by the former, and the regimental color by the latter gentleman. At the moment before
the heights were gained, and when the deadly struggle raged
so fiercely as to make it almost impossible to tell friend from
foe, the two lieutenants became separated from their battalion,
and found themselves with the four serjeants whose duty it
was to support them, attacked by a body of Russians, whose
commanding officer had led them against the colors. A desperate conflict ensued; the four serjeants quickly fell under a
shower of balls. The Queen's color, carried by Mr. Lindsey,
was torn into stripes, being pierced by a cloud of bullets. The
staff was shot in two ; still the gallant officers persevered, and
succeeded in cutting their way through the enemy who surrounded them. They were ably assisted, and at the right moment, by Captain Drummond, the adjutant of the regiment,
whose horse was at that moment shot under him. Captain
Lindsey, seeing the danger to which the colors were exposed,
rushed to the relief, and, with a revolver-pistol, shot three of
the assailants. The successful bearers of the standard escaped
almost miraculously, and succeeded in planting their colors on
the heights, which had been then but just won from the Russians, Mr. Lindsey having actually climbed the steep face of
the hill with the aid of the broken staff, while he exultingly
waved what remained of it, with her Majesty's colors, over
his head. Neither this gallant gentleman, nor his equally
distinguished companion, Mr. Thisthethwaite, received any
hurt.

Colonel Heygarth's escape was also a singular instance of the
chances of the battle-field. When he received his first wound,
he was in such extreme close quarters with the enemy that
his shoulder, which was shot through, was burned by the discharge of a Russian musket. While lying on the field, close
to the river's bank, which he had but just ascended, and in an
unconscious state, another shot fractured his leg, and, in the
struggle produced by this concussion, he rolled over and down
the bank into the stream of the Alma. The sudden shock and
the coldness of the water staunched the blood which was flowing from the arteries of the shoulder, and so saved his life,
although, in scrambling out of the water, he received another
wound from a ball, which grazed his head.

Colonel Steele, Lord Raglan's military secretary, was for some
time supposed to have fallen. Lord Raglan, in the heat of the
fight, ordered him to ride to the brigade of Guards, and give

the order to advance, intending, of course, that the order being given, he should return to his place with the staff. The moment was, however, too exciting for the hot blood of the military secretary, and having given the order of his chief, he rushed forward himself with his old battalion, and did not again present himself to Lord Raglan until he came to announce that the field was won, and to ask forgiveness for the breach of orders of which he had been guilty, in joining the brilliant charge of the Guards, which so largely aided in gaining the battle.

A surgeon writes: "I have seen some curious wounds from the course taken by the balls. One man, who fell by my side, roared out, 'O doctor, I am killed,' but on tearing open his clothes, I found the ball had not gone deeper than the skin. A cannon-ball passed close to me, and over the head of a man who was lying on the ground; you could see the round shot passing by you like a swift bowling at cricket. The Russians had an ugly trick of lying on the ground, pretending to be wounded, and firing at us as soon as we passed; so our men massacred them right and left."

MARCHING FOR SEBASTOPOL.

On the morning of September 23, two days after the battle, the Allied army left the blood-stained heights of Alma, and commenced their march towards Sebastopol. Soon after dawn the French assembled all their drums and trumpets on the top of the highest of the hills they carried, and a wild flourish and roll, repeated again and again, and broken by peals of sound from the bugles of the infantry, celebrated their victory ere they departed. It was spirited, stirring, and thrilling music; and its effect, as it swelled through the darkness of early morning, down over the valley, was most impressive and exciting. The watch-fires were still burning languidly as the sleepers roused themselves, all wet with dew, and prepared to leave the scene of their triumphs. The fogs of the night crept slowly up the hill-sides, and hung in uncertain folds around their summits, revealing here and there the gathering columns of our regiments, in dark patches on the declivities, or showing the deep black-looking squares of the French battalions, already in motion towards the south. Dimly seen in the distance, the fleet was moving along slowly by the line of the coast, the long lines of smoke trailing back on their wake.

At 3 P.M., the beautiful valley of the Katcha River came in sight; its opposite side formed by a ridge of hills clad with verdure, and with a small forest of shrubs, through which,

here and there, shone the white walls of villas and snug cottages. Altogether that valley was too fair a picture of rural
comfort and happiness for the ruthless hand of man to lay
waste.

"The Katcha is a small and rapid rivulet, with banks like
those of the Alma. We found the whole course was marked
by neat white cottages, and that it watered the most delicious
vineyards and gardens, amid which their habitations were
placed; but there were no inhabitants visible. Wheeling over
the bridge, we turned eastward towards the little village of
Eskel, on the left bank. The first building on the road was
the Imperial Post-house, with its sign-post of a double-headed
eagle, and an illegible inscription. The usual wooden direction-
post, with a bluish ribbon painted round it diagonally on a
white ground, informed us that we were on our way to Sebastopol, distant about ten miles. The place was abandoned, and
the house destitute of the smallest particle of furniture. The
road now assumed the character of an English by-way in De-
vonshire or Hampshire. Low walls at either side were sur
mounted by fruit trees laden with apples, pears, peaches, apri-
cots, all ripe and fit for use, and at their feet clustered grapes
of the most delicate flavor. The first villa we came to was
the residence of a physician or country surgeon. It had been
ruthlessly destroyed by the Cossacks. A verandah, laden
with clematis, roses, and honeysuckle in front, was filled with
broken music-stools, work-tables, and lounging-chairs. All
the glass of the windows was smashed. Every thing around
betokened the hasty flight of the inmates. Two or three side-
saddles were lying on the grass outside the hall-door; a parasol
lay near them, close to a Tartar saddle and huge whip. The
wine-casks were broken, and the contents spilt, the barley and
corn of the granary were thrown about all over the ground,
broken china and glass of fine manufacture were scattered
over the pavement outside the kitchen, and amid all the desolation and ruin of the place a cat sat blandly at the threshold,
winking her eyes in the sunshine at the new-comers. No pen
can describe the scene within. Mirrors, in fragments, were
lying on the floor; the beds had been ripped open, and the
feathers littered the rooms a foot deep; chairs, sofas, fauteuils,
bedsteads, book-cases, picture-frames, images of saints, women's
needle-work, chests of drawers, shoes, boots, books, bottles,
physic jars, all smashed or torn in pieces, lay in heaps in every
room. Even the walls and doors were hacked with swords.
The very genius of destruction had been at work, and had re
veled in mischief. The physician's account-book lay open on
a broken table; he had been stopped in the very act of debit-

ing a dose to some neighbor, and the entry remained unfinished. Besides his account-book, lay a volume of "Madame de Sevigny's Letters," in French, and a "Pharmacopœia," in Russian. A little bottle of prussic acid lay so invitingly near a box of bonbons that I knew it would be irresistible to the first hungry private who had a taste for almonds, and I accordingly poured out the contents to prevent the possible catastrophe. Our men and horses were soon reveling in grapes and corn, and we pushed on to Eskel, and established ourselves in a house, which had belonged to a Russian officer of rank; at least many traces of the presence of one were visible. Every house and villa in the place was a similar scene to that which I have in vain tried to describe. The better the class of the residences the more complete and pitiable the destruction. Grand pianos and handsome pieces of furniture, covered with silk and damasked velvet, rent to pieces with brutal violence, were found in more than one house ; but one of the instruments retained enough of its vital organs to breathe out *God save the Queen*, from its lacerated brass ribs, and it was made to do so accordingly— aye, under the very eye of a rigid portrait of his Imperial Majesty the Czar, which hung on the wall above! These portraits of the autocrat were not uncommon in the houses ; nearly as common as pictures of saints with gilt and silver glories around their heads. The houses, large and small, consist of one story only, and magnitude is gained by lateral extension. Each house stands apart, with a large patch of vineyard around it, and a garden of fruit-trees, and is fenced in from the road by a stone-wall, and a line of poplars or elms. A porch, covered with vines, protects the entrance. The rooms are clean and scrupulously white-washed. Large outhouses, with wine-presses, stables, etc., complete the farmer's establishment."

At the village of Eskel, Lord Raglan bivouacked for the night, he himself occupying a handsome villa, all the furniture of which had been destroyed by the Cossacks. Orders were given to prevent the soldiers destroying the vineyards or eating the fruit ; but, of course, it was quite impossible to guard so extensive and tempting a region as the valley of the Katcha from thirsty and hungry men. The soldiers fared on the richest of grapes, and the choicest pears and apples ; but they did not waste and spoil as the French did at Marnaschei, lower down the river. A guard was set over the Greek Church of the village, and nothing was plundered ; nothing was taken, except such things as hay, barley, fowls, and things absolutely necessary for the men and horses. Had the owners been there, they would have been paid full value.

The retreating Russians encamped at this village on the night of the battle of Alma, in a fatigued and dispirited condition. At 12 o'clock the same night there was an alarm that the English and French were coming. Up got the whole army of the Russians, pell-mell, and snatching up whatever they could, they rushed off in disorder across the country. A part of the army went towards Bakshiserai. They were said to consist of about 20,000 men, and to be under the command of Prince Menchikoff in person.

On the evening of the next day, (the 24th,) the English forces encamped on the high left bank of the Balbec River or Creek, six miles from the Katcha, and four from Sebastopol, having taken up a position considerably above the direct line of march, to escape the fire of a Russian battery on the opposite bank, lower down. The French were posted on the hills in advance. The combined fleet at this time lay at the mouth of the Katcha, from which large reïnforcements were being landed.

TAKING POSSESSION OF BALAKLAVA.

Lord Raglan and Marshal St. Arnaud, not deeming it important to maintain communication with the Katcha, commenced a flank movement to the left the next day, (Sept. 25th;) and the following day, after some sharp skirmishing with a Russian division, Lord Raglan took possession of Balaklava without opposition. The town is small, decayed, and unimportant; but the harbor, though narrow and closely shut in by hills, afforded a secure shelter for several large English men-of-war, and at the same time presented convenient facilities for the landing of such war munitions as were needed in carrying on the siege.

DEATH OF MARSHAL ST. ARNAUD.

Though it will interrupt the narrative for a moment, it is in place here to speak of the death of Marshal St. Arnaud. He had been suffering from severe illness for some time previous to the expedition to the Crimea; grew rapidly worse after the battle of the Alma; resigned his command into the hands of General Canrobert on the 25th of September, and died on the 29th. His body was conveyed to France, and on the 14th of November was interred at Paris with great military pomp. His private character, it appears, was far from a model for imitation; but he had behaved gallantly as a soldier, and the Emperor, therefore, ordered for him a splendid funeral, and also gave a handsome annuity to his widow.

The expedition to the Crimea is supposed to have originated mainly with Arnaud, who was impatient of delay, and desirous, perhaps, to add to his military distinction already acquired in Africa. He eagerly sought a conflict with the Russians at the Alma; and his plan seems to have been, after having broken and scattered the army under Menchikoff, to march immediately upon Sebastopol, while feebly garrisoned, and carry it by storm. But death interfered, and perhaps materially changed the result of the siege. If he had lived to participate in it, the operations would doubtless have been more bold, if not more successful, than they have proved to be under Lord Raglan and General Canrobert.

A characteristic anecdote is told of a French officer in connection with Marshal St. Arnaud. One day, after the siege had fairly commenced, and the exceeding difficulties of the undertaking began to be developed, he was taking a survey of the frowning fortifications of Sebastopol. Dropping his glass, he exclaimed, "St. Arnaud, lucky dog, *he is dead!*"

THE SIEGE OF SEBASTOPOL.

The position of Sebastopol may be seen by a glance at the map accompanying this volume, which will convey a better idea of it than could any written description.

FORCE OF THE COMBATANTS.

At the commencement of the siege, Sebastopol contained a garrison of 34,000 men, under the command of General Nochimoff, who declared that he would defend the place to the last man and the last bullet; 30,000 men were encamped at Bokshiserai, under Prince Menchikoff; and reïnforcements soon arrived from the principalities, sufficient to swell the Russian force to about 90,000 men, including soldiers and marines. The force of the Allies at the same time, on sea and on shore, was nearly, or quite, 100,000, and during the siege, reïnforcements were constantly arriving, consisting of the wounded from the hospitals, who were sufficiently recovered to resume service; and a combined force from England and France, chiefly from the latter country, of some 50,000 men. Death, however, made such rapid havoc among the soldiers, that all the reïnforcements hardly sufficed to keep up the original number.

The siege artillery of the Allies was truly formidable, con-

sisting of 400 field and siege guns; and for these, 800,000 shot
and shells were provided, besides an immense quantity of
gabions, fascines, and other materials for fortification. The
Russians had 800 guns in their different forts, and 100 field
pieces with Menchikoff's army.

The Russians, to guard against a direct attack from the sea,
had sunk seven large war-vessels at the entrance of the harbor,
and some weeks afterwards another, thus effectually closing it
against the fleets of the Allies. Some weeks later, an English
officer conceived a plan for removing these vessels by sub-
marine explosion, something similar to the operations of M.
Maillefert, on the rocks at Hurlgate. Twenty-four iron cylin-
ders were constructed, each to contain 1000 pounds of powder,
and shipped for the Crimea; but as yet we have received no
account of a commencement of operations upon the sunken
vessels, and we presume the work is found to be impracticable,
on account of the destructive sweep of the Russian guns.

THE POSITION OF THE ALLIES AROUND SEBASTOPOL.

The position of the Allies was well defended from the land-
ward. Their extreme right leaned on the slope of the mountains east of Balaklava, which run down like immense walls to
Aloushta; the body of the right wing was at Karma, and the
outposts stationed on the Black River. The centre occupied
the road leading from Radikoi to Sebastopol, and from Bakshiserai to Balaklava. The body of the left wing was at Karani;
the outposts at Khutor. The French were on the left from the
southern fort; the English on the right, from the southern fort
to the ruins of Inkermann. The English were thus in position
to draw supplies from Balaklava, and the French were furnished with like facilities by two small bays to the north of
Cape Chersonesus. The Turks were placed in reserve, to act
according to circumstances.

The Allied armies were in position about the 1st of October.
On the 2d, 5th, and 11th, the garrison of Sebastopol made
sorties, and destroyed some small works, but without any very
important result. On the 7th, the Russians, hovering on the
outskirts of the Allies' position, made a strong demonstration
on the north-west extremity of the camp, but were kept in
check by artillery, and retired without giving battle.

OPENING FIRE UPON SEBASTOPOL.

The siege batteries of the Allies were finished by the 7th of
October, and guns and munitions in position by the 15th. In

the intermediate time from the arrival of the Allies to
this date, nothing of a remarkable character occurred beyond
a few skirmishes with the Cossacks, and a division or two
of Menchikoff on the outskirts of the army, or an occasional sortie from the town, in all which the Russians were
easily repulsed.

On the 17th, however, the siege commenced in earnest, and
with such results as will make it a memorable day in the history of the conflicts of the Crimea.

<h2>THE ATTACK ON LAND.</h2>

The firing commenced by signal from the French and English batteries at 6.30 A.M., and the cannonade was tremendous for two hours.

At 8.30 the fire was slackened on both sides, but in a few
minutes re-commenced with renewed energy, the whole town
and the line of the batteries being enveloped in smoke.

At 8.40 the magazine of the French battery at the extreme
right blew up with a tremendous explosion, killing and wounding 100 men. The Russians cheered, fired with renewed vigor,
and nearly silenced the fire of the French, who had to suspend
operations to repair damages.

A lull on both sides at 10.30, but with a vigorous re-firing
half an hour after.

At 1.25 P.M. another magazine in the French lines blew
up, and by this time the English fire had demolished the
Round Tower, but could not silence the works around it.

At 1.40 a great explosion occurred in the centre of Sebastopol; but the fire of the Russians at that point did not abate
in consequence. The cannonade continued on both sides, with
occasional intermissions, until dark.

The loss of the French was 200, principally by explosions;
and the batteries on the extreme left were silenced. The loss
of the English was comparatively trifling, and from the commencement of the siege up to this time did not exceed 100.
The loss of the Russians was about 500.

The attack at sea.—At the urgent solicitation of Lord Raglan
and General Canrobert, it was agreed by Admirals Dundas
and Hameline, commanders of the Allied fleets, that the whole
of the ships should assist the land attack by engaging the sea
batteries on the north and south of the harbor. The French
occupied the right, and the English the left.

At 12.45, the French line-of-battle ships ran up in most
magnificent style, and engaged the batteries on the sea-side, in
coöperation with the fire of the Allies on the land. The scene

was stunning, tremendous, indescribable; the Russians reply
ing to the attacks by sea and land, though suffering greatly.

At 2 P.M., the English vessels commenced, and engaged the
batteries on the other side, and the firing became terrific. At
the distance of six miles, the sustained sound was that of a
furious locomotive at full-speed, but with an infinitely grander
roar. It was a dead calm, so that the smoke hung in thick
clouds about both ships and batteries, frequently hiding the
combatants from each other.

From 2 P.M. till dark, the cannonade raged furiously. Three
of the English ships were badly handled, and the loss on their
side was 46 killed and 250 wounded. On board the Sanspareil,
eight or nine men were swept away at a forecastle gun, but the
two remaining went on loading as if nothing had happened.
The loss of the French was not so large as that of the English.
The Russian Admiral, Raniloff, was killed.

At dark, all the ships returned to their anchorage. The
change was magical from the hot sun, mist, smoke, explosions,
shot, shell, rockets, and the roar of ten thousand guns, to the
cool, still, starlight-sky, reflecting in long tremendous lines the
lights at the mast-heads of the ships, returning in profound
silence.

The combined fleet seems to have been placed in a position
to suffer a good deal of damage, without being able to act very
effectively upon the batteries of the town; and from the tone
of Admiral Dundas's dispatch, giving an account of the
action, it may be inferred that both admirals went into the
engagement reluctantly.

During the night of the 7th, the Russians mounted new
guns, made repairs, and briskly opened fire early the next
morning. Their fire was superior to that of the English, firing
three shots to their two. The French, for that day, were *hors
du combat*, having been too much damaged by the disasters of
the previous day.

At 10 A.M. of the 18th, the Russians were discovered to be
creeping up in a fog, to attack the rear on the Balaklava, but
were dispersed by the fire of the Turks.

On the night of the 20th, the Russians made a sortie, and
attempted to spike the French guns; and most of those who
entered the batteries were killed. On that day, Nochimoff, the
commander of Sebastopol, was wounded in the head by a shell,
and was reported dead, but subsequently recovered.

From the opening fire to the 23d of October, the cannonade
was almost incessant, and during that time, the town was frequently on fire from hot shot and the bursting of shell.

From this time no remarkable incident is to be recorded until

THE BATTLE OF BALAKLAVA,

FOUGHT OCTOBER 25.

TERRIBLE AND FATAL CHARGE OF THE LIGHT CAVALRY—A VICTORY ALMOST AS FATAL AS A DEFEAT.

AT half-past seven o'clock in the morning, an orderly came galloping in to the head-quarters camp from Balaklava, with the news that at dawn a strong corps of Russian horse, supported by guns and battalions of infantry, had marched into the valley, and had already nearly dispossessed the Turks of the redoubt, No. 1, (that on Canrobert's Hill, which was farthest from the English lines,) and that they were opening fire on the redoubts Nos. 2, 3, and 4, which would speedily be in their hands unless the Turks offered a stouter resistance than they had done already.

Orders were dispatched to Sir George Cathcart, and to H.R.H. the Duke of Cambridge, to put their respective divisions, the 4th and the 1st, in motion for the scene of action, and intelligence of the advance of the Russians was also furnished to General Canrobert. Immediately on receipt of the news, the General commanded General Bosquet to get the 3d division under arms, and sent a strong body of artillery and some two hundred Chasseurs d'Afrique to assist us in holding the valley. Sir Colin Campbell, who was in command of Balaklava, had drawn up the 93d Highlanders a little in front of the road to the town, at the first news of the advance of the enemy. The marines on the heights got under arms; the seamen's batteries and marines' batteries, on the heights close to the town were manned, and the French artillerymen and the Zouaves* prepared for action along their lines. Lord Lucan's little camp was the scene of great excitement. The men had not had time to water their horses; they had not broken their fast from the evening of the day before, and had barely saddled at the first blast of the trumpet, when they were drawn up on the slope behind the redoubts in front of their camp to operate on the enemy's squadrons. When the

---

* The Zouaves are by many supposed to be natives of Algeria, but such is not the case, though their dress is of the same picturesque character as that of the Turcas or Spahis, who form a part of the French army in Africa. In the wars with the Arabs of that country they have been trained to great muscular force and agility, and astonished the Russians at Alma by the cat-like facility with which they made their way up the heights on that occasion, where they supposed no man could maintain a footing.

5

Russians advanced, the Turks fired a few rounds at them, got frightened at the distance of their supports in the rear, looked round, received a few shots and shell, and then "bolted." Turks on the Danube were very different beings from Turks in the Crimea, as it proved the Russians of Sebastopol were not at all like the Russians of Silistria.

Soon after eight Lord Raglan and his staff turned out and cantered towards the rear of our position. The booming of artillery, the spattering roll of musketry, were heard rising from the valley, drowning the roar of the siege guns in front before Sebastopol. A French light infantry regiment advanced with admirable care and celerity towards the ridge near the telegraph-house, which was already lined by companies of French infantry, while mounted officers scampered along its broken outline in every direction.

General Bosquet a stout, soldier-like looking man, who reminds one of the old *genre* of French generals, as depicted at Versailles, followed with his staff and a small escort of Hussars, at a gallop. Faint white clouds rose here and there above the hill from the cannonade below. Never did the painter's eye rest on a more beautiful scene than was to be seen from the ridge. The fleecy vapors still hung around the mountain tops, and mingled with the ascending volumes of smoke; the patch of sea sparkled freshly in the rays of the morning sun, but its light was eclipsed by the flashes which gleamed from the masses of armed men below.

Looking to the left towards the gorge, compact masses of Russian infantry were seen, which had just debouched from the mountain passes near the Tchernaya, and were slowly advancing with solemn stateliness up the valley. Immediately in their front was a regular line of artillery, of at least twenty pieces strong. Two batteries of light guns were already a mile in advance of them, and were playing with energy on the redoubts, from which feeble puffs of smoke came at long intervals. Behind these guns, in front of the infantry, were enormous bodies of cavalry. They were in six compact squares, three on each flank, moving down *en echelon* towards the English forces, and the valley was lit up with the blaze of their sabres and lance points, and gay accoutrements. In their front, and extending along the intervals between each battery of guns, were clouds of mounted skirmishers, wheeling and whirling in the front of their march like autumn leaves tossed by the wind. The Zouaves close by, were lying like tigers at the spring, with ready rifles in hand, hidden chin deep by the earth-works which run along the line of these ridges on our rear; but the quick-eyed Russians were manœuvering on the other side of the valley, and did not expose their columns to attack. Below the Zouaves could be seen the Turkish gunners in the redoubts, all in confusion as the shells burst over them. "Just as I came up," says an English eye-witness, "the Russians had carried No. 1 redoubt, the farthest and most elevated of all, and their horsemen were chasing the Turks across the interval which lay between it and redoubt No. 2. At that moment the cavalry, under Lord Lucan, were formed in glittering masses—the light brigade, under Lord Cardigan, in advance; the heavy brigade, under Brigadier-General Scarlett, in reserve. They were drawn up just in front of their encampment, and were concealed from the view of the enemy by a slight 'wave' in the plain. Considerably to the rear of their right, the 93d Highlanders were drawn up in line, in front of the approach to Balaklava. Above and behind them, on the heights, the marines were visible through the glass, drawn up under arms, and the gunners could be seen ready in the earth-works, in which were placed the heavy ships' guns. The 93d had originally been advanced somewhat more into the plain, but the instant the Russians got possession of the first redoubt they opened fire on them from their own guns, which inflicted some injury, and Sir Colin Campbell 'retired' his men to a better position. Meantime the enemy advanced his cavalry rapidly. To our inexpressible disgust we saw the Turks in redoubt No. 2 fly at their approach. They ran in scattered groups across towards redoubt No. 3, and towards Balaklava; but the horse-hoof of the Cossack was too quick for them, and sword and lance were busily piled among the retreating herd. The yells of the pursuers and pursued were plainly audible. As the lancers and light cavalry of the Russians advanced; they gathered up their skirmishers with great speed and in excellent order—the shifting trails of men, which played all over the valley like moonlight on the water, contracted, gathered up, and the little *peloton* in a few moments became a solid column. Then up came their guns, in rushed their gunners to the abandoned redoubt, and the guns of No. 2 redoubt soon played with deadly effect upon the dispirited defenders of No. 3 redoubt. Two or three shots in return from the earth-works, and all is silent. The Turks swarm over the earth-works, and run in confusion towards the town, firing their muskets at the enemy as they run. Again the solid column of cavalry opens like a fan, and resolves itself into a 'long spray' of skirmishers. It laps the flying Turks, steel flashes in the air, and down goes the poor Moslem quivering on the plain, split through fez and musket-guard to the chin and breast-belt. There is no support for them. It is evident the

Russians have been too quick for us. The Turks have been
too quick also; for they have not held their redoubts long
enough to enable us to bring them help. In vain the naval
guns on the heights fire on the Russian cavalry; the distance
is too great for shot or shell to reach. In vain the Turkish
gunners in the earthen batteries which are placed along the
French intrenchments strive to protect their flying countrymen; their shot fly wide and short of the swarming masses.
The Turks betake themselves towards the Highlanders, where
they check their flight and form into companies on the flanks
of the Highlanders.

As the Russian cavalry on the left of their line crown the
hill across the valley, they perceive the Highlanders drawn up
at the distance of some half-mile, calmly waiting their approach.
They halt, and squadron after squadron flies up from the rear,
till they have a body of some 1500 men along the ridge—lancers,
and dragoons, and hussars. Then they move *en echelon* in two
bodies, with another in reserve. The cavalry who have been
pursuing the Turks on the right are coming up to the ridge
beneath us, which conceals our cavalry from view. The heavy
brigade in advance is drawn up in two lines. The first line
consists of the Scots Greys and of their old companions if
glory, the Enniskillens; the second of the 4th Royal Irish, on
the 5th Dragoon Guards, and of the 1st Royal Dragoons. The
light cavalry brigade is on their left, in two lines also. The
silence is oppressive; between the cannon-bursts one can hear
the champing of bits and the clink of sabres in the valley
below. The Russians on their left drew breath for a moment,
and then in one grand line dashed at the Highlanders. The
ground flies beneath their horses' feet; gathering speed at every
stride, they dash on towards that thin red streak topped with a
line of steel. The Turks fire a volley at eight hundred yards,
and run. As the Russians come within six hundred yards,
down goes that line of steel in front, and out rings a rolling
volley of Minié musketry. The distance is too great; the
Russians are not checked, but still sweep onwards with the
whole force of horse and man, through the smoke, here and
there knocked over by the shot of our batteries above. With
breathless suspense every one awaits the bursting of the wave
upon the line of Gaelic rock; but ere they come within a
hundred and fifty yards, another deadly volley flashes from
the levelled rifles, and carries death and terror into the Russians.
They wheel about, open files right and left, and fly back faster
than they came. " Bravo, Highlanders! well done," shout the
excited spectators; but events thicken. The Highlanders and
their splendid front are soon forgotten; men scarcely have a

moment to think of this fact, that the 93d never altered their formation to receive that tide of horsemen. 'No,' said Sir Colin Campbell, 'I did not think it worth while to form them even four deep!' The ordinary British line, two deep, was quite sufficient to repel the attack of these Muscovite cavaliers. Our eyes were, however, turned in a moment on our own cavalry. We saw Brigadier-General Scarlett ride along in front of his massive squadrons. The Russians—evidently *corps d'elite*—their light blue jackets embroidered with silver lace, were advancing on their left, at an easy gallop, towards the brow of the hill. A forest of lances glistened in the rear, and several squadrons of gray-coated dragoons moved up quickly to support them as they reached the summit. The instant they came in sight, the trumpets of our cavalry gave out the warning blast which told us all that in another moment we should see the shock of battle beneath our very eyes; Lord Raglan, all his staff and escort, and groups of officers, the Zouaves, French generals and officers, and bodies of French infantry on the height, were spectators of the scene, as though they were looking on the stage from the boxes of a theatre. Nearly every one dismounted and sat down, and not a word was said. The Russians advanced down the hill at a slow canter, which they changed to a trot and at last nearly halted. Their first line was at least double the length of ours—it was three times as deep. Behind them was a similar line, equally strong and compact. They evidently despised their insignificant-looking enemy, but their time was come. The trumpets rang out again through the valley, and the Greys and Enniskilleners went right at the centre of the Russian cavalry. The space between them was only a few hundred yards; it was scarce enough to let the horses "gather way," nor had the men quite space sufficient for the full play of their sword-arms. The Russian line brings forward each wing as our cavalry advance, and threatens to annihilate them as they pass on. Turning a little to their left, so as to meet the Russian right, the Greys rush on with a cheer that thrills to every heart—the wild shout of the Enniskilleners rises high and clear through the air at the same instant. As lightning flashes through a cloud, the Greys and Enniskilleners pierced through the dark masses of the Russians. The shock was but for a moment. There was a clash of steel and a light play of sword-blades in the air, and then the Greys and the red-coats disappear in the midst of the shaken and quivering columns. In another moment we see them emerging and dashing on with diminished numbers, and in broken order, against the second line, which is advancing against them as fast as it can to retrieve the for tune of the charge. It was a terrible moment. God help them! they are lost!' was the exclamation of more than one man, and the thought of many. With unabated fire the noble hearts dashed at their enemy. It was a fight of heroes. The first line of Russians which had been smashed utterly by our charge, and had fled off at one flank and towards the centre, were coming back to swallow up our handful of men. By sheer steel and sheer courage, Enniskillener and Scot were winning their desperate way right through the enemy's squadrons, and already gray horses and red coats had appeared right at the rear of the second mass, when, with irresistible force, like one bolt from a bow, the 1st Royals, the 4th Dragoon Guards, and the 5th Dragoon Guards rushed at the remnants of the first line of the enemy, went through it as though it were made of pasteboard, and, dashing on the second body of Russians as they were still disordered by the terrible assault of the Greys and their companions, put them to utter rout. This Russian horse in less than ten minutes after it met our dragoons was flying with all its speed before a force certainly not half its strength. A cheer burst from every lip; in the enthusiasm, officers and men took off their caps and shouted with delight, and thus keeping up the scenic character of their position, they clapped their hands again and again. Lord Raglan at once dispatched Lieutenant Curzon, Aide-de-Camp, to convey his congratulations to Brigadier-General Scarlett, and to say 'well done.' The gallant old officer's face beamed with pleasure when he received the message. 'I beg to thank his Lordship very sincerely,' was his reply. The cavalry did not long pursue their enemy. Their loss was very slight, about 35 killed and wounded in both affairs. Major Clarke was slightly wounded, and had a narrow escape from a sabre-cut at the back of his head. Lieut-Colonel Griffiths retired after the first charge, having been wounded at the back of the head. Cornet Pendergast was wounded in the foot. There were not more than four or five men killed outright, and our most material loss was from the cannon playing on our heavy dragoons afterwards, when covering the retreat of our light cavalry.

In the Royal Horse Artillery, we had a severe, but I am glad to say, a temporary loss. Captain Maude, who directed the service of his guns with his usual devotedness and dauntless courage, was struck in the arm by a shell which burst at his saddle-bow and killed his horse. To the joy of all the army it is ascertained that he is doing well on board ship. After the charge, Captain, the Hon. Arthur Hardinge, came galloping up to Lord Raglan with the news of what the cavalry had done. He had been sent with orders to Lord Lucan, and at the moment of the charge he had joined the Greys and dashed with them into the Russian columns. He was an object of envy to all his friends on the staff while he described in animated language the glorious events of those brilliant five minutes.

At 10 o'clock the Guards and Highlanders of the First Division were seen moving towards the plains from their camp The Duke of Cambridge came up to Lord Raglan for orders, and his Lordship, ready to give the honor of the day to Sir Colin Campbell, who commanded at Balaklava, told His Royal Highness to place himself under the direction of the Brigadier. At 10.40 the Fourth Division also took up their position in advance of Balaklava. The cavalry were then on the left front of our position facing the enemy; the Light Cav· alry Brigade was on the left flank forward; the Heavy Cavalry Brigade *en echelon* in reserve, with guns on the right; the 4th Dragoons and 5th Dragoons and Greys on the left of the brigade, the Enniskillens and 3d Dragoons on the right. The Fourth Division took up ground in the centre; the Guards and Highlanders filed off towards the extreme right, and faced the redoubts, from which the Russians opened on them with such guns as had not been spiked.

At 10.50 General Canrobert, attended by his staff, and Brigadier-General Rose, rode up to Lord Raglan, and the staffs of the two Generals and their escorts mingled together in praise of the magnificent charge of our cavalry, while the chiefs apart conversed over the operations of the day, which promised to be one of battle. The Russian cavalry, followed by our shot, had retired in confusion, leaving the ground covered with horses and men. In carrying an order early in the day, Mr. Blunt, Lord Lucan's interpreter, and son of our Consul in Thessaly, had a narrow escape. His horse was killed ; he seized a Russian charger as it galloped past riderless, but the horse carried him almost into the Russian cavalry, and he only saved himself by leaping him into a redoubt among a number of frightened Turks who were praying to Allah on their bellies. I should mention here that the Turks who had been collected on the flanks of the 93d, fled at the approach of the Russians without firing a shot! At 10.55, a body of cavalry, the Chasseurs d'Afrique, passed down to the plain, and were loudly cheered by our men. They took up ground in advance of the ridges on our left."

THE DISASTROUS CAVALRY CHARGE.

"And now occurred the melancholy catastrophe which fills us all with sorrow. It appears that the Quartermaster-Gene

ral, Brigadier Airey, thinking that the Light Cavalry had not
gone far enough in front when the enemy's horse had fled, gave
an order in writing to Captain Nolan, 15th Hussars, to take to
Lord Lucan, directing his Lordship 'to advance' his cavalry
nearer to the enemy. A braver soldier than Captain Nolan
the army did not possess. He was known to all his arm of the
service for his entire devotion to his profession; and his name
must be familiar to all who take interest in our cavalry, for his
excellent work, published a year ago, on our drill and system
of re-mount and breaking horses. I had the pleasure of his
acquaintance, and I know he entertained the most exalted
opinions respecting the capabilities of the English horse soldier.
Properly led, the British Hussar and Dragoon could, in his
mind, break square, take batteries, ride over columns of infantry, and pierce any other cavalry in the world as if they were
made of straw. He thought they had not had the opportunity
of doing all that was in their power, and that they had missed
even such chances as they had offered to them—that, in fact,
they were in some measure disgraced. A matchless horseman
and a first-rate swordsman, he held in contempt, I am afraid,
even grape and canister. He rode off with his orders to Lord
Lucan. He is now dead and gone. God forbid I should cast
a shade on the brightness of his honor; but I am bound to
state what I am told occurred when he reached his Lordship.
I should premise that as the Russian cavalry retired, their
infantry fell back towards the head of the valley, leaving men
in three of the redoubts they had taken, and abandoning the
fourth. They had also placed some guns on the heights over
their position, on the left of the gorge. Their cavalry joined
the reserves, and drew up in six solid divisions, in an oblique
line, across the entrance to the gorge. Six battalions of infantry were placed behind them, and about thirty guns were drawn
up along their line, while masses of infantry were also collected
on the hills behind the redoubts on our right. Our cavalry
had moved up to the ridge across the valley, on our left, as the
ground was broken in front, and had halted in the order I have
already mentioned. When Lord Lucan received the order
from Captain Nolan and had read it, he asked, we are told,
'Where are we to advance to?' Captain Nolan pointed with
his finger to the line of the Russians, and said, 'There are the
enemy, and there are the guns, sir, before them; it is your
duty to take them,' or words to that effect, according to statements made since his death. Lord Lucan, with reluctance, gave
the order to Lord Cardigan to advance upon the guns, con-
ceiving that his orders compelled him to do so. The noble
Earl, though he did not shrink, also saw the fearful odds against

him. Don Quixote, in his tilt against the windmill, was not near so rash and reckless as the gallant fellows who prepared without a thought to rush on almost certain death. It is a maxim of war, that "cavalry never act without a support," that "infantry should be close at hand when cavalry carry guns, as the effect is only instantaneous," and that it is necessary to have on the flank of a line of cavalry some squadrons in column, the attack on the flank being most dangerous. The only support our light cavalry had was the reserve of heavy cavalry at a great distance behind them, the infantry and guns being far in the rear. There were no squadrons in column at all, and there was a plain to charge over before the enemy's guns were reached, of about a mile and a half in length. At 11.10 our Light Cavalry Brigade rushed to the front, the whole force numbering a little over 600.

The whole brigade scarcely made one effective regiment, and yet it was more than could be spared. As they passed towards the front, the Russians opened on them from the guns in the redoubt on the right, with volleys of musketry and rifles. They swept proudly past, glittering in the morning sun, in all the pride and splendor of war. The beholders could scarcely believe the evidence of their senses. Surely that handful of men are not going to charge an army in position? Alas! it was but too true; their desperate valor knew no bounds; and far, indeed, was it removed from its so-called better part—discretion. They advanced in two lines, quickening their pace as they closed towards the enemy. A more fearful spectacle was never witnessed than by those who, without the power to aid, beheld their heroic countrymen rushing to the arms of death. At the distance of 1200 yards, the whole line of the enemy belched forth, from thirty iron-mouths, a flood of smoke and flame, through which hissed the deadly balls. Their flight was marked by instant gaps in the gallant ranks, by dead men and horses, by steeds flying wounded or riderless across the plain. The first line is broken—it is joined by the second—they never halt or check their speed an instant. With diminished ranks, thinned by those thirty guns, which the Russians had laid with the most deadly accuracy, with a halo of flashing steel above their heads, and with a cheer, which was many a noble fellow's death-cry, they flew into the smoke of the batteries; but ere they were lost from view, the plain was strewed with their bodies, and with the carcases of their horses. They were exposed to an oblique fire from the batteries on the hills on both sides, as well as to a direct fire of musketry. Through the clouds of smoke could be seen their sabres flashing as they rode up to the guns, and

dashed between them, cutting down the gunners as they stood
We saw them riding through the guns; and soon again,
to our frenzied delight, we saw them returning, after breaking through a column of Russian infantry, and scattering them
like chaff, when the flank fire of the battery on the hill swept
them down, scattered and broken as they were. Wounded
men and dismounted troopers flying towards us told the tale;
demi-gods could not have done what we failed to do. At the
very moment when they were about to retreat, an enormous
mass of lancers was hurled on their flank. Colonel Shewell,
of the 8th Hussars, saw the danger, and rode his few men
straight at them, cutting his way through with fearful loss.
The other regiments turned, and engaged in a desperate encounter.

With courage too great almost for credence, they were
breaking their way through the columns that enveloped them,
when there took place an act of atrocity without parallel in
the modern warfare of civilized nations. The Russian gunners, when the storm of cavalry passed, returned to their guns.
They saw their own cavalry mingled with the troopers who
had just ridden over them, and, to the eternal disgrace of the
Russian name, the miscreants poured a murderous volley of
grape and canister on the mass of struggling men and horses,
mingling friend and foe in one common ruin.

It was as much as our heavy cavalry brigade could do to
cover the retreat of the miserable remnants of that band of
heroes, as they returned to the place they had so lately quitted
in all the pride of life. At 11.35 A.M., not a British soldier,
except the dead and dying, was left in front of the bloody
Muscovite guns. Of the 607 Light Dragoons, Lancers, and
Hussars, who rode so gallantly in the storm of battle, only
198 could be mustered at 2 P.M., and above 400 were killed,
wounded, and missing. Lord Lucan was slightly wounded;
and Lord Cardigan, who led the charge at the head of the
Light Dragoons, received a lance through his clothes. This
gallant brigade, a majority of whom had so suddenly met a
bloody death, were the flower of the whole army, and many
a heart is saddened by their untimely fate.

While this affair was going on, the French cavalry made a
most brilliant charge at the battery on our left, which was firing on our men, and cut down the gunners; but they could
not get off the guns, and had to retreat with a loss of two cap-
tains and fifty men out of their little force of 200 Chasseurs.
The heavy cavalry, in columns of squadrons, moved slowly
backwards, covering the retreat of the broken men. The
ground was left covered with our men, and with hundreds of

Russians, and we could see the Cossacks busy searching the dead. The Russians were finally compelled to retreat up the gorge, successively abandoning Nos. 1, 2, and 3 redoubts, and blowing up the magazine of No. 2 as they left it. The cannonade ceased at 1.15 P.M., and the two armies retained their respective positions. Balaklava still remained in our possession, in spite of the most desperate efforts of the enemy to drive us from our position. Our loss was above 500 in all. Another such victory would ruin us."

LETTERS FROM THE COMBATANTS.

A corporal of the 5th Dragoons, one of the regiments engaged in the terrible charge of the 25th, writes home as follows :

"Dear Father and Mother: I am glad to tell you that we had an engagement with the Russians on the 25th of this month. We turn out in marching ordei every morning at four o'clock; it is quite dark then, so we stand to our horses till about one hour after daylight, because we expected an attack before this, as they have been gathering their army about three miles from our camp, this last fortnight They had before the action 34,000 men. Well, on the morning of the 25th, just as daylight was breaking, the cannon commenced firing from our batteries on the hills, and about seven o'clock we advanced just opposite our batteries under the hill. We could not see our enemies, but they kept firing at our artillery, and shell was flying over our heads and dropping all round us. Our artillery had to retire, as they had no more ammunition; so after a while the Turks started, left the batteries, and run down the hill as hard as ever they could. Well, the enemy got possession of our batteries, and we could see them bringing their guns up the hill; and in a few minutes the shot and shell was coming pretty fast; they were firing six-pounders at us, and we could see the balls coming; we shouted out, 'Look out, boys;' they came with such force against the ground that they would rise and go for half a mile before they would touch the ground again. Us and the Greys lost some horses there. We had to retire out of the range of the guns. We had no infantry up at the time, except the Highlanders; for the Turks had all run away, so their cavalry came galloping over the hills. Some of them went to attack the Highlanders, who formed square, and popped them off nicely, so they retired from them. In the mean time, another lot of cavalry came to attack us; I suppose they thought we should run. At first we thought they were our Light Brigade, till they got about twenty yards from us; than we saw the difference. We wheeled into line; they stood still, and did not know what to do. The charge sounded, and away we went into the midst of them. Such cutting and slashing for about a minute, it was dreadful to see; the rally sounded, but it was no use, none of us would come away until the enemy retreated; then our fellows cheered as loud as ever they could. When we were in the midst of them my horse was shot; he fell, and got up again, and I was entangled in the saddle; my head and one leg were on the ground. He tried to gallop on with the rest, but fell again, and I managed to get loose. While I was in that predicament a Russian lancer was going to run me through, and I could not help myself. Macnamara came up at the time, and nearly severed his head from his body, so thank God I did not get a scratch. I got up, and ran to where I saw a lot of loose horses; I got one belonging to one of the Enniskilleners, and soon was along with the regiment again. When I had mounted again, I saw a Russian who had strayed from the rest; he rode up to try and stop me from joining the regiment again. As it happened, I had observed a pistol in the holster pipe, so I took it out, and shot him in the arm; he dropped his sword; then I immediately rode up to him and run him through the body; the poor fellow dropped to the ground. Lord Lucan said, when we charged, that we were into them, and the devil could not get us away from them. Lord Raglan sent his compliments to General Scarlett, and said that the heavy brigade behaved gallantly. We had two men killed; Corporal Taylor was one, and Ealing was the other, and fourteen wounded. In the evening they wanted to give the Light Division a chance, and sent them to retake the guns. The poor fellows went, and not half of them came back. The Donalys are safe. We expected an attack this morning, but they did not advance. We expect to be engaged to-morrow, but we don't care a pin about them as long as we have plenty of our infantry; that day there was none there but cavalry and artillery."

A French Zouave before Sebastopol, thus details his rather singular experience:

"MY DEAR FATHER: I have been leading of late the life of a poacher. I am every day on the look out for a Russian, being attached to a company of *francs tireurs*, or riflemen. Our duty is to fire at the Russian artillerymen and to protect our own, who have no reason to be dissatisfied with us yet. I can not say the same of the Russians, who appear to suffer greatly from our rifles. To give you an idea of our mode of acting, we set out at two in the morning, fully accoutred, with a supply of ammunition and biscuit. On our arrival in the trenches, we are provided with bags, a shovel, and a pickaxe. At a given signal, we jump over the parapets with the agility of stags, and take refuge in some sheltered spot under the forts, where we dig a kind of rabbit-hole to hide in. We place our bags as a protection on the side facing the enemy, and we then set to work. We remain in this sort of tomb the entire day; we leave it at dark, often exposed to a shower of grape shot. You will naturally ask, dear father, what we have to do all that time. I can assure you that we have plenty to do. We load and fire in rapid succession, and every shot tells on a Russian artilleryman. The other day two officers were standing on a piece of timber placed on the top of a tower opposite my station for the purpose of having a view of our works. With two shots I brought down those gentlemen, and at the same moment the batteries let fly a discharge of balls, shells, and grape shot, which fortunately passed over my head."

BADLY CUT UP—THE SURGEONS AT WORK.

"The Greys have again distinguished themselves beyond praise, suffering, however, severely in the affair of the 25th. They charged right through the Russian cavalry, who num-bered about five to one; got surrounded by them, made another charge, and cut themselves out by sheer fighting. Colonel Griffith got shot in the head; Brevet-Major Clarke a sabre-cut at the back of his neck; Cornet Prendergast shot right through the foot; Cornet Handley stabbed in the side and arm, being at one time surrounded by four Cossacks, three of whom he shot with his revolver, and the fourth was cut down by his sergeant. I saw this young gallant fellow a few hours after, and he was then getting ready to rejoin his regiment from the temporary hospital, not finding his two wounds of sufficient consequence to keep him from his post. The Colonel did the same, after getting his head dressed. Major Clarke did not, I believe, leave the field. I also saw Lieutenant Eliot, 5th Dragoon Guards, riding into Balaklava, his face so covered with blood, and his head bound up, that we could not ·ecognize him. The gallant Captain White, too, of the 17th Lancers, was lying on his back when we came up to him. with a round shot right through his leg, with Sir W. Gordon dreadfully cut about the head, both receiving, however, every attention and care from Surgeon Kendall. In this garden and temporary hospital could be seen men with every description of wound, from the sabre-cut to the grape and canister shot. One poor fellow's leg was taken off while we were there, nor can one easily forget the shocking scenes, the result of such a day's fighting. The surgeons (Brush and his assistant, Chapple,) of the Greys, were working away with their sleeves turned up, arms bloody, faces the same, looking more like butchers than surgeons, so hard they worked all day.

SORTIE THE NEXT DAY.

On the 26th, the Russians, elated by the easy success gained over the Turks the day previous, ventured an attack upon the British lines. Toward noon three large columns, numbering nine thousand infantry, with a numerous artillery, were seen advancing along a ravine directly on the encampment of the 2d British Division. A brisk fire of eighteen guns was opened upon them, and at the same time a volley of shells tore open their ranks with great carnage. A Lancaster gun was also brought to bear upon them, belching forth a shower of grape; and a few rockets, dexterously discharged into their midst, transformed the panic which had commenced into a complete rout. Regiment after regiment started in pursuit of the flying foe at a rattling pace, eager to settle scores with them for many a false and wearisome night alarm. Many of the fugitives were killed during the flight, and the carnage was only staid by the Russians taking refuge within the walls of Sebastopol. General Gortchakoff, who commanded the sortie, was wounded in the hip; and about eighty prisoners were brought in by the skirmishers. The Russian loss was about four hundred, that of the British less than a quarter of that number.

THE SIEGE CONTINUED.

The state of the besieged was now getting desperate. The fire of the Allies had become more and more effective; their lines of batteries having from a range of one thousand two hundred or one thousand five hundred yards at the commencement, approached to within three hundred yards of the walls. The town was almost a heap of ruins; there was no rest either night or day for the soldiers; no time to bury the dead; and the stench arising from their decaying bodies infected the whole atmosphere; and fires from hot shot and shells were of frequent occurrence. To add to their miseries, the Allies had destroyed the aqueduct which supplied water to the town, and it had to be obtained from wells outside the walls, where women and children came early every morning, and were permitted to return without molestation.

On the 28th a terrible calamity occurred. A shell from the camp of the Allies struck upon the roof of the hospital in Sebastopol, shattered its walls, set it on fire, and it is said that two thousand wounded Russians perished in the flames. It is believed that the Allies did not intentionally fire upon the building, or else supposed the hospital flag had been raised over the principal magazine of the fortress, with the view of thus saving it from destruction.

We now come to the most important event of the siege.

THE BATTLE OF INKERMANN.

The bloodiest page in the great war drama is now to be given. We should have to go far back in history to find the record of a battle so fiercely contested as that of Inkermann. No instance is called to mind, this side of Thermopylæ, where an invincible handful so successfully withstood the crushing force of overwhelming numbers. For eight terrible hours, 14,000 of the Allies thrust back, with great slaughter, 60,000 Russians, inspired by patriotism, religious fanaticism, and ' the stimulus of intoxication.

For a day or two previously to the 5th of November, the Russians, who already possessed a large force within the prolonged fortifications, and a large force toward the rear, in the neighborhood of Balaklava, had been observed to receive reinforcements, estimated at 30,000 or 40,000, which, added to Liprandi's corps on the Russian left, of 35,000 or more, and the garrison, would probably justify General Canrobert's estimate of 100,000 men, in one way and another, arrayed against the Allies on the memorable 5th of November. To augment the weight of the force brought down to crush the besiegers, the now useless army of the Danube had been withdrawn from Moldavia, leaving Bessarabia still defended by its special army · but not, it is supposed, entirely exhausting the reinforcements to be brought from the interior. The effort of Menchikoff to throw his strength into a succession of powerful, and, if possible, decisive blows, is shown by the advance of Dannenberg's army in the very lightest order, augmenting the numbers about Sebastopol, without much regard either to their equipment or provision. The aim was to bear down by accumulated pres- sure; and it was with such a view that the batteries resumed the bombardment of the Allies in their besieged camp; a strong force from the garrison moved out to act with Dannenberg's army, and Liprandi made a feint that might have been, had it succeeded, a penetrating attack toward the rear; and, as it was, it did engage the attention of a portion of the British and French forces. Thus the Allies were to be occupied all round, while the weak, unintrenched and unfortified point in their position toward the valley of the Inkermann was to be pene- trated by a force of great weight and momentum.

It had rained incessantly the night before, and the early morning gave no promise of any cessation of the heavy showers which had fallen for the previous four-and-twenty hours. To wards dawn, a heavy fog settled down on the heights and on the valley of the Inkermann, and as day began to dawn, was so thick that one could scarcely see two yards before him.

At 4 o'clock, the bells of the churches in Sebastopol were heard ringing drearily through the cold night air, but the oc- currence has been so usual, that it excited no particular atten- tion. During the night, however, a sharp-eared sergeant, on an outlying picket of the Light Division, heard the sound of wheels in the valley below, as though they were approaching the position up the hill. He reported the circumstance to Major Bunbury; but it was supposed that the sound arose from ammunition carts or arabas going into Sebastopol by the Ink- ermann road. No one suspected for a moment that enormous masses of Russians were creeping up the rugged sides of the heights over the valley of Inkermann on the undefended flank of the Second Division. There all was security and repose. Little did the slumbering troops in camp imagine that a subtle and indefatigable enemy were bringing into position an over- whelming artillery, ready to play upon their tents at the first glimpse of daylight.

The Russians had well chosen the point of attack; it was the only ground where the English camp was exposed to sur- prise; for a number of ravines and unequal curves in the slope of the hill, toward the valley, lead up to the crest and summit, against the adverse side of which their flank was resting, with- out guns, entrenchments, abattis, or outlying defense of any kind. A battery was thrown up with sand-bags and gabions and fascines on the slope of the hill over Inkermann on the east, but no guns were mounted there, for Sir De Lacy Evans thought that two guns in such a position, without any works to support them, would only invite attack and capture. This officer is severely censured for not having made more efficient preparations to repel an attack upon his position.

It was a little after 5 o'clock this morning when Brigadier-General Codrington visited the outlying pickets of his own brigade of the Light Division. Having heard the report that "all was well," he turned his horse's head, and had proceeded but a few paces, when a sharp rattle of musketry was heard down the hill, to the left of the Light Division. The well-informed correspondents of the *London Times* and *Morning Herald*, who were on the ground, give a graphic description of the scenes that followed.

The Russians were advancing in force upon us! Their gray great-coats rendered them almost invisible even when close at hand. The pickets of the 2d Division had scarcely made out the advancing line of infantry, who were clambering up the steep sides of the hill through a drizzling shower of rain, when they were forced to retreat by a close sharp volley of musketry, and were driven up toward the brow of the hill, contesting every step of it, and firing as long as they had a round of ammunition on the Russian advance. The pickets of the Light Division were assailed soon afterward, and were also obliged to retreat and fall back on their main body, and it was evident that a very strong sortie had been made upon the right of the position of the Allied armies, with the object of forcing them to raise the siege, and, if possible, of driving them into the sea.

About the same time that the advance of the Russians on our right flank took place, a demonstration was made by the cavalry, artillery, and a few infantry in the valley against Balaklava, to divert the attention of the French on the heights above, and to occupy the Highland Brigade and Marines, but only an interchange of a few harmless rounds of cannon and musketry took place, and the enemy contented themselves with drawing up their cavalry in order of battle, supported by field artillery, at the neck of the valley, in readiness to sweep over the heights and cut our retreating troops to pieces should the assault on our right be successful.

A steamer with very heavy shell-guns and mortars was sent up by night to the head of the creek at Inkermann, and caused much injury throughout the day by the enormous shells she pitched right over the hill upon our men. Every thing that could be done to bind victory to their eagles—if they have any —was done by the Russian generals. The presence of their Grand Duke, Michael Nicholavitch, who told them that the Czar had issued orders that every Frenchman and Englishman was to be driven into the sea ere the year closed, cheered the common soldiers, who regard the son of the Emperor as an emanation of the divine presence. They had abundance of a coarser and more material stimulant, which was found in their canteens and flasks; and, above all, the priests of the Greek Catholic Church "blessed" them ere they went forth upon their mission, and assured them of the aid and protection of the Most High. A mass was said for the army, and the joys of Heaven were freely offered to those who might fall in the holy fight, and the favors of the Emperor were largely promised to those who might survive the bullets of a heretical enemy.

The men in our camp had just begun to struggle with the rain in endeavoring to light their fires for breakfast, when the alarm was given that the Russians were advancing in force. Brigadier-General Pennefather, to whom the illness of Sir De Lacy Evans had given, for the time, the command of the 2d Division, at once got the troops under arms. One brigade, under Brigadier-General Adams, consisting of the 41st, 47th, and 49th regiments, was pushed on to the brow of the hill to check the advance of the enemy by the road through the brushwood from the valley. The other brigade, (Brigadier-General Pennefather's own,) consisting of the 30th, 55th, and 95th regiments, was led to operate on their flank. They were at once met with a tremendous fire of shell and round shot from guns which the enemy had posted on the high grounds in advance of our right, and it was soon found that the Russians had brought up at least forty pieces of heavy artillery to bear upon us.

Owing to the fog they took but a blind aim, yet nevertheless their shot and shell flew in all directions for the space of nearly twenty minutes, while the cannonade in rear of the line at Balaklava was also redoubled; so that it seemed impossible to say which would prove the true and which the feint attack, or whether they were both true or both feints. The latter opinion was adopted by many, who said that the enemy would never dare attack us in our intrenchments, but rather distract our attention while a sortie was made from the town upon the trenches. As if to confirm this surmise, the instant the canonnade in the rear re-commenced, all forts, redoubts, and batteries round Sebastopol opened with a tremendous roar, which seemed to shake the earth.

The scene at this moment was awful. The whole camp, except to the sea, seemed encircled by fire, as flash after flash lit up the foggy air in all directions. The uproar was perfectly deafening; for our batteries began to reply, and both sides firing shell increased the din two-fold. The shower of

6

these terrible explosives, which rained into the camp like hail, baffles description. No place was safe from them. They killed men and tore the tents to pieces on places which we had hith-erto considered as utterly out of range. Every minute or so they were compelled to throw themselves upon their faces as the terrible missiles came roaring through the air, and pitching within a few yards, sent their fragments humming over the spot where the men crouched close to the earth. For about ten minutes the stunning noise, confusion, and incessant bursting of shells made the whole place seem perfectly unearthly. The horror of the scene was increased by the obscurity of the morn-ing. It was not six o'clock, the darkness and fog were still thick, and through the heavy air the broad red flashes of the guns and their tremendous reports seemed ten times louder than ever. For all that could be seen or told to the contrary, the Russian batteries seemed within fifty yards of us on all sides. Of course, the troops remained under arms, but did not attempt to move until the sharp report of the musketry told where the real attack was to be met.

Meantime the alarm had spread through the camps. Sir George Cathcart, with the greatest promptitude, turned out as many of his division as were not employed in the trenches, and led the portions of the 20th, 21st, 46th, 57th, 63d, and 68th Regiments, which were available, against the enemy, directing them to the left of the ground occupied by the columns of the 2d Division. It was intended that one brigade, under Brigadier-General Torrens, should move in support of the brigade under Brigadier-General Goldie; but it was soon found that the enemy were in such strength that the whole force of the division, which consisted of only 2200 men, must be vigorously used to repel them. Sir George Brown had rushed up to the front with his brave fellows of the Light Division—the remnants of the 7th Fusileers, of the 19th Regi-ment, of the 23d Regiment, of the 33d Regiment, and the 77th and the 88th Regiments, under Brigadiers Codrington and Buller. As they began to move across the ground of the 2d Division, they were at once brought under fire by an unseen enemy. The gloomy character of the morning was unchanged. Showers of rain fell through the fogs, and turned the ground into a clammy soil, like a freshly-ploughed field; and the Russians, who had, no doubt, taken the bearings of the ground ere they placed their guns, fired at random indeed, but with too much effect on our advancing columns. While all the army was thus in motion, the Duke of Cambridge was not behind-hand in bringing up the Guards under Brigadier Ben-tinck—all of his division now left with him, as the Highland

ers are under Sir Colin Campbell at Balaklava. These
splendid troops with the greatest rapidity and ardor rushed to
the front on the right of the 2d Division, and gained the
summit of the hills, toward which two columns of the Russians
were struggling in the closest order of which the nature of the
ground would admit. The 3d Division, under Sir R. England, was also got under arms as a reserve, and one portion of
it, comprising the 50th, part of the 28th and of the 4th Regiments, were engaged with the enemy ere the fight was over.

And now commenced the boldest struggle ever witnessed
since war cursed the earth. It has been doubted by military
historians if any enemy have ever stood a charge with the
bayonet; but here the bayonet was often the only weapon
employed in conflicts of the most obstinate and deadly character. We have been prone to believe that no foe could ever
withstand the British soldier wielding his favorite weapon, and
that at Maida alone did the enemy ever cross bayonets with
him; but at the battle of Inkermann not only did we charge
in vain—not only were desperate encounters between masses
of men maintained with the bayonet alone—but we were
obliged to resist bayonet to bayonet the Russian infantry again
and again, as they charged us with incredible fury and determination.

It was six o'clock when all the head-quarter camp was roused
by roll after roll of musketry on the right, and by the sharp
report of field-guns. Lord Raglan was informed that the enemy was advancing in force; and soon after seven o'clock he
rode toward the scene of action, followed by his staff, and accompanied by Sir J. Burgoyne, Brigadier-General Strangways,
R. A., and several aides-de-camp. As they approached the
volume of sound, the steady, unceasing thunder of gun, and
rifle, and musket, told that the engagement was at its height.
The shell of the Russians, thrown with great precision, burst
so thickly among the troops, that the noise resembled the continuous discharges of cannon, and the massive fragments inflicted
death on every side. One of the first things the Russians did,
when a break in the fog enabled them to see the camp of the
2d Division, was to open fire on the tents with round shot
and large shell, and tent after tent was blown down, torn to
pieces, or sent into the air, while the men engaged in camp
duties, and the unhappy horses tethered up in the lines, were
killed or mutilated.

Colonel Gambier was at once ordered to get up two heavy
guns (18 pounders) on the rising ground, and to reply to a fire
which our light guns were utterly inadequate to meet. As he

was engaged in this duty, and was exerting himself with Capt. Daguilar to urge them forward, Col. Gambier was severely but not dangerously wounded, and was obliged to retire. His place was taken by Lieutenant-Colonel Dickson, and the conduct of that officer in directing the fire of those pieces, which had the most marked effect in deciding the fate of the day, was such as to elicit the admiration of the army, and as to deserve the thanks of every man engaged in that bloody fray. But long ere these guns had been brought up, there had been a great slaughter of the enemy, and a heavy loss of our own men. Our generals could not see where to go. They could not tell where the enemy were—from what side they were coming, and where going to. In darkness, gloom, and rain, they had to lead our lines through thick, scrubby bushes and thorny brakes, which broke our ranks and irritated the men, while every pace was marked by a corpse or man wounded from an enemy whose position was only indicated by the rattle of musketry, and the rush of ball and shell.

Sir George Cathcart, seeing his men disordered by the fire of a large column of Russian infantry which was outflanking them, while portions of the various regiments composing his division were maintaining an unequal struggle with an overwhelming force, rode down into the ravine in which they were engaged, to rally them. He perceived at the same time that the Russians had actually gained possession of a portion of the hill in rear of one flank of his division, but still his stout heart never failed him for a moment. He rode at their head encouraging them, and when a cry arose that the ammunition was failing, he said coolly, "*Have you not got your bayonets?*" As he led on his men, it was observed that another body of men nad gained the top of the hill behind them on the right, but it was impossible to tell whether they were friends or foes. A deadly volley was poured into our scattered regiments. Sir George cheered them and led them back up the hill; but a flight of bullets passed where he rode, and he fell from his horse close to the Russian columns. The men had to fight their way through a host of enemies, and lost fearfully. They were surrounded and bayoneted on all sides, and won their desperate way up the hill, with diminished ranks, and the loss of near five hundred men. Sir George Cathcart's body was afterwards recovered, with a bullet-wound in the head, and three bayonet-wounds in the body. In this struggle, where the Russians fought with the greatest ferocity, and bayoneted the wounded as they fell, Colonel Swyny, of the 63d, a most gallant officer; Lieut. Dowling, 20th; and Major Wynne, 68th;

met their death; and Brigadier Goedie, of the 57th Regiment, received the wounds of which he has since died.

The conflict on the right was equally uncertain and equally bloody. In the Light Division, the 88th got so far into the front, that they were surrounded and put into utter confusion, when four companies of the 77th, under Major Straton, charged the Russians, broke them, and relieved their comrades. The fight had not long commenced, ere it was evident that the Russians had received orders to fire on all mounted officers. Sir G. Brown was struck by a shot, which went through his arm and struck his side. I saw with regret his pale but sternly composed face, as his body was borne by me on a litter, early in the day, his white hair flickering in the breeze; for I knew that we had lost the services of a good soldier that day. Further to the right, a contest, the like of which, perhaps, never took place before, was going on between the Guards and dense columns of Russian infantry of five times their number. The Guards had charged them and driven them back, when they perceived that the Russians had outflanked them. They were out of ammunition, too. They were uncertain whether there were friends or foes in the rear. They had no support, no reserve, and they were fighting with the bayonet against an enemy who stoutly contested every inch of ground, when the corps of another Russian column appeared on their right, far in the rear. Then a fearful *mitraille* was poured into them, and volleys of rifle and musketry. The Guards were broken; they had lost twelve officers, who had fell in the field; they had left one half of their number on the ground, and they retired along the lower road of the valley. They were soon reïnforced, however, and speedily avenged their loss. The French advanced about ten o'clock, and turned the flank of the enemy.

The 2d Division, in the centre of the line, were hardly pressed. The 41st Regiment, in particular, were exposed to a terrible fire; and the 95th were in the middle of such disorganizing volleys that they only mustered sixty-four men when paraded at two o'clock. In fact, the whole of the Division numbered only 300 men when assembled by Major Eman, in rear of their camp, after the fight was over. The regiments did not take their colors into the battle; but the officers neverthe-less were picked off wherever they went, and it did not require the color-staff to indicate their presence. Our ambulances were soon filled; and, ere nine o'clock, they were busily engaged in carrying loads of men, all covered with blood, and groaning, to the rear of the line. About 9½ o'clock, Lord Raglan and his staff were assembled on a knoll, in the vain hope of getting a glimpse of the battle which was raging below them Here Gen.

Strangways was mortally wounded, and I am told that he met his death in the following way : A shell came right in among the staff ; it exploded in Captain Somerset's horse, ripping him open ; a portion of the shell tore off the leather overalls of Captain Somerset's trowsers, it then struck down Captain Gordon's horse and killed him at once, and then blew away General Strangway's leg, so that it hung by a shred of flesh and a bit of cloth from the skin. The poor old General never moved a muscle of his face. He said merely, in a gentle voice, "*Will any one be kind enough to lift me off my horse?*" He was taken down and laid on the ground, while his life-blood ebbed fast, and at last he was carried to the rear. But the gallant old man had not sufficient strength to undergo an operation, and in two hours he had sunk to rest, leaving behind him a memory which will ever be held dear by every officer and man of the army.

The fight about the battery before alluded to was most sanguinary. It was found that there was no banquette to stand upon, and that the men inside could not fire upon the enemy. The Russians advanced mass after mass of infantry. As fast as one column was broken and repulsed, another took its place. For three long hours about 8500 British infantry contended against at least four times their number. No wonder that, at times, they were compelled to retire. But they came to the charge again. The admirable devotion of the officers, who knew they were special objects of attack, can never be too highly praised. Nor can the courage and steadiness of the few men who were left to follow them in this sanguinary assault on the enemy be sufficiently admired. At one time, the Russians succeeded in getting up close to the guns of Capt. Wodehouse's and of Capt. Turner's batteries, in the gloom of the morning. Uncertain whether they were friends or foes, our artillerymen hesitated to fire. The Russians charged them suddenly, bore all resistance down before them, drove away or bayoneted the gunners, and succeeded in spiking some of the guns. Their columns gained the hill, and for a few moments the fate of the day trembled in the balance ; but Adam's Brigade, Pennefather's Brigade, and the Light Division, made another desperate charge, while Dickson's guns swept their columns, and their Guards, with undiminished valor and steadiness, though with a sadly-decreased front, pushed on again to meet their bitter enemies. The rolling of musketry, the clash of steel, and the pounding of guns were deafening ; and the Russians, as they charged up the heights, ye'' d like demons. They advanced, halted, advanced again, . ece ved and returned a close and deadly fire; but the Minié is .he king of weapons—Inkermann proved it.

The regiments of the 4th Division and the Marines, armed

with the old and much-belauded Brown Bess, could do nothing
with their thin line of fire against the massive multitudes of the
Muscovite infantry; but the volleys of the Minié rifle cleft them
like the hand of the destroying angel, and they fell like leaves
in autumn before them. About ten o'clock, a body of French
infantry appeared on our right, a joyful sight to our struggling
regiments. The Zouaves came on at the *pas de charge.* The
French artillery had already begun to play with deadly effect on
the right wing of the Russians. Three battalions of the Chasseurs d'Orleans (I believe they had No. 6 on their buttons)
rushed by, the light of battle on their faces. They were accompanied by a battalion of Chasseurs Indigènes—the Arab Se-
poys of Algiers. Their trumpets sounded above the din of
battle, and when we watched their eager advance right on
the flank of the enemy, we knew the day was won. Assailed
in front by our men—broken in several places by the impetuosity of our charge, renewed again and again—attacked by the
French infantry on the right, and by artillery all along the
line, the Russians began to retire, and, at twelve o'clock, they
were driven pell-mell down the hill towards the valley, where
pursuit would have been madness, as the roads were all covered
by their artillery. They left mounds of dead behind them.
Long ere they fled, the Chasseurs d'Afrique charged them most
brilliantly over the ground, difficult and broken as it was, and
inflicted great loss on them; while the effect of this rapid
attack, aided by the advance of our troops, secured our guns,
which were only spiked with wood, and were soon rendered fit
for service. Our own cavalry, the remnant of the Light Brigade,
were moved into a position where it was hoped they might be
of service; but they were too few to attempt any thing, and
while they were drawn up they lost several horses and some
men. One officer, Cornet Cleveland, was struck by a piece
of shell in the side, and has since expired. There are now
only two officers left with the fragment of the 17th Lancers—
Captain Godfrey Morgan and Cornet George Wombwell. At
twelve o'clock, the battle of Inkerman seemed to have been
won; but the day, which had cleared up for an hour previously
so as to enable us to see the enemy and meet him, again became
obscured. Rain and fog set in, and as we could not pursue the
Russians, who were retiring under the shelter of their artillery,
we had formed in front of our lines, and were holding the battle-field so stoutly contested, when the enemy, taking the advantage of our quietude, again advanced, while their guns pushed
forward and opened a tremendous fire upon us. General Canrobert, who never quitted Lord Raglan for much of the early
part of the day, at once directed the French to advance and

outflank the enemy. In his efforts he was ably seconded by General Bosquet, whose devotion was noble. Nearly all his mounted escort were down beside and behind him. General Canrobert was slightly wounded. His immediate attendants suffered severely. The renewed assault was so admirably repulsed, that the Russians sullenly retired, still protected by their crushing artillery. The Russians, about 10, made a sortie on the French lines, and traversed two parallels before they could be resisted. They were driven back at last with great loss, and as they retired they blew up some of the mines inside the Flagstaff Fort, evidently afraid that the French would enter pell-mell after them. At one o'clock the Russians were again retiring. At 40 minutes past one, Dickson's two guns smashed their artillery, and they limbered up, leaving five tumbrils and one gun-carriage on the field.

THE FEROCITY OF THE COMBATANTS.

The battle of Inkermann, says another eye-witness, admits of no description. It was a series of dreadful deeds of daring, of sanguinary hand-to-hand fights, of despairing rallies, of desperate assaults—in glens and valleys, in brushwood-glades and remote dells, hidden from all human eyes, and from which the conquerors, Russians or British, issued only to engage fresh foes, till our old supremacy, so rudely assailed, was triumphantly asserted, and the battalions of the Czar gave way before our steady courage and the chivalrous fire of France.

An English officer who participated in and was severely wounded in the battle, but who has subsequently returned to London, bears still more emphatic testimony to the fury of the contest. I have, he says, already read the accounts forwarded by newspaper correspondents—I have already seen the enumeration of the Russians slain; but, on my conscience, I believe no description, no enumeration, has at all reached the mark. I was in every battle of the Peninsula—I have seen horrors enough for any one man's life; but never, never, did I witness any thing approaching to the carnage, the fury, the fiendish deviltry of that drizzling morning of the 5th. I saw whole ranks battle with their musket-stocks at men who played at quarter-staff; I saw them hang on each other like gnashing bull-dogs, and roll on the ground over and over again, stabbing, tearing, cutting, and mangling like men who had lost every characteristic of humanity, and acquired more than tiger ferocity.

AFTER THE BATTLE—A TERRIBLE PICTURE.

Here is a picture which must have frozen the blood of the spectator:

"Toward evening I walked over the battle-field; but I can never describe to your readers what it was like. Its horrors beggar all description—12,000 dead and wounded English, French, and Russian, lay upon the heights, and the groans and screams of agony were rising up from all parts. Alma was a mere skirmish to it. What made the scene worse was, that the Russians, from the ships in the harbor and the fortifications to the north, were throwing a perfect storm of shell all over the field, killing their own and our wounded.

Later the same evening, I took a second survey of the scene. A considerable number, some 800 or 1000 Russian killed and wounded, were lying among our tents, and here also were many, too many, corpses of Zouaves and French Infantry of the line. All our wounded had been removed, and the wounded of the enemy were being gathered in. The kindness and attention of our fellows to their helpless enemies was beyond all praise. They brought them water, got knapsacks to put under their heads, and borrowed blankets in which to cover them from the raw night air; here and there small groups of them stood absorbed in pity round some prostrate foe, to whom their kindness came too late, and who, shot either through the head or lungs, gasped out his existence in painful sobs, or terminated it in a horrible convulsion which made your blood curdle to hear.

A little above the line of tents was the brow of the hill overlooking Inkermann Lights. Here was the spot where the Allied artillery engaged that of the enemy after the retreat, and here the sight was sickening, indeed. There is nothing so awful as the spectacle of the bodies of those who have been struck down by round shot or shell. One poor fellow of the 95th had been struck by two 24-pounders in the head and body. A shell afterward burst on him and tore him to pieces, and it was only by the fragments of cloth, with the regimental buttons adhering, that you could tell the rough bloody mass which lay in the road had ever been a human being. But it is useless to dwell on these sickening details; suffice to say that here, among the carcasses of some 200 killed and wounded horses, lay the bodies of our brave English and French artillerymen, all more or less frightfully mutilated. Some had their heads taken off at the neck, as if with an axe; others their legs gone from the hips; others their arms, and others, again, who were hit in the chest or stomach, were literally as smashed as if they had been crushed in a machine. But it was not alone the Allies who lay here ; on the contrary, there were ten Russian corpses for one of theirs ; but the latter were all killed by musketry before the artillery came up. On this spot the Russians kept dropping shells the whole night; but their vindictive efforts were in vain : all who lay within reach of their missiles had suffered the last which they were to endure on earth.

Passing up the road to Sebastopol between heaps of Russian dead, you came to the spot where the Guards had been compelled to retire from the defense of the wall above Inkermann Valley. Here our dead were nearly as numerous as the enemy's. Across the path, side by side, lay five Guardsmen, who were killed by one round shot as they advanced to charge the enemy. They lay on their faces, in the same attitude, with their muskets tightly grasped in both hands, and all had the same grim, painful frown upon their features, like men who were struck down in the act of closing with their foes. Beyond this, the Russian Guardsmen and line regiments lay as thick as leaves, intermixed with dead and wounded horses. The latter, with fractured limbs, were now and then rising, and, after staggering a few steps, rolling over among the corpses, snorting and plunging fearfully.

Up to the right of the wall was the way to the two-gun battery. The path lay through thick brushwood ; but the path was slippery with blood, and the brushwood was broken down and encumbered with the dead. The scene from the battery was awful—awful beyond description. I stood upon the parapet at about nine at night, and felt my heart sink as I gazed upon the scene of carnage around. The moon was at its full, and showed every object as if by the light of day. Facing me was the Valley of Inkermann, with the Chernaya like a band of silver flowing gracefully between the hills, which for varied and picturesque beauty might vie with any part of the world. Yet I shall never recall the memory of Inkermann Valley with any but feelings of loathing and horror; for around the spot from which I surveyed the scene lay upwards of 5000 bodies. Many badly wounded also lay there; and their low, dull moans of mortal agony struck with horrible distinctness upon the ear; or, worse still, the hoarse, gurgling cry and vehement struggles of those who were convulsed before they passed away. Around the hill small groups of men, with hospital-stretchers, were searching out for those who still survived; and others again, with lanterns, busily turning over the dead, looking for the bodies of officers who were known to be killed, but who had not been found. Here also were English women, whose husbands had not returned, hurry‑ ing about with loud lamentations, turning the faces of our dead to the moonlight, and eagerly seeking for what they feared tc find. These latter were far more to be pitied than the inani mate forms of those who lay slaughtered around. The ambu lances, as fast as they came up, received their load of sufferers, and even blankets were employed to convey the wounded to the rear. Outside the battery the Russians lay two and three deep. Inside the place was literally full with bodies of Russian Guardsmen, 55th and 20th. The fine, tall forms of our poor fellows could be distinguished at a glance, though the gray great-coats, stained with blood, rendered them alike externally. They lay as they fell, in heaps ; sometimes our men over three or four Russians, and sometimes a Russian over three or four of ours. Some had passed away with a smile on their faces, and seemed as if asleep ; others were horribly contorted, and with distended eyes and swollen features, appeared to have died in agony, but defying to the last. Some lay as if pre‑ pared for burial, and as though the hands of relatives had arranged their mangled limbs, while others, again, were in almost startling positions, half-standing, or kneeling, clutching their weapons, or drawing a cartridge. Many lay with both their hands extended toward the sky, as if to avert a blow, or utter a prayer, while others had a malignant scowl of mingled fear and hatred, as if, indeed, they died despairing. The moon‑ light imparted an aspect of unnatural paleness to their forms ; and, as the cold, damp wind swept around the hills, and waved the boughs above their upturned faces, the shadows gave a horrible appearance of vitality ; and it seemed as if the dead were laughing, and about to rise. This was not the case on one spot, but all over the bloody field.

The loss of the Allies in the day's battle was about 5000 ; that of the Russians not far from 15,000. The proportionate loss of officers by the Allies was excessive. From their con‑ spicuous uniforms, they are always a fair mark for the Russian sharp-shooters, and these latter apparently neglect no opportu‑ nity of picking them off. The Russian officers, on the con‑ trary, are not distinguishable from common soldiers by their dress."

ENGLISH OFFICERS — HAIR-BREADTH ESCAPES, AND MORTAL DISASTERS.

The Duke had his horse completely smashed under him by a round-shot, and the fall of the animal bruised his leg severely. Beyond this he was not hurt. Major Macdonald, a so, as at Alma, had his horse killed under him. In fact, nearly all the staff-officers were either wounded or had their horses killed. Perhaps there never was an infantry action in which so many chargers and artillery horses were destroyed. Altogether, with staff, we lost about 150, the French about 100, and the Russians nearly 400 horses. Their mangled bodies quite covered the ground. Lord Raglan and staff were in the front of the troops, and in the very thickest of the fire. So hot was the cannonade and musketry round his lordship, that no one can understand how he escaped uninjured An eight-inch shell came roaring and hissing along the ground, passed between the legs of Lord Raglan's horse, and exploded behind him and the staff. They were covered for the moment with dust and smoke, but fortunately escaped unhurt. Major-General Strangways was killed close beside Lord Raglan. When raised from the ground he was perfectly calm and collected, and appeared not to suffer in the least. His thigh was fractured near the hip-joint, and the brave old soldier looked at the mangled limb with perfect composure, saying he knew the wound was mortal. He died in about half an hour after the amputation was performed. Sir George Cathcart, who was only a few paces in front of Lord Raglan, was shot through the heart, and fell from his horse a dead man. Colonel Seymour, who was with him, instantly dismounted, and was endeavoring to raise the body, when he himself received a ball which fractured his leg. He fell to the ground beside his general, and a Russian officer and five or six men running in, bayoneted him, and cut him to pieces as he lay helpless. General Cathcart's corpse was also bayoneted in five or six places. I have mentioned in my letter of this morning, the cold-blooded cruelty with which the enemy treated all the wounded who fell into their hands. In not one solitary instance, as far as can yet be ascertained, was a man spared.

REGIMENTS BADLY CUT UP.

The Coldstream Guards, when they returned from the two-gun battery, leaving about 100 wounded behind, were maddened to perceive that the instant the enemy occupied the place they commenced massacring all the poor defenseless objects. The conduct of the Coldstream Guards should immortalize their name. They fought literally to the death. They went into action with 16 officers and about 400 men, and out of this small number had 8 officers killed, 5 wounded, and upwards of 200 rank and file killed and wounded. The Grenadiers and Fusilers also performed prodigies. On the whole, the brigade of Guards lost 13 officers killed, 15 wounded, and

580 rank and file, out of about 1600 men engaged. The Coldstreams charged the enemy at the point of the bayonet eleven times. At each time the Russians crossed bayonets, and fought fiercely, but were slaughtered like sheep by our gallant fellows. The three' battalions of Guards now barely mustered 1000 effective men. After the Guards, the 2d and 4th divisions have suffered most. The 95th and 30th regiments are the principal sufferers, having lost most of their officers and men. The unfortunate 23d regiment of the Light Division, which was so terribly cut up at Alma, has again lost heavily. The 20th and 55th Regiments, of the 4th division, have lost many men and officers, as well as the 41st, 47th, and 49th Regiments, of the 2d Division.

RUSSIAN BRUTALITIES.

A private letter says: " I can not mention without horror the atrocious conduct of the Russian soldiers to such of our wounded as were passed by them in the repeated changes of ground during the engagement. Nearly every officer and soldier was bayoneted on the ground, and some even mutilated to a great extent. Captain Sir R. L. Newman, of the Grenadier Guards, who was wounded in the leg, received so many bayonet thrusts, and was otherwise so mutilated, that the body was scarcely recognizable. The adjutant of the 95th Regiment was killed under circumstances of similar atrocity. The lieutenant-colonel of the 47th Regiment was surrounded and taken prisoner, dragged from his horse, and bayoneted on the spot. Lieutenant-Colonel Carpenter, of the 41st Regiment, was being conveyed wounded from the field by four of his men, when the Russians surrounded him; the men left him to his fate, when one Russian bayoneted him in the back, another clubbed his musket, and struck him on the head with the intention of dashing his brains out, but by great good fortune the blow only rendered him insensible, in which state he was found, and it is hoped he will yet recover. Captain Crosse, 88th, was wounded in the leg, and surrounded by six Russians, who came to dispatch him. Drawing his revolver, he shot three of them dead upon the spot, wounded the fourth, and the other two took to their heels. Great numbers of wounded soldiers were treated in the same manner."

FATALITY OF THE MINIE RIFLE.

Our Minié bullets have mangled the Russians in the same awful manner as at Alma. Nearly all our dead were killed

by shot and shell. Some of them were so mangled as barely
to be recognizable for human remains. It is awful to stand on
one of the heights and look over the field. The ground is
hidden by the corpses. Round the little battery which was
taken and retaken so often, are 2500 dead Russians. For
about fifty yards around the outside of the battery, the corpses
literally lie two and three deep. Many of the wounded were
afterward killed by the shells which the Russians threw from
the forts to the north of the harbor.

PERSONNEL OF THE RUSSIAN SOLDIERS.

The Russian soldiers were infinitely inferior in appearance
to those we met at Alma. In all that relates to discipline and
courage, our late antagonists were far superior. They were all
clean, but ragged in the extreme. None had knapsacks, but
merely a little canvas-bag of that disgusting, nauseous-looking
stuff they call their bread. No other provisions were found
on any. The knapsacks, I presume, were left behind, in order
that they might scale the heights on our left with greater
facility. Every man wore strong, well-made Wellington boots,
of a stout but rough-looking brown leather. On none, that I
have heard of, were found either money or books. On many
were miniatures of women, and locks of hair. They appear to
have been veteran troops, as a large number bore the scars of
previous wounds. The dead officers, as at Alma, were with
difficulty to be distinguished from the men. Their officers
behaved very well.

It is said that the Russian soldiers had been liberally supplied with liquor previous to the commencement of the attack
of the 5th. Their continued and loud shouting, and the impetuosity of their attack, render it probable that they were
under the influence of some artificial stimulus of the sort. In
the canteens, also, of many of the killed on the field was found
a mixture of raki and water. The men who have fallen into
our hands, though generally of short stature, are of sturdy
frames, with broad chests and well-developed, muscular legs.
Their clothing is well made and warm ; and, though coarse in
texture, an amply sufficient protection against the weather
The voluminous folds of their great-coats, the sleeves of which
are doubled back nearly as far as the elbows, while the skirts
descend to the ankles—throw the " skimping" ordnance great-
coats issued to our troops completely in the shade as regards
comfort and warmth. To prevent the length of the coat incon-
veniencing the wearer when walking, the skirt all around is
made by a very simple contrivance to loop up above the knees.

So, also, the coat can be worn loose like a cloak, or drawn in at the waist. The men carry with them mittens of thick black cloth, the four fingers being together in one, the thumb in another division of the glove.

A GALLANT DEED.

Suddenly the smoke cleared away, and we discovered the Russian infantry in great force within ten yards of us. I shall never forget the aspect of these fellows, dressed in their long gray coats and flat glazed caps, firing most deliberately at our poor gunners, and picking them down like so many crows. We at this time were under a very heavy fire of shot and shell. Major Townsend saw at once the critical position of his guns, and most wisely gave the order to retire, as we were quite unsupported; but too late—the enemy's skirmishers had come up to the guns. However, five out of the six escaped; and one of our men seeing the last, as was then supposed, certain to be taken, judiciously spiked it. The gun belonged to a division of our battery, to which was attached young Miller, one of our lieutenants; and poor Major Townsend, turning round his horse, seeing what was likely to occur, cried out, " You won't disgrace me." The words were hardly out of his mouth when a shell burst in among us, and one unfortunate fragment struck him in the head, and literally crushed it to pieces, of course killing him immediately. Miller drew his sword, and single-handed, galloped his horse towards the gun, riding down one and cutting down a second Russian. He alone turned aside a dozen of the enemy, and we recovered the gun. Was not this a most plucky thing to do? He returned with his gun, without having received even a scratch.

GETTING ACCUSTOMED TO BULLETS, AND TAKING THINGS COOLLY.

When we got under fire of the enemy's large guns, we deployed into line and lay down, and remained one hour in this recumbent position, with shot, shell, grape, canister, and every infernal invention for the destruction of human life, flying over and into us, and all about us, fired from 32, 24, and 18 pounders. Just when we lay down, an 18-pound shot struck and went through one of my front rank men, carrying away his pouch and ammunition; he was the third man on my right, and I thought that things were becoming serious. We lay still for half an hour before any of our artillery came up, and when they did open fire, (as you may imagine,) nine and six-pounders could not do much against heavy guns, securely posted in a commanding position, and well-worked. After lying down for about ten minutes, I began to get a little accustomed to the whiz of the shot and the screech of the canister, etc., over my head ; and, consoling myself with the idea that if there was one of them meant for me, I could not possibly avoid it, I took out my opera-glass and watched the proceedings of the enemy. In a very short time I knew every gun that would bear on my position, and you may imagine my feelings when I saw those guns discharged. The intervals between the discharge and the arrival of the shot (which was sure to pitch somewhere near me) were not, I confess, the happiest moments of my life. I can't describe the feeling exactly. It was not fear, and still it was something of the same nature, I suppose; at all events, it was very unpleasant. If you wish to have my autograph you had better keep this, as not a day and scarcely an hour passes without some deadly missile passing close to us, and perhaps some day one of them may take a fancy to my head, and then you will not hear any more from " your own correspondent at the seat of war." Just this moment two shell burst close to where I am sitting, and one of the men has brought me a very ugly-looking fragment of one of them. I am writing this on my knee, under a stone wall, thrown up for the defense of the picket. My back is nearly broken, and I am perfectly bothered and confused by the incessant firing from our lines and the town, which is now going on for its sixth day. I think the Russian fire is slackening, but this may be fancy. I shall now go for a change, to see if there are any Russians moving about in our neighborhood.

A DRAGOON CAPTAIN'S SENSATIONS IN A CAVALRY CHARGE

" You have, I presume, devoured all the accounts which have been sent home as to our glorious charge. Oh! such a charge! Never think of the gallop and trot which you have often wit nessed in the Phœnix Park when you desire to form a notion of a genuine blood-hot, all-mad charge, such as that I have come out of—with a few lance-prods, minus some gold lace, a helmet chain, and Brown Bill's (the charger's) right ear. From the moment we dashed at the enemy, whose position and so forth, you doubtless know as much about as I can tell you, I knew nothing, but that I was impelled by some irresistible force onward, and by some invisible and imperceptible influence, to crush every obstacle which stumbled before my good sword and brave old charger. I never in my life experienced such a sublime sensation as in the moment of the charge.

Some fellows talk of its being 'demoniac.' I know this, that it was such as made me a match for any two ordinary men, and gave me such an amount of glorious indifference as to life, as I thought it impossible to be master of. It would do your Celtic heart good to hear the most magnificent cheer with which we dashed into what P—— W—— calls 'the gully scrimmage.' Forward—dash—bang—clank, and there we were in the midst of such smoke, cheer, and clatter, as never before stunned a mortal's ear. It was glorious! Down, one by one—aye, two by two—fell the thick-skulled and ever-numerous Cossacks, and other lads of the tribe of old Nick. Down, too, alas! fell many a hero with a warm Celtic heart, and more than one fell, screaming loud for victory. I could not pause. It was all push, wheel, phrensy, strike, and down, down, down they went. Twice I was unhorsed, and more than once I had to grip my sword tighter, the blood of foes streaming down over the hilt, and running up my very sleeve.

"I can not depict my feelings when we returned. I sat down completely exhausted and unable to eat, though deadly hungry. All my uniform, my hands, my very face were bespattered with blood. It was that of the enemy! Grand idea! But my feelings, they were full of that exultation which it is impossible to describe. At least twelve Russians were sent wholly out of the 'way of the war' by my good steel alone, and at least as many more put on the passage to that peaceful exit by the same excellent weapon. So also can others say. What a thing to reflect on! I have almost grown a soldier philosopher, and most probably will, one of these days, if the bullets which are flying about so abundantly give me time to brush up."

HORSE INCIDENTS.

Fictionists are shabby judges of true bravery. No novel ever had a sham hero who comes up to the realities I have witnessed. One of my troop, for instance, had his horse shot under him in the *melée.* "Bloody wars!" he roared, "this won't do;" and right at a Russian he ran, pulled him from his horse by the sword-hand in the most extraordinary manner, then deliberately cutting off his head as he came down, vaulted into the saddle, and turning the Russian charger against its late friends, fought his way. This took less time to do than I to tell it. I saw another of our fellows, unhorsed and wounded, creep under a Russian charger, and run the sword up his belly. The animal plunged and fell on his slayer, crushing him to pieces.

7

SULTAN OF TURKEY.

ALEXANDER II.

R. A. WILLIAMS & N.Y.

LOUIS NAPOLEON.

QUEEN VICTORIA.

CANTONNIER OF THE REGIMENT.

RUSSIANS ATTACKING A BATTERY.

CHARGE OF

ID CAVALRY

CHARGE OF LIGHT CAVALRY AT BALAKLAVA.

FIELD AFTER A SORTIE.

A STORM IN THE BRITISH CAMP BEFORE SEBASTOPOL.

READING NEWS FROM HOME.

GENERAL WINDHAM.

MARSHAL PELISSIER.

PRINCE GORTSCHAKOFF.

FLORENCE NIGHTINGALE.

A FRENCH RUSE.

The French are very good soldiers, and very kind and
good natured. They will do any thing for the English. They
fight to the last man for the English. The Russians came on
us several times in the middle of the night, and we all had to
turn out. But the French laid a plot for them, and they have
never disturbed us since in the night. The French made it up
with some of our riflemen and Highland regiments; and they
moved from their camps about a mile nearer the Russians, and
kindled a great many fires. So the Russians thought to have
a fine grab when they saw the fires. They came up as usual.
The French retreated a certain distance from the fires. Upon
which the Russians came up, and saw nobody there. They
then came on further from the fires ; the French could see them
quite plainly between them and the fires. The French now
went to work, and fired into them, and shot a great many as
they retreated. The Rifles, and Highland regiments then came
up behind them, and gave them a great beating, and then the
cannon fired upon them, and made a terrible slaughter among
them.

Thus far we have faithfully detailed the Battles of the Crimea,
with all their terrible and singular incidents. But the end is
not yet. We may be called upon to add another chapter to
the great War Drama now being enacted in that region.

THE SIEGE CONTINUED.

BOTH besiegers and besieged had suffered so severely by the
terrible conflict of Inkermann, which took place on the 5th of
November, that, by common consent and common necessity,
active hostilities were in a great measure suspended. In fact,
no important action has occurred since then up to the middle
of December; yet the siege during this time was signalized by
a variety of skirmishes and interesting incidents, a summary of
which we give in order of time.

Nov. 9.—Four days had elapsed since the battle of Inkermann, and the Russians had begun to recover their spirits. A
French officer writing on that day says, " You may judge of
the efficiency of the Russian artillery when I tell you that,
while I was dating the letter I am writing, I reckoned forty-twc
shots from the town, which we did not return ; for at this late
hour, half past eight P.M., we take care not to waste our pow-

der like the Russians, forty-two shots in less than one minute! This may appear fabulous, but is nevertheless true; the Russians from time to time being seized with fits of rage, which they give vent to by firing at random volleys of artillery. It is in the evening, or immediately before day, these fits come on. Yesterday, we heard in the city sacred music, hymns, and loud huzzas. There are strange doings at Sebastopol."

Nov. 10.—A cold rain was falling all day, but the besiegers continued their siege works without intermission.

Nov. 11.—Powerful reïnforcements were arriving daily to both armies, and the works were carried on with vigor in every direction.

Nov. 12—About seven P.M., in the midst of a severe storm, the besieged opened a most tremendous fire of artillery, field batteries and musketry. Viewed from the camp, the spectacle was truly grand and imposing. As usual, the Russians threw away their ammunition. The only loss was a French captain, who was supposed to have fallen into an ambuscade or been taken prisoner.

THE GREAT STORM OF NOVEMBER 14—THE WAR SPIRIT SUC
CUMBING TO THE ELEMENTS—WHOLESALE SHIPWRECK
OF THE ALLIED FLEETS.

After a violent rain, a hurricane like those of the West-Indies arose about eight o'clock A.M., when all the siege works were suspended. Men had the greatest difficulty in keeping on their legs. The tents were carried away or destroyed. A melting snow, with compact hail-stones, covered the ground. It was a Russian winter-day in all its hideousness. The fire of the besieged and the besiegers was suspended. Every body mustered courage to struggle against the fury of the elements. The hurricane proceeded from the south-west, and the guard of the trenches, coming to relieve those on duty during the night, were near being blown into Sebastopol. The hurricane continued with the same intensity until five o'clock P.M., and only subsided during the night.

At sea, the storm was most disastrous to the ships of the Allies, forty-six transports and other vessels being destroyed, and many more injured. The British lost eighteen, and the French twelve, off Balaklava, besides fifteen or sixteen which were dismasted. About eighteen or more English vessels were also lost or dismasted at Eupatoria or at the Katcha. Five French line-of-battle ships lost their rudders, and suffered other injuries; the British ships Sampson, Retribution, and Vesuvius also sustained considerable injury. The whole were sent to Constantinople for repairs. A Turkish line-of battle ship went ashore and became a complete wreck at Balaklava, and the flag-ship of the Turkish Admiral was dismasted.

The loss of the Prince, a splendid British ship of two thousand five hundred tons, was a serious calamity to the whole army. She had on board forty thousand suits of clothing, with under-garments, socks, gloves, and a multitude of other articles of the kind, (said to have been a present of Prince Albert to the army,) vast quantities of shot and shell, and, not least in consequence, the medical stores sent out in consequence of the deficiencies which formerly existed. Every thing was lost, and of a crew of one hundred and eighty, only six were saved. She was carried from her moorings on to the rocks with such force, that in ten minutes there was hardly a piece a yard long remaining. The cargo embraced the whole of the winter clothing for the British army. By the loss of the Prince, and also of the Resolute, laden with powder and shells, the British army was for the time being deprived of the means of continuing the siege. The cargo of the Prince was valued at £500,000.

Many lives were lost by the wreck of the other vessels, and quite a number of the poor fellows who were washed ashore, were made prisoners by the Russians, and a few carried into Sebastopol. The Sampson, Firebrand, and other steamers kept off the Russians by the fire of their heavy guns. Some Cossacks came down to the beach and got near enough to fire on some of the men-of-war's boats, killing one man in the Queen's launch and wounding others. One fellow rode close up to a stranded vessel and made a thrust of his lance at a man on board; however, he did not observe that the water deepened very suddenly at the vessel's side; and as he rode in to make his thrust, the horse tumbled over in a hole, and the Cossack, in the great delight of the crew, was nearly drowned, and got to shore half dead under a heavy fire of laughter. A drosky, with two gentlemen in it, drove down to the beach, and came alongside another transport. The gentlemen addressed the crew very civilly, and through the medium of a Swedish boy, who understood what they said, invited them to come on shore. "We are," said they, "Christians like yourselves, and (laying their hands on that organ) we have hearts as well as Englishmen. Don't be drowned. Come on shore, and we'll treat you well." "What do they say?" asked the mate. The boy interpreted. "Just tell them to go to ——, and be off out of that, or I'll soon make them," was the reply. They simply went back to Sebastopol. The Sampson and Firebrand shelled so severely the ranks of some Cossacks, who came down to plunder the wrecks and actually fired on the men-of-war's boat as they pulled in to save the men, that they were driven back precipitately. The shots were so well directed as to strike in the midst of groups of ten or twelve, scattering them in every direction.

The Russians also suffered in their harbor from the storm, and set fire to one of their wrecked vessels. Most of their large buildings were unroofed, and their bridge of boats broken. In the memory of men such a hurricane has not desolated the Crimean shores.

From the storm up to November 18, no firing took place beyond an occasional shot.

A SERIES OF SHARP ENCOUNTERS.

Nov. 20.—A smart affair occurred on the night of the 20th between the British Rifle Brigade and about three hundred Russians, who had established themselves in some caverns and stone huts, in a ravine between the first and second parallels The Rifles advanced, and very soon forced the enemy to retreat, after a brisk fire, in which they killed and wounded a considerable number of the Russians with comparatively little loss to themselves. The enemy fell back on their main body; and when the Rifles had established themselves for the night in the caves which the enemy had occupied, they were assailed by a strong column of Russians, who fired volleys of musketry and rifles against their small force continuously, and were only kept at bay by the deadly return of the Miniés. The action ended in the complete repulse of the Russian columns. The English loss was seven killed, and eighteen or nineteen wounded.

On the night of the 22d, there was a brisk affair between the Chasseurs de Vincennes and the Russian Riflemen in front of the Flagstaff battery earth-work; and the Russians dispelled all absurd myths about their being in want of powder and ball, by a most tremendous cannonade. Assaults and counter-assaults continued, amid a furious fire, which lighted up the skies with sheets of flame from nine o'clock at night until four o'clock in the morning. The French actually penetrated behind the outer entrenchments and established themselves for a time within the 'enciente,' but as there were no preparations for a general assault, they withdrew. Vollies of musketry and salvos of cannon roared through the camp during the whole night, but few lost their rest in consequence, for these affairs had become a nightly occurrence.

The fight between the French and Russian Riflemen, aided

by artillery, was renewed on the night of the 25th. The object of contention was a mud fort near the Quarantine Battery, which the French persisted in holding, although useless. *Nov.* 29.—Storm, wind, and rain. The Russians had much strengthened their defenses. They had scarped the ground in front of all their batteries, constructed strong abattis in front of the lines, thrown up numerous earth-works, and made sunken batteries before all their redoubts, and a long scarp of slopes. During the night, a particularly strong sortie was made on the French. Hearing a noise, a French rifleman crept forward and saw a column of Russians, two thousand strong, forming in the rear of the battery. The French, therefore, seven hundred strong, silently mounted the parapet of their own battery, and received the Russians with a deadly volley, then leaping down, attacked them with the bayonet, and compelled them to retreat.

Nov. 30.—A heavy fire on the French during the night. The Grand Duke Michael, with a very large staff, was observed making a reconnoisance at a distance of one thousand yards. The Grand Duke was recognizable by the profound respect paid to him by all; wherever he went, hats were taken off and heads uncovered. He was also detected by the presence of a white dog which always accompanies him. He is a fine, stout young fellow enough, but did not look in particularly good humor at what he saw through his telescope.

THE ORDER OF THE ENTERTAINMENT,

in the latter part of November, is thus described : " During the day the Russians fire on the British about one gun every five minutes; the English look-out man cries, 'Tower,' 'Redan,' or 'Garden Battery,' and the shot is returned; but the fire on the French is much more lively, and is kept up with some effect on their earth-work and parallel.

Every night, about nine o'clock, the Flagstaff, Quarantine, and Wall Batteries open a furious cannonade, which lasts from twenty to forty-five minutes, as hard as the men can load, right into the French lines, and then follows instantly a sally, the result of which is invariably the same. The Russians push a strong column out of the place, rush toward the first line, drive in the pickets and riflemen, get up to the first parallel, sometimes into it, occasionally beyond it and close to the second parallel, when they are received as they advance, by the French covering parties, with a deadly fire ; they halt and fire in return ; are charged by the French, who rout and pursue them into the town, but who are obliged to retire by the flank fire of the batteries and street guns. In this way the French

lose forty or fifty men, but the loss of the Russians in these
sorties must be considerable. Frequently about daybreak the
Russians repeat the performance.

THE MISERIES OF LIFE IN CAMP.

Under date of Sebastopol, November 25, the correspondent
of the *London Times* furnishes a sad picture of the miseries
to which the soldiers are exposed in camp: " The siege has
been for many days practically suspended, our batteries are
used up and silent, and our army are much exhausted by the
effect of excessive labor and watching, and by the wet and
storm to which they have been so incessantly exposed. It is
now pouring rain, the skies are black as ink, the wind is
howling over the ragged tents, in which the water is sometimes
a foot deep; the trenches are turned into dykes; the men
have not either warm or water-proof clothing, and are out for
twelve hours at a time in the trenches; they are plunged into
the inevitable miseries of a winter campaign—and not a soul
seems to care for their comfort, or even their lives. These are
hard truths, but the people of England must hear them. They
must know that the wretched beggar who wanders about the
streets of London in the rain, leads the life of a prince compared
with the British soldiers who are fighting out here for their
country, and who, we are complacently assured by the
home authorities, are the best-appointed army in Europe.
They are well fed, indeed, but they have no shelter, no rest,
and no defense against the weather. The tents, so long exposed to the blaze of a Bulgarian sun, and now continually
drenched by torrents of rain, let the wet through like sieves,
and are perfectly useless as protections against the weather."
Under these circumstances a great deal of sickness, fever,
dysentery, and diarrhea prevailed, and as many as three hundred
and fifty a day were sometimes on the sick-list. The cholera,
too, which had followed up the army more or less from the
time of leaving Varna, broke out with great virulence on the
night of November 28, and was carrying off the poor fellows
at the rate of sixty per day. On a single night, eighty-five
fell victims to the disease.
Efforts were making, however, to render the soldiers more
comfortable by the erection of sheds and huts, large quantities
of planks having been landed for the purpose. A large number of small wooden houses were also shipped from England,
some time in December, to be set up in the Crimea to shelter the
troops. Fresh supplies of clothing have also been sent. The
provisions for the comfort of the French army seem to have

been made on a much better scale than those for the English, and the soldiers have suffered less.

The Turks are in a most wretched condition. A letter dated Balaklava, December 3, says : The Turkish garrison at this place are dying off at the rate of some one hundred and fifty a day. It is not at all uncommon to see the corpses of these unfortunate beings, who have been stricken down by cholera on their way to hospital, lying along the road-side. Besides this dreadful disease, typhus fever and dysentery are making terrible havoc among their ranks. In spite of all our efforts, the dying Turks have made of every lane and street a *cloaca*, and the forms of human suffering which meet the eye at every turn, and once were wont to shock us, have now made callous, and have ceased even to attract passing attention. Raise up the piece of matting or coarse rug which hangs across the doorway of some miserable house, from within which you hear wailings and cries of pain, and prayers to the Prophet, and you will see in one spot and in one instant a mass of accumulated woes that will serve you with nightmares for a lifetime. The dead, laid out as they died, are lying side by side with the living, and the latter present a spectacle beyond all imagination. The commonest necessaries of a hospital are wanting ; there is not the least attention paid to decency or cleanliness—the stench is appalling—the fetid air can barely struggle out to taint the atmosphere, save through the chinks in the walls and roofs ; and, for all I can observe, these men die without the least effort being made to save them. There they lie just as they were let gently down on the ground by the poor fellows, their comrades, who brought them on their backs from the camp with the greatest tenderness, but who are not allowed to remain with them. The sick appear to be tended by the sick, and the dying by the dying.

Dec. 1.—The state of the roads having prevented the arrival of supplies, a part of the British forces had been put temporarily on a short allowance.

Dec. 2.—Continued rain. The besiegers began to erect huts for shelter. Deserters say that the condition of the Russians in the field is worse than that of the Allies. Much bell-ringing and rejoicing heard in Sebastopol during the night, supposed to be caused by the arrival of provisions.

Dec. 5.—The Russians made a sortie against the French lines, when eight divisions of French, under General Forri, repulsed them with much loss.

Dec. 7.—The besiegers' batteries were reëstablished, and the Allies sufficiently entrenched and provisioned to remain throughout the winter.

Dec. 13.—A Russian dispatch states that up to this date nothing of importance had occurred before Sebastopol. Some small sorties had been successful ; in one of them the Russians captured some small mortars and spiked others of a larger size. The fires of the Allies continued feeble.

INCIDENTS OF THE SIEGE, ETC.

A naval officer writes : " We received the news a short while since from the reports of a French officer, who was taken prisoner, but managed to escape, that, in addition to our killing the Russians, they are killing themselves. He says, ' When I came to the market-place, (or what used to be the market place,) I saw a pair of gallows erected, and three hundred Poles and Russians led out to be hung. This they do if any refuse to work the guns, or if they utter a word in objection. The others the officers keep to their guns with the point of the bayonet.' A few days ago, a Russian officer of the rank of captain deserted, and he said that the Poles would come on our side against the Russians as soon as we stormed the place. I suppose you heard that a blue-jacket, of the ——, two Royal Artillerymen, and one Royal Marine Artilleryman, deserted and joined the Russians. The captain, on hearing this, had the magazine shifted immediately ; and it was lucky he did, for on the next day the shot and shell came pitching on the place where the magazine had been like so many hailstones. I am happy to say that the fellow was a Yankee. By this time he has got his deserts, I think ; for two days ago he ventured out at the head of a party of Russians, as leader, and when these were driven back he was taken by us. When captured, he was in Russian uniform, cross-belted and all."

A private in the 4th Dragoon Guards writes : " There were the Greys and First Royals up at this time, and we charged them—they had nothing else for it, so they charged at the same time. O God! I can not describe it ; they were so superior in numbers that they ' outflanked' us, and we were in the middle of them. I never certainly felt less fear in my life than I did at that time, and I hope that God will forgive me, for I felt more like a devil than a man. We fought our way out of them as only Englishmen can fight ; and the 4th, 5th, and 6th were there up with us. I escaped without a scratch, thank God, though I was covered with blood ; my horse was not even wounded ; but oh ! the work of slaughter that then began—'twas truly awful, but I suppose it was necessary. We cut them down like sheep, and they did not seem to have power to resist. The plain is covered and covered with dead Russians, and of course we left some of our poor comrades on the field."

A medical officer in the Crimea writes : "Many of our senses are considerably altered by our campaigning. Smell, from colds, is quite gone, a great blessing in this country ; taste, from want of practice, considerably blunted; sight, from sleeping with one eye open, and looking out for number one and shells, very acute. Although many have escaped from the fire of the enemy, we have all bled in our country's cause, as we are devoured by insects of the most vulgar description, which in former days we associated with paupers and other tribes belonging to the unwashed ; but in this respect the British officer has descended from his high estate, and when we remember him in all the pride of gold and red cloth, it would be difficult to recognize him in the faded and tattered object seated by the bivouac fire, smoking his pipe contentedly, and dreaming of home and happier days.

"One of the most wonderful things I think is to see the way in which our riflemen go about in small detached parties, crawling along on the ground up the side of a hill, till they appear to be within three hundred yards of the enemy, and thus they lie on their bellies till a chance offers, when crack goes a Minié, and down falls a Russian. I was informed most creditably, that one of these brave fellows a few days since, thought he would go and do a little business on his own account, got away from his company, and crawled up close to a battery under shelter of a hill, lay on his back and loaded, and turned over and fired; when after killing eleven men, a party rushed out, and he took to his heels, but sad to say, a volley, fired after him by this party, levelled him with the earth, and he was subsequently picked up with thirty-two balls in his body."

MISCELLANEOUS ITEMS.

General Liprandi is deprived of his command for a fault committed at Inkermann, on the 5th of November.

Since the siege began, twenty British soldiers have deserted to the Russians. Some of them had been flogged in their own camp, and probably for that reason concluded to try Russian fare. If the accounts we receive of the treatment of Russian soldiers be correct, they will, most likely, repent the step they have taken.

The carriage of Menchikoff, taken at the battle of the Alma, was afterwards exhibited as a curiosity at Constantinople, and is said to be the identical vehicle in which he drove through that city during his insolent embassy of last year. This is what Emerson might call a species of "compensation."

Lord Raglan and General Canrobert, on demanding a formal surrender of Sebastopol, required the women, children, and sick to be sent away, and flags to be hoisted upon the hospitals. The Chasseurs de Vincennes, French riflemen, will be long remembered by the Russians. They signalized themselves during the siege, by their skill in sharp-shooting, by picking off every Russian artilleryman who ventured to show himself at the embrasures.

The noble devotion of Miss Florence Nightingale, and her band of English sisters, who some time in November started on their mission of mercy, to nurse the sick and wounded soldiers in the hospitals near Constantinople, ought to be held in grateful remembrance by all whose sympathies are excited by human suffering, and who can appreciate the self-sacrificing goodness which encounters every risk and welcomes every labor or trial that may relieve it.

When the armies were drawn up at Alma, the French officer who was in attendance on Lord Raglan, for the purpose of communicating with the Marshal, made some observation upon the appearance of the French wing, to the right of the English. "Yes," said Lord Raglan, glancing at his empty sleeve, "France owed me an arm, and she has paid me."

GENERAL PROSPECTS OF THE SIEGE.

The Russian defenses on the south are estimated at one hun dred guns stronger than when the siege began, while, on the other hand, the British have erected a very powerful new battery, not yet opened, on an eminence north of the valley of Inkermann, and commanding every house in Sebastopol, besides being another step toward the complete investiture of the place. By this time the Allies must have received from 15,000 to 20,000 additional troops, besides an abundance of supplies. It is affirmed, but is probably an exaggeration, that the French army will be augmented to twelve divisions, or 120,000 men, which, with the English and Turkish reïnforcements, will make the strength of the Allies 200,000 men, an army which, it is considered, will equal any that Russia can bring into the field. The contingent of Omer Pacha's force, to be sent to the Crimea, is now called 45,000. He was to embark in a few days.

Russian deserters say that provisions and ammunition were be coming scarce in Sebastopol, but there was no famine for either.

PROGRESS OF THE WAR.

JAN. 14th.—The Russians made a most daring sally out, after a few rounds of artillery, and charged with full bayonets, so that the two parties fought hand to hand. Many of the Russians fell, and several of the French were killed. This is about the first instance that the Russians have been known to stand to the bayonet.

JAN. 20th.—The Russians commenced a sharp fire from the tower called Malakoff on the English batteries, but without doing material injury, although kept up for two days.

JAN. 22d.—The Russians made a sortie on the English batteries, and were repulsed after a brisk fire of two days.

JAN. 25th.—The French opened a brisk fire on Sebastopol from six batteries stationed near the Bay of Chersonese. The firing continued to the 28th, every shot during the three days, committing frightful havoc. The barracks of the Russians, on which the fire was especially directed, had to be evacuated.

JAN. 28th.—Sunday was celebrated by an extremely heavy fire of musketry between the Russians and the French covering-parties and sharp-shooters.

JAN. 31st.—Another sortie by the Russians, who were repulsed without material loss by the Allies.

FEB. 1st and 2d.—A demonstration was made by the Russians, but they were driven back with great loss, by the French volunteers.

FEB. 13th.—The Russians made a sortie during the night, but it was not formidable; only five of the French were killed.

FEB. 14th.—Another night-sortie by the Russians, in which the French lost thirty-five men.

FEB. 17th.—The town of Eupatoria was attacked on the eastern side, by eighty pieces of artillery, six regiments of cavalry, under the command of General Korff, and twelve regiments of infantry, consisting of about 25,000 men, under the orders of General Osten Sacken. The combat lasted from 5½ o'clock until 10 o'clock in the morning. The Russians were vigorously repulsed. Their loss is estimated at 500 killed, and the wounded in proportion. The Turks had 88 killed, 250 wounded, and lost 70 horses. Selim Pasha, General of the Egyptian division, and Col. Rustem Bey, were killed. Eighteen French were killed or wounded on shipboard. The attack has not been renewed by the Russians.

The steamers at anchor in the roadstead contributed energetically to the defense of the town.

Since the affair of the 17th February, the Russians have not made any new attempt upon Eupatoria, although many villages are still in flames near the scene of action. More guns have been landed, and additional forces thrown in. The town is in a good state of defense. The battle consisted mainly of a heavy fire of artillery, under cover of which the Russians made two or three attempts to carry the town. They bivouacked on the field without tents or fires, the night after the battle, notwithstanding the weather was intensely cold; the next day they commenced retiring on Simpheropol.

The Russians, in their attack on Eupatoria, suffered a very material loss, which acted as a peremptory check upon their further movements. The French official account of the battle states that the Russians lost 500 killed and 2000 wounded—their artillery lost 300 horses; while others, who walked over the field, estimate the loss of the Russians at 300 killed and 700 wounded; and of the Turks, 80 killed and 200 wounded.

FEB. 19th.—The French mining party succeeded in nearly destroying the Flag-Staff Battery of Sebastopol. General Campbell and General Bosquet made a reconnoissance in force, but a thick fall of snow coming on, it resulted in no engagement.

FEB. 22d and 23d.—The Russians succeeded in erecting a redoubt on the left flank of the fortifications of Sebastopol.

FEB. 23d and 24th.—The French attacked the redoubt and works around the Malakhoff tower, and succeeded in destroying them after some sharp fighting. The French loss is estimated at 100 wounded. No account of the Russian loss has reached us, but it must have been considerable from the desperate character of the encounter. The affair was serious, and gave evidence of the superiority of the French troops over the Russian.

DEATH OF THE EMPEROR NICHOLAS.

MARCH 2d.—The Emperor Nicholas expired to-day at one o'clock. The Emperor had been ill for several days, and complained of oppression of the head and chest. His physicians gave no hopes of his recovery from the first moment of his seizure. An announcement of his speedy dissolution found him calm and fortified for the event; asking his attendant, when "he should become paralyzed?" Not receiving a definite answer, he asked Dr. Carrell, " When shall I suffocate ?" He took the last sacrament, and bid farewell to his wife and family, and blessed them, and the last words he spoke were addressed to the Empress, and were: "Tell Frederick (the King of Prussia) to continue attached to Russia, as he has hitherto been, and never to forget his father's words." He was in his fifty-ninth year at the date of his death, and had reigned Czar of Russia and Finland twenty-nine years, three months, and one day.

On the news reaching Berlin, the Court placed itself in mourning, and orders were issued that the whole Prussian army shall wear the symbols of mourning four weeks. The general feeling in the Prussian capital seemed to be one of regret. At Vienna, the intelligence caused much agitation. An order of the day, by the Emperor of Austria, directs that, "in acknowledgment of the services rendered with noble eagerness by the Emperor Nicholas, during a time of unfortunate trials," the Nicholas regiment of Cuirassiers shall always preserve that name as a souvenir for the Austrian army.

The Emperor Nicholas is succeeded by his eldest son, Alexander, who has issued a manifesto, in which he promises to adhere to the policy of his father. We give the concluding portion: "As the deceased devoted himself incessantly to the welfare of his subjects, so do we, also, on ascending the thrones of Russia, and of Poland and Finland, inseparable from each other, take a solemn oath before God to regard the welfare of our empire as our only object. May Providence, which has selected us for so high a calling, be our guide and protector, that we may maintain Russia on the highest standard of power and glory, and in our person accomplish the incessant wishes and views of Peter, of Catharine, of Alexander, and of our father! May the zeal of our subjects assist us therein! We invoke and command the oath of allegiance to us and to the heir to our throne, our son Alexandrovitch!"

The Grand Duke Constantine has been reconciled with his brother Alexander, and has taken the oath of fidelity to his person and heir. The greatest enthusiasm was manifested during the ceremony. The officers of the house, and the authorities of St. Petersburg and elsewhere, had likewise taken the oaths to the Emperor and the Crown Prince, and the whole garrison was to do so on the 3d.

MARCH 4th.—Sardinia declared war against Russia, and revoked the *exequators* of all Russian diplomatic agents or consuls in the Sardinian States. Prince Menchikoff is recalled from the Crimea, and Prince Gortchakoff invested with the chief command, General Osten-Sacken to be the second in command. General Rüdiger was summoned from the command of the army of Poland to take the direction of the Ministry of War, in the place of Prince Dolgorouki.

MARCH 5TH.—To-day Skender Beg left Eupatoria, with 300 irregular cavalry and 100 Tartar bashi-bazouks, to make a reconnoissance, and he was met by four strong squadrons of Russian regular cavalry. Notwithstanding the disproportion of numbers, an obstinate struggle ensued. Skender Beg was compelled to retreat, retiring slowly, and fighting inch by inch of ground. In this affair, the Russians lost about thirty men. The Tartars had made five prisoners, but they afterwards escaped. Skender Beg had only eleven men killed and two wounded. He himself received a very severe wound.

MARCH 8TH.—Commander Armytage, of the British steam-vessel "Viper," destroyed the Martello Tower, at Djemiteia, and dispersed its garrison. He burnt the fort and barracks, spiked the guns, and destroyed the ammunition, successfully putting to flight the Cossacks, without any casualty on board the "Viper."

MARCH 14TH.—General Osten Sacken announces that, not withstanding the fire of the Allied artillery, he has succeeded in erecting a new redoubt in front of the Kormiloff bastion.

MARCH 16TH.—The French troops carried a line of ambuscades occupied by the Russian sharp-shooters. At the same time, the Russians made a sortie on the extreme left of the English line, which was repulsed. The Russians had fifty men put *hors du combat,* and withdrew in disorder.

MARCH 17TH.—Another severe struggle for the possession of the rifle pits before the Malakoff Tower, between the Russian and French troops. The latter, after gallantly contesting every inch of ground, were compelled to abandon the pits to the Russians, who immediately occupied them, under protection of the heavy guns of the Malakoff Tower. The Russians indulged in a severe rifle practice, and considerably annoyed the Zouaves. Loss of the French is reported as 2 officers and 29 men dead, and 3 officers and 133 men wounded.

MARCH 18TH.—The Russians, in pushing ahead some advanced works, were to-day vigorously attacked by the French, and driven from their position with the loss of a large number.

MARCH 20TH.—Prince Gortchakoff arrived, and took command of the army at Sebastopol.

MARCH 22D AND 23D.—The Russians made a series of sorties on the French line, and fought with desperate bravery, but were eventually repulsed with great slaughter. The English camp was under arms, expecting a general attack on their line; but it was not attempted. The English soldiers do not relish these night-attacks, but the circumstances attending these sorties evince the greatest coolness and bravery on the part of all engaged. The following extract, from a letter written

by the surgeon of an English regiment, will give the reader
an idea of the result of one of these nocturnal sorties:

"I was up till half-past three o'clock this morning with wounded Frenchmen
The Zouaves will soon be exterminated at the rate they are losing men. These
night-attacks are horrid affairs; there are always mistakes: last night, the French
on the left of their advanced works mistook Russians for English, and the English
on the extreme right thought the Russians were French. Some fellows of the
Ninety-seventh, who brought in poor Captain Vicars, (since dead,) would insist in
telling me that the French had fired into our troops; the Russian dead in our
trench was of course the strongest reply. A number of Greeks and Armenians
fought with the Russians last night. The French killed a Greek officer whom
they declare to be seven feet high—a giant. There is now lying dead in our
trench an officer, supposed at first to be a Russian; but his papers show him to
be a Greek. He had thirty-five gold pieces on his person. The dead on the
Mamelon Hill are nearly as thick for about the fourth of an acre as they were at
Inkermann. We have sorties and skirmishes every night, and I am kept constantly on the *qui vive*, being so near to the Mamelon attack."

The loss of the Russians is estimated at 700 killed and 1500
wounded. General Canrobert admits the loss of the French
to have been 200 killed and 500 wounded. The English and
Turkish troops took no active part in these sorties, it being
deemed a point of honor by General Bosquet for his division
of Zouaves to drive the Russians from the rifle pits, and to
repel the attack on their part of the French line.

MARCH 23D.—An agreement was entered into for a suspen-
sion of hostilities for three hours, in order to bury the dead, during which time French, English, and Russian officers were walking about, saluting each other courteously as they passed, and
occasionally entering into conversation; and a constant interchange of little civilities, such as offering and receiving segar-
lights, was going on in each little group. Some of the Russian
officers were evidently men of high rank and breeding. Their
polished manners contrasted remarkably with their plain and
rather coarse clothing. They wore, with few exceptions, the
invariable long gray coat over their uniforms. The French
officers were all *en grande tenue*, and offered a striking contrast
to many of the English officers, who were dressed *à la* Balaklava, and wore uncouth head-dresses, cat-skin coats, and non-
descript paletots. During the burial of the dead, a certain
amount of lively conversation sprung up, in which the Russian
officers indulged in a little badinage. Some of them asked
the Allied officers, "When they were coming in to take the
place?" Others, "When the Allies thought of going away?"
Some congratulated the Allies upon the excellent opportunity
they had of getting a good look at Sebastopol, as the chance
of getting a nearer view, except on similar occasions, was not,
in their opinion, very probable. At one time, a Russian with
a litter stopped by a dead body, and put it into the litter. He

looked round for a comrade to help him. A Zouave at once advanced with much grace, and lifted it. General Bosquet, and several officers of rank of the Allied army, visited the trenches during the armistice, and staff-officers were present, to see that the men did not go out of bounds. The armistice was over about three o'clock. Scarcely had the flag disappeared behind the parapet of the Mamelon before a round shot from the English battery went slap through one of the embrasures of the Russian work, and dashed up a great pillar of earth inside. The Russians at once replied, and the noise of cannon soon reëchoed through the ravines.

APRIL 6TH.—Russians made a sortie on the English line. They were met and repulsed in gallant style, without material loss on either side.

APRIL 9TH.—The Allies commenced bombarding Sebastopol. The cannonade lasted twelve hours, without making any visible impression, notwithstanding that five hundred heavy guns were actively served. It is reported that the beseiged lost 833 men during the bombardment of to-day.

APRIL 10TH.—The cannonading of yesterday was resumed, but without any beneficial result to the Allies.

APRIL 11TH.—Continuation of the bombardment. A breach made in the bastion between the Russian works and the Quarantine Fort. It is reported that three Russian batteries have been dismounted.

APRIL 12TH.—Bombardment continued by the Allies. Omar Pasha landed at Kamiesch with 15,000 men, and will assist at the assault upon Sebastopol.

APRIL 13TH.—The Allies continue the cannonading without gaining material advantage. They declare their loss to be im material, while that of the Russians amounts to thousands of killed and wounded.

APRIL 14th.—The Russians made a sortie from the Flagstaff battery on the left of the French. They fought desperately, and at first drove the French from their position. A sanguinary fight took place, in which the bayonet and the musket-stock were used in a pell-mell struggle ; but soon the French asserted their supremacy, and, in spite of the fierce charge of the Russians, succeeded in driving them back. The loss of the French was considerable ; namely, six officers killed, nine officers wounded, and three hundred men put *hors du combat.*

APRIL 15th.—Lieutenant Mitchell, R.A., and Lieutenant Preston, 88th Regiment, were killed while on duty in the trenches. The fire of the Russians is not so heavy to-day. Every night, one English and one French man-of-war runs in close to the south side of Sebastopol, and discharges a broadside, doing considerable damage. The Redan Battery, Garden Batteries, Round Battery, and Barrack Battery were worked with activity throughout the day. The fire of the Allies on the Mamelon tower is so heavy and constant that the Russians can not get up guns to it. Gen. Bigot died last night from the effects of his wound.

APRIL 16th.—The cannonade on both sides was very heavy throughout the day.

APRIL 17th.—The cannonading still kept up on both sides without any definite results. About five hundred Russian cavalry, escorting a large staff, made a reconnoissance of the Allied position in the valley of Balaklava.

APRIL 21st.—The firing from the Allied army is somewhat slackened, and the bombardment is nearly suspended. A fire occurred in Sebastopol, caused, doubtless, by the explosion of shells from the naval forces. It was extinguished without doing much damage. The French did their best to keep it alive by constant discharges of shell from their Picket-house Battery. The firing was very heavy—almost as vigorous, indeed, as that on the second evening of the bombardment, when twenty-three shells were counted twinkling up among the stars as they swept down from the French batteries upon the Russian works.

APRIL 27th.—The 77th Regiment made a successful attack on the rifle-pits in front of the Redan tower, and after a severe hand-to-hand struggle, succeeded in driving the Russians from it. Loss considerable on both sides.

MAY 1st.—The Russians made a sortie from the Flagstaff Battery, and exploded five mines, entirely destroying the works of the Allied army. The Allies opened a heavy fire against the Schwartz redoubt, but were compelled to retrace their steps by a heavy fire of grape. The encounter was of a sanguinary character, and the loss very severe. The Russians admit the loss of 300 killed and 540 wounded.

MAY 5th.—Some well-directed shells from Sebastopol blew up two powder-magazines in the French eight-gun battery.

MAY 6th.—The fire of a battery near the Flagstaff bastion caused the explosion of a magazine in the Allied camp.

MAY 7th to 12th.—Nothing of a decisive character has been effected by either of the contending armies. Skirmishes and night-sorties continue with more or less loss. The bombardment of the city is not conducted with the vigor of former days.

MAY 14th.—A private letter from the Crimea furnishes the following account of a mistake which occurred. It says: " We have had terrible work here. Last night, the 18th Regiment fired on the 68th by mistake. The Russians made an attack on the advanced batteries, and were repelled by the 68th and Rifles. The Russians returned in a short time with reïnforcements, again attacked the batteries, and a fearful

struggle then took place. The reserves were then sent up —
the 9th, 18th, and 44th — and when they got into the advanced
trench, both sides were so covered with mud that we could not
tell Russian from English; so the reserve opened fire, but it
was unfortunately on the poor 68th. They then charged on
them, when they found out their mistake, but not till a good
many of the 68th had fallen. However, the Russians had it
hot and warm afterwards. The poor fellows who are wounded
in advance of the trench are obliged to lie there all day till
dark, as the Russians fire on any of the Allies who go to bring
them in. Many of the wounded might recover, if brought in,
but they lie and bleed to death."

MAY 19th.—General Pelissier assumed the supreme command
of the French army; Gen. Canrobert retiring from the chief
command to that of the command of the first division of the
French Crimean army.

May 22d and 23d—The following dispatch of Gen. Pelissier to
the French Minister of War fully explains the celebrated night
attack.

"HEAD-QUARTERS BEFORE SEBASTOPOL, May 26.

"MONSIEUR LE MERÉCHAL : Since the storming of the Russian
counter-approaches in front of the Central Bastion, on the night
of the 2d of May, and the occupation of that important
work by our troops, the enemy to impede our progress, and
take our attacks in flank, turned their attention to the Quarantine side, and erected there new lines of counter-approach.
They formed the plan by connecting by a gabionade the ambuscades at the extremity of the bay, those of the cemetery, and
to connect the work by a continuous covered way with the
right lunette of the Central Bastion. In the night between the
21st and 22d, by an enormous effort of labor, skillfully concealed, they commenced laying out that vast *place d' armees*, so
threatening for our left attack, and so convenient for enabling
the enemy to assemble large bodies of men and make considerable sorties.

"The danger of this Russian work was evident. I saw at
once its extent, and ordered General De Salles, commander of
the First Corps, to carry that position, and turn the enemy's
new works against themselves.

"The General of Division, Paté, was charged with the operation. Two attacks were organized—one on the ambuscades at
the bottom of the bay; the other on the ambuscades of the cemetery by the south-east angle of that inclosure : they were to
be simultaneous.

"After having carried the new gabionades of the enemy, the
object was to maintain ourselves in advance, with sufficient
solidity to protect the work, and to transform the Russian work

to our own use. The combat took place on the night between
the 22d and 23d of May ; it commenced at nine o'clock in the
evening.

"Our left attack consisted of three companies of the 10th
battalion of Chasseurs-à pied, three battalions of the 2d Regiment of the Foreign Legion, and one battalion of the 98th of
the Line.

"The right attack consisted of picked companies of the 1st
Regiment of the Foreign Legion, supported by two battalions
of the 28th Line, with a battalion of the 18th and two battalions
of Voltigeurs of the Garde, as reserve.

"The enemy were there in great force to receive us. We
estimated at more than twenty battalions the force of the enemy our brave soldiers had to attack and defeat. According to
prisoners there were twenty-six battalions.

"The action commenced on a signal given by General Paté,
with inexpressible impetuosity. In a few minutes all the ambuscades on our right were in our hands. The veterans of the
Foreign Legion had carried every thing before them, and, supported by the 28th of the Line, they established themselves in
front of the Russian works, covering our workmen. But formidable masses of Russians soon issued from the Quarantine
ravine, joined in the combat, and disputed the ground with an
extraordinary obstinacy. Five times the most distant ambuscades were taken and re-taken by the Russians and our troops.
These bayonet *mêlées* were terrible.

"As the dawn broke, the Russians had ceased fighting, and
our battalions returned to the trenches, leaving the ground
covered with the enemy's slain.

"On the left attack the ambuscades were carried with the
same impetuosity. There, also, the Russians returned to the
charge with extraordinary tenacity. Numerous assaults were
made at the point of the bayonet; but after two hours, the
enemy, discouraged, beat a retreat, and our engineers installed
themselves solidly in the Russian gabionade, which became
definitively our conquest.

"On the following night I ordered a second attack, expecting
full success from this new effort of our brave infantry.

"Four of these battalions were charged to cover our conquest
on the extreme left. The six others were to re-take on the right
the gabionade running parallel with the great wall of the cemetery, to beat the enemy, and allow our engineers to make the
works definitively our own.

"The action commenced at the same hour as on the previous
evening. The ambuscades were turned and carried; the enemy, driven back on all sides, retreated, keeping up a skirmishing fire, which gradually ceased. The engineers immediately

set to work, despite a fire of grape and every sort of missile from the place.

"Our success has therefore been complete. The considerable work upon which the enemy had counted to arrest our attacks is in our hands; their gabions cover us; their own ambuscades are turned against themselves. Those which we could not combine in our system have been destroyed.

"Yesterday, upon the reïterated demand of General Osten-Sacken, a flag of truce was hoisted, and an armistice concluded for carrying off the dead. We handed over more than 1200 corpses to the enemy.

"According to the number of dead given up to the enemy, and the results ascertained from recent affairs, we are assured that the losses of the Russians are at least four times our own; they give to these engagements the proportions of a battle. These calculations are, however, under those made by prisoners and deserters.

"Our artillery gave proof of extraordinary vigor and skill. It constantly swept with its fire the ravine where the enemy assembled their reserves.

"The Commander-in-Chief,   PELISSIER."

MAY 24th.—Last night the French attempted to drive the Russians from a position that annoyed them considerably. The French fire was returned by the Flag-staff, the Garden, and the battery in the middle of Sebastopol. It was an extraordinary sight. A thick white cloud of smoke hung over the French batteries and that part of the town which was answering their fire. Bright flashes of fire gleamed through this smoke every second, as guns were fired or shells exploded. There was no cessation in the firing for an hour, when there was a slight lull, and immediately volleys of musketry were heard, which continued without intermission for some time. About 10.15 there was an explosion in the Russian batteries. It seemed as if there had been a train of powder loose on the ground, as there was suddenly a long bright sheet of flame seen lighting up the wall of smoke. About 10.30 there was another similar explosion. The number of shells that were fired from both sides was enormous. There were generally five or six in the air at one time. The French fired a great many "bouquets"—not the bouquets that are popular among young ladies, but a flight of shells, which separate in the air and fly about in all directions. The expedition sailed this morning—it is supposed to Kertch; the English part of it under Sir George Brown, as on the first occasion. He has four regiments of Highlanders this time.

MAY 25th.—An Allied expedition of 15,000 men of all

arms, and five batteries of artillery, transported by a fleet of French and English vessels, have made themselves masters of the Sea of Azoff.

The fleets steamed rapidly up to Kamiesch, where the army landed under cover of the guns of the steam-frigates, and immediately ascended the heights without opposition, while the steamers of light draught of water pushed on towards Kertch and Yanikale; and the Russians, apparently taken by surprise at the rapidity of these movements, and at the imposing appearance of the expedition, blew up their fortifications on both sides of the Straits, mounting not less than 50 guns, (new, and of heavy calibre,) which have fallen into possession of the Allies, and retired after having destroyed three steamers and several other heavily-armed vessels, as well as large quantities of provisions, ammunition, and stores, thus leaving the Allies masters of the entrance into the Sea of Azoff, without having sustained any loss whatever. The Russians lost 160,000 sacks of oats, 360,000 sacks of corn, and 100,000 sacks of flour. A carriage-factory and a foundry were burnt down; three steamers, one of which was a war-steamer, were sunk by the Russians themselves. Some thirty transport-ships were destroyed, and at least as many taken. In the different explosions, about 100,000 kilogrammes of powder were destroyed. A great store of shells and cannon balls no longer exists.

MAY 26th.—The French batteries continue to bombard the city, and the Russians return the compliment with their shell, but without effecting much injury to the French battery. A correspondent of the Austrian *Military Zeitung* thus describes Sebastopol:

" The southern side of our town is scarcely to be recognized ; 500 houses have been totally destroyed. The beautiful tneatre no longer exists. The streets are everywhere rooted up by shot, and the pavement is totally destroyed, while at every corner stand whole pyramids of the enemy's cannon-balls, and exploded shells, which were daily collected before the opening of the fire. In many streets five or six such pyramids are to be seen, each of them from eight to ten feet high. Nevertheless business is continued, and booths are opened for the sale of goods. Prices, however, are enormously raised, and sugar costs one silver rouble per pound. The supply of meat is more than abundant, but bread is exceedingly scarce."

MAY 30th.—The flotilla of the Allies has returned from the Sea of Azoff. It destroyed 106 Russian merchantmen at Berdiaansk. The expedition has captured 90 guns of different calibre. The Russians have only one small steamer in the Sea of Azoff.

MAY 31st.—On the refusal of the military authorities of Genitchi, situate on the northern extremity of the tongue of land of Arabat, to give up the government stores and 90 vessels laden with provisions for the Russian army in the Crimea, the squadron, under the orders of Captain Lyons, bombarded the place, drove out the troops, and destroyed all the stores.

The Russians have thus lost, in four days, an immense quantity of provisions, four war-steamers, and 240 vessels employed exclusively in provisioning the troops in the Crimea.

JUNE 4th.—The British and French fleets were close to Cronstadt. The Russian ships were nearly all dismantled in harbor; only three steamers were serviceable. Admiral Dundas has been in the Merlin to get a nearer view of the fortifications, and to satisfy himself as to the propriety of an attack; he thinks it impracticable. New works have been added since last year.

Sixteen Russian merchantmen, most of them loaded with timber, have been captured and destroyed near Cronstadt, and others run ashore and burned.

JUNE 6th.—The Allies in force opened a fire along the whole range of their position on Sebastopol. The cannonading was continued during the day; 547 guns and mortars were brought in play.

JUNE 7th.—The English Naval Brigade continued their fire on the Redan Tower, and in a short time it gave unmistakable evidence of the rough treatment it had received, the jaws of its embrasures gaping, and its fire being irregular and interrupted. About 3 o'clock the fire of the Allies was renewed, with an access of fury, and continued until the capture of the Mamelon Tower and the Quarries. The following account of which, by an eye-witness, is subjoined:

" Between five and six, Lord Raglan and his staff took up a conspicuous position on the edge of the hill, where it commands the English four-gun battery, and looks straight into the teeth of the Redan. Sir Colin Campbell was observed to plant himself on the next summit still nearer to the enemy, commonly called the Green Hill. His appearance drew some fire, and the shells dropped and flashed close by, but without disconcerting his purpose of having a thorough good look-out place. About half-past six the head of the French attacking column came into view from these two spots, as it climbed its arduous road to the Mamelon. A rocket instantly went off as the signal of our diversion, and as instantly the small force of our men detached for the post of honor made a rush at the Quarries. After one slight check they drove out the Russians, and turning round the gabions commenced making themselves snug. The French went up the steep to the Mamelon in most beautiful style and in loose order, and were seen running, climbing, scrambling like skirmishers up the slopes on to the body of the work amid a plunging fire from the Russian guns, which, owing to their loose formation, did them as yet little damage. The Zouaves were upon the parapets firing down into the place from above; the next moment a flag was up as rallying-point and defiance, and was seen to sway hither and thither, now up, now down, as the tide of battle raged round it; and now like a swarm they were in the heart of the Mamelon, and a fierce hand-to-hand encounter here with the musket, there with the bayonet, was evident. It was seven minutes and a half from the commencement of the enterprise. Then there came a rush through the angle where they had entered, and there was a momentary confusion outside. Groups, some idle, some busy, some wounded, were collected on the hither side, standing in shelter, and now and then to the far corner a shell flew from the English battery facing it. But hardly had the need of support become manifest, and a gun or two again flashed from the embrasure against them, than there was another run in, another sharp bayonet-fight inside, and this time the Russians went out, spiking their guns. Twice the Russians made head against the current, for they had a large mass of troops in reserve, covered by the guns of the Round Tower. Twice they were forced back by the onsweeping flood of French, who fought as if they had eyes upon them to sketch the swift event in detail. For ten minutes or so the quick flash and roll of small-arms had declared that the uncertain fight waxed and waned inside the inclosure. Then the back-door, if one may use a humble metaphor, was burst open. The noise of the conflict went away down the descent on the side towards the town, and the arena grew larger. It was apparent that the Russians had been reïnforced by the space over which the battle spread. When the higher ground again became the seat of action, then there came the second rush of the French back upon their supports, for the former one was a mere reflux or eddy of the stream. When rocket after rocket went up ominously from the French General's position, and seemed to emphasize by their repetition some very plain command, we began to get nervous. It was growing darker and darker too, so that with our glasses we could with difficulty distinguish the actual state of affairs. At last, through the twilight, we discerned that the French were pouring in. After the interval of doubt, our ears could gather that the swell and babble of the fight was once more rolling down the inner face of the hill, and that the Russians were conclusively beaten. 'They are well into it this time,' says one to another, handing over the glass. The musket flashes were no more to be seen within it. There was no more lightning of the heavy guns from the embrasures. A shapeless hump upon a hill, the Mamelon was an extinct volcano

" Then, at last, the more hidden struggle of our own men in the hollow on the left came uppermost. 'How are our fellows getting on?' says one. 'Oh! take my word for it, they're all right,' says another. And they were right, so far as the occupation and retention of the quarries was concerned, but had, nevertheless, to fight all night, and repel six successive attacks of the Russians, who displayed the most singular pertinacity and recklessness of life. As it grew dark, our advanced battery under the Green Hill made very pretty practice and pretty spectacle, by flipping shells over our men's heads at the Russians. Meanwhile the fall of the Mamelon and the pursuit of the flying foe, did not by any means bring the combat to an end on the side of the Allies. The Zouaves, emboldened by their success, and enraged by their losses, carried their powers a step too far, and dreamt of getting into the Round Tower by a *coup de main.* A new crop of battle grew up over all the intervening hollow between it and the Mamelon, and the ripple of musket-shots plashed and leaped over the broad hill-side. The combatants were not enough for victory there too, but they were enough for a sanguinary and prolonged contest. The tower itself, or rather the inglorious stump of what was the Round Tower, took and gave shot and shell and musketry with the most savage ardor and rapidity. The fire of its musketry was like one sheet of flame rolling backwards and forwards with a dancing movement. Our gunners, observing the duration and aim of the skirmish, redoubled their exertions, and flung their shells into the Round Tower with admirable precision, doing immense mischief to the defenders. From Gordon's battery and the second parallel they streamed and plunged into the enciente up to which the Zouaves had won their way unsupported, heralded every now and then by the prompt and decisive ring of a round shot. The Russian defense, rather than their defenses, crumbled away before the tremendous fire ; but on the other hand, the attack not being fed, as it was not designed, began to languish, and died gradually away. It was a drawn battle so far ; but there may be another story to-morrow."

12 P.M.—The French are putting the new front of their position in a state of defense, and employing an immense number of hands. Our men are still in their warm berth in the Redan, repelling the attacks of the Russians. There was but one embrasure left in a comfortable state in the Redan at the end of the evening, and the quarries are too close under it for heavy guns to be brought to bear.

JUNE 8th.—During the night repeated attacks, six in all, were made upon our men in the quarries, who defended their new acquisition with the utmost courage and pertinacity, and at a great sacrifice of life, against superior numbers, continually replenished. The strength of the party told off for the attack was in all only 1000, of whom 600 were in support. At the commencement 200 only went in, and another 200 followed. More than once there was a fierce hand-to-hand fight in the position itself, and our fellows had frequently to dash out in front and take their assailants in flank. The most murderous sortie of the enemy took place about three in the morning; when the whole ravine was lighted up with a blaze of fire, and a storm of shot thrown in from the Strand Battery and every other spot within range. The Russian gunners were not very active through the night; indeed, there was little for them to do, and they are evidently shy of throwing away ammunition. The French were losing no time in the Mamelon, in which, by the bye, they found only seven guns, five of them spiked. When morning dawned, the position held by both parties was one of expectation. The French were in great force within and on the outer slopes of the Mamelon, and also in possession of two out of the three offsets attached to the Mamelon on the Sapoune hill. On the rear of the Mamelon their efforts to entrench themselves were being occasionally interrupted by shells from the ships in harbor, and from a battery not hitherto known to exist, further down the hill. On our side 365 rank and file and 35 officers had been killed and wounded. On the French side nearly double the number of officers, and a total of not less than 1500 men, probably more. It has been stated as high as 3700, but there must be error in the statement.

JUNE 18th.—The English troops attacked the Redan Tower, and the French the Malakoff Tower, at daylight, but were repulsed by the Russians with great slaughter. The Allied troops carried the outworks of the Redan, but found that the Russians had prepared a deep trench, which it was impossible to pass without either scaling-ladders or planks. The assailants were here exposed to a most murderous fire, after sustaining, it is said, a loss of from 4000 to 5000 men, and having 40 officers killed. The casualties were much augmented by the guns on the Malakoff enfilading the outworks of the Redan, added to which the men-of-war in the harbor were laid broad-side on, and by their fire on the retiring troops caused fearful havoc, there being no cover or shelter whatever from the storm of projectiles.

The losses of the Allied troops are believed to be greater than in any former action of the war. Sir John Campbell, Colonel Yea of the 7th, Colonel Shadforth of the 57th, and many other officers of distinguished gallantry, fell in the English ranks, while the French have lost two general officers and a vast number of men in all branches of the service.

In order to convey a correct idea of the attack of the 18th
June, we extract the following from the private letter of an
English officer who took part in it. He says:
"It is no use my attempting to tell you what was done or
doing on the 18th. We failed, I fear, altogether, and with
great loss. There was a complicated plan of attack, of the
success of which I always had doubts. Had 70,000 men been
let loose at the place at an appointed time, and at all points,
with no other word of command than go ahead at a certain
signal, I do believe the place would have been taken with a
loss of from 7000 to 10,000 in killed and wounded; and this
would have been about the proportionate loss in such a number in any hard-fought engagement. Still the loss in such a
mode of attack might have been less than even our loss on the
18th, for the Russians might not have withstood the onset of
such a host; but when they saw driblets of only 400 men
coming here and there, and straight at their strongest points,
they naturally felt confidence in their superiority of numbers
and position. During the flag of truce, a Russian officer,
speaking to one of ours of the attack of the Redan, said: "How
could you think of attacking such a place with 400 men? Your
men are indeed lions, but your officers must be donkeys."
The English Naval Brigade suffered considerably in the
attack on the Redan; 14 were killed and 47 wounded, out of
the small number composing it. When the men retreated,
overwhelmed by the storm from the enemy's battery, several
officers and men were left behind wounded, and endured fearful agonies for hours, without a cup of water or a cheering
voice to comfort them.
JUNE 19TH.—To-day an armistice was demanded for a few
hours in order to bury the dead. After some delay it was
acceded to by the Russians, who were rather reluctant to grant
an armistice, when they had no occasion to go outside their
lines for their dead or wounded. It was a very hot day, and
of all the places in the world where heat displays its utmost
power, a trench before Sebastopol is the most intolerable. An
eye-witness thus describes the heart-rending scene:
"It was agonizing to see the wounded men who were lying
there under a broiling sun, parched with excruciating thirst,
racked with fever, and agonized with pain — to behold them
waving their caps faintly, or making signals towards our lines,
over which they could see the white flag waving, and not to
be able to help them. They lay where they fell, or had scrambled into the holes formed by shells; and there they had been
for thirty hours — oh! how long and how dreadful in their
weariness! An officer told me that one soldier who was close
to the abattis, when he saw a few men come out of an embra-

sure, raised himself on his elbow, and fearing he should be un-
noticed and passed by, raised his cap on a stick and waved it
till he fell back exhausted. Again he rose, and managed to
tear off his shirt, which he agitated in the air till his strength
failed him. His face could be seen through a glass, and my
friend said he could never forget the expression of resignation
and despair with which the poor fellow at last abandoned his
useless efforts, and folded his shirt under his head to await the
mercy of Heaven. Whether he was alive or not when our men
went out, I can not say; but five hours of thirst, fever, and
pain, under a fierce sun, would make awful odds against him.
The red-coats lay sadly thick over the broken ground in front
of the abattis of the Redan, and blue and gray coats were
scattered about, or lay in piles in the rain-courses before the
Malakoff."

The Russians assisted their enemy in gathering in the dead
and dying, asking many questions as regards the assault, etc.
Their "pumping" inclination, however, was so marked, as in
most cases to defeat itself. The whole sad duty was soon performed, and the truce brought to an end. After the armistice,
the Russians made another sortie in force against the advanced
works of the Allies, and were, after some severe fighting, repulsed with inconsiderable loss. The Second Brigade (English)
succeeded in taking the cemetery and one house near the town,
which they held for some days—not, however, without considerable daily loss of men and material.

JUNE 24TH.—No move of importance has occurred in the
siege operations since the 19th. Both armies are pushing forward their works with vigor. Major-General Estcourt, Adju-
tant-General of the English Army, died to-day of cholera.

JUNE 28TH.—Field-Marshal Lord Raglan, G. C. B., Commander-in-chief of the English Army in the Crimea, died to-day,
and the command of the army devolved on Lieutenant-General
James Simpson.

JULY 3D.—Occasional sorties by the Russians disturb the
Allies, and impede the progress of their sapping operations.
The event of the day has been the funeral procession of the
late Lord Raglan, from the head-quarters' house to the " Cara-
doc," which was waiting at Kazatch Bay, to convey the remains
to England.

JULY 4TH.—The heightening of the Allied parapets in front
of the Malakoff is progressing, notwithstanding the heavy
Russian fire on the working parties.

JULY 7TH.—The fire from the Russian batteries was particularly active during the day, and was confined to mortar practice, which successfully defeated the projects of the Allies in
pushing forward their mining operations.

JULY 10TH. — A powerful fire was opened this morning against the Redan tower, by the Allies, and continued during the day, but without material benefit.

AUGUST 16TH—The long-threatened attack of the Russians on the Tchernaya was commenced to-day, and resulted in a severe repulse to their arms. The action commenced before daylight by a heavy column of Russians under the command of General Liprandi, and composed of the 6th and 17th Divisions, with the 4th and 7th Divisions in reserve, attacking the advanced posts of the Sardinians.

The ground occupied by them is on commanding hills on the right of the position, on the left bank of the Souhaia river, where it forms its junction with the Tchernaya, with two advanced posts on the opposite side. These were held with very determined gallantry for a considerable time, but being separated from their supports by the river, and not having the protection of artillery, they were compelled to leave the most advanced one.

About the same time the 5th and 12th Divisions, to which was added a portion of the 17th, advanced against the bridge of Traktir, held by one battalion of French infantry of the line, who were for a short time obliged to yield and fall back upon the main supports; with these, however, they quickly re-took the bridge at the point of the bayonet.

Again the Russians attacked with persevering courage, and were enabled to follow up their advantage by gaining the heights which rise precipitously on each side of the road; their success was but momentary; they were driven back across the river, leaving the ground covered with dead and wounded.

The Russian general, in no way daunted by the failure of his two attempts, ordered a second column, of equal force to the first, to attack; they advanced with such impetuosity, covered by the fire of their numerous artillery, that a third time the bridge was carried, and the heights above it crowned, but they were again repulsed, and retired in great confusion into the plain, followed by the bayonets of our gallant allies.

The general officer who commanded the Russian column, and who is supposed to be General Read, was killed, and in his possession were found the orders for the battle, signed by Prince Gortchakoff, who commanded in person.

The action is most glorious to the arms of the French and the Sardinian troops. To meet the force of the Russians the former had but 12,000 infantry, and four batteries of artillery engaged; the latter had 10,000 men in position, 4500 actually engaged, and 24 pieces of cannon.

The Russian force consisted of from 50,000 to 60,000 men, with 160 pieces of artillery, and cavalry to the amount of 6000.

The loss sustained by the Russians is estimated at between 5000 and 6000 men, including 600 prisoners, while on the part of the Allies it does not amount to more than 1000 men.

AUGUST 24TH.—The French attacked the Russians, and took from them an ambuscade, established on the glacis of the Malakoff. Five hundred Russians made a sortie in order to recover it, but they were repulsed with the loss of about 300 men. The work was then turned against the Russians.

AUGUST 28TH.—A shell from the Russian works struck a tumbril discharging powder for the French battery near the Mamelon, and exploded, instantly killing forty men and wounding many others. The weight of powder exploded was about seven tons, or 1400 rounds of ten pounds each.

AUGUST 31ST.—The Russian Infantry made an attack on the 5th parallel of the English works, leaped into the trench, and took possession, but were repulsed with considerable loss.

SEPTEMBER 3D.—The Russians attacked the French works in front of the Mamelon and for the space of twenty minutes kept up an "infernal" fire of musketry, followed by considerable shell practice. The sortie was a desperate one and the loss heavy; the French had at least 300 men put *hors du combat.* After an hour's hand-to-hand fighting, the Russians retired, leaving their quota of dead and dying on the field.

FALL OF SEBASTOPOL.

ON Saturday, the 8th of September, 1855, within a few days of the anniversary of the landing of the allied forces in the Crimea, and 316 days after the opening of the besieging batteries against Sebastopol, on the 17th of October, 1854, a final and victorious assault was made upon the southern part of the town. Before night the French flag waved in triumph upon the Malakoff Tower, which had fallen before the indomitable courage and perseverance of the assailants; and within a few hours more the Russian garrison had evacuated the Karabelnaia suburb and the southern portion of the fortress, after blowing up the magazines and principal works, setting fire to the town in many places, and then endeavoring to withdraw by the bridge across the harbor from this terrific scene of devastation and defeat. So fell Sebastopol. The catastrophe surpasses in horrible interest all the preceding scenes of this gigantic contest. The columns of the allied armies, combined in a fourfold attack, struggled all day with equal valor, though with unequal success, against the principal points marked out for assault. The extreme right of the French attack was directed against the work called the Little Redan, which was at first carried by the impetuosity of the French, though they were subsequently driven back by the fierce resistance of the Russians. The second and principal assault of the French army was against the Malakoff, which was carried by storm, and determined by its fall the fate, not only of the day, but of the siege. A third attack was made by the British forces on the Great Redan, and although the salient angle of this formidable work was at one moment carried and occupied by the English troops, they were subsequently driven out of it by the fire of the Russian batteries which commanded it. The French columns on the left also assailed, in the fourth place, the Central Battery, but failed to establish themselves in the work. No doubt every man who attacked the defenses of Sebastopol on that eventful day fought with the same undaunted gallantry and the same determination to carry the place or to perish in the attempt; and, although the results of these several attacks were unequal, all were animated by the same spirit and contributed to the great result. The first prize of this glorious victory belongs of right to the French, since the Malakoff Tower, the key of the main position, fell before the vigor of their assault. The Russians on their side defended the place with the utmost determination, and on more than one point they had the advantage over the besiegers. No sooner were the outer works taken, which laid the town and the port at the mercy of the allied forces, than the men-of-war and steamers in the harbor were all set on fire, blown up, sunk, or destroyed, either by the fire of the allied batteries or by the orders of the Russian authorities. Such was the fate of the Russian Black Sea fleet, on which the Imperial government had expended incalculable sums of money and incessant labor—that fleet which two years ago threatened the very existence of the Turkish empire.

The following graphic description of the Assault and Fall of Sebastopol is from the pen of the *London Times*' correspondent in the English Camp:

THE DAY OF THE ASSAULT—THE REDAN.

SATURDAY, SEPTEMBER 8TH.—The weather changed suddenly yesterday. This morning it became bitterly cold. A biting wind right from the north side of Sebastopol blew intolerable clouds of harsh dust into our faces. The sun was obscured; the sky was of a leaden wintry gray. Early in the morning a strong force of cavalry, under the command of Colonel Hodge, was moved up to the front and formed a chain of sentries in front of Cathcart's Hill and all along our lines. No person was allowed to pass this line, unless he was a staff officer or was provided with a pass. Another line of sentries in the rear of them was intended to stop stragglers and idlers from Balaklava, and the object in view was probably to prevent the Russians gathering any intimation of our attack from the unusual accumulation of people on the look-out hills. If that were so, it would have been better to have kept the cavalry more to the rear, and not to display to the enemy a line of hussars, lancers, and dragoons along our front. At 11.30 the Highland Brigade, under the command of Brigadier Cameron, marched up from Kamara and took up its position in reserve at the right attack, and the Guards, also in reserve, were posted on the same side of the Woronzoff Road. The first brigade of the fourth division served the trenches of the left attack the night before, and remained in them. The second brigade of the fourth division was in reserve. The Guards, who served the trenches of the left attack, and only marched out that morning, were turned out again after arriving at their camp. The third division, massed on the hill-side before their camp, were also in reserve, in readiness to move down by the left attack, in case their services were required. General Pelissier during the night collected about 30,000 men about the Mamelon to form the storming columns for the Malakoff and Little Redan and to provide the necessary reserves. The French were reinforced by 5000 Sardinians, who marched up from the Tchernaya last night. It was arranged that the French were to attack the Malakoff at noon, and as soon as their attack began, that we were to assault the Redan. At the same time a strong column of French was to make a diversion on the left and menace the line of the Bastion du Mat. The cavalry sentries were posted at 8.30. At 10.30 the second division and the light division moved down to the trenches, and were placed in the advanced parallels as quietly and unostentatiously as possible. About the same hour General Simpson and staff moved down to the second parallel of the Green Hill Battery. Sir Harry Jones, too ill to move hand or foot, nevertheless insisted on being carried down to witness the assault, and was borne to the parallel on a litter, in which he remained till all was over. It was a bitter cold day, and a stranger would have been astonished at the aspect of the British Generals as they viewed the assault. The Commander-in-Chief, General Simpson, sat in the trench, with his nose and eyes just facing the cold and dust, and his cloak drawn up over his head to protect him against both.	General Jones wore a red night-cap, and reclined on his litter ; and Sir Richard Airey, the Quartermaster-General, had a white pocket-handkerchief tied over his cap and ears, which detracted somewhat from a martial and belligerent aspect.	The Duke of Newcastle was stationed at Cathcart's Hill in the early part of the day, and afterwards moved off to the right to the picket-house, over the Woronzoff road.	All the amateurs and gentlemen were in a state of great excitement, and dotted the plain in eccentric attire—which recalled one's old memories of Cowes, and yachting and sea-bathing—were engaged in a series of subtle manœuvres to turn the flank of unwary sentries, and to get to the front, and their success was most creditable to their enterprise and ingenuity.	The Tartars, Turks, and Eupatorians were singularly perturbed for such placid people, and thronged every knoll which commanded the smallest view of the place.	At 10.45 General Pelissier and his staff went up to the French Observatory on the right.	The French trenches were crowded with men as close as they could pack, and we could see our men through the breaks in the clouds of dust, which were most irritating, all ready in their trenches.	The cannonade languished purposely towards noon; but the Russians, catching sight of the cavalry and troops in front, began to shell Cathcart's Hill and the heights, and disturbed the equanimity of some of the spectators by their shells bursting with loud "thuds" right over their heads.	A few minutes before 12 o'clock the French, like a swarm of bees, issued forth from their trenches close to the doomed Malakoff, swarmed up its face, and were through the embrasures in the twinkling of an eye.	They crossed the seven metres of ground which separated them from the enemy at a few bounds—they drifted as lightly and quickly as autumn leaves before the wind, battalion after battalion, into the embrasures, and, in a minute or two after the head of their column issued from the ditch, the tri-color was floating over the Korniloff Bastion. The musketry was very feeble at first; indeed, our allies took the Russians quite by surprise, and very few of the latter were in the Malakoff; but they soon recovered themselves, and from twelve o'clock till past seven in the evening, the French had to meet and defeat the repeated attempts of the enemy to regain the work and the Little Redan, when, weary of the fearful slaughter of his men, who lay in thousands over the exterior of the works, the Muscovite general, despairing of success, withdrew his exhausted legions, and prepared, with admirable skill, to evacuate the place.	Of the French attack on the left I know nothing, but that, if intended in earnest, it was not successful, and was followed by some loss to our allies.	As

9

soon as the tri-color was observed waving over the parapet of the Malakoff through the smoke and dust, four rockets were sent up from Chapman's attack one after another, as a signal for our assault on the Redan. They were almost borne back by the violence of the wind, and the silvery jets of sparks they threw out, on exploding, were nearly invisible against the raw gray sky.

When the order was received on the 7th, the general remark was—"This looks like another 18th of June." In fact, the attacking columns were not strong enough, the supports were not strong enough, and were also too far behind, and the trenches did not afford room for a sufficient number of men. Now, it will be observed that, where we attacked the Redan with two divisions only, a portion of each being virtually in reserve, and not engaged in the affair at all, the French made their assault on the Malakoff with four divisions of the second corps d'armée, the first and fourth divisions forming the storming columns, and the third and fifth being the support, with reserves of 10,000 men. The French had probably not less than 30,000 men in the right attack on the 7th of September. The divisional orders for the Second Division were very much the same as those for the Light Division. The covering party consisted of 100 men of the Third Buffs, under Captain John Lewes, who highly distinguished himself, and 100 men of the Second battalion of the Rifle Brigade, I believe under the command of poor Captain Hammond. The scaling ladder party consisted of 160 of the 3d Buffs, under Captain Maude, whose gallantry was very conspicuous throughout the affair, in addition to the 160 of the 97th, under the gallant and lamented Welsford. The part of the force of the Second Division consisted of 260 of the 3d Buffs, 300 of the 41st, (Welsh,) 200 of the 62d, and a working party of 100 men of the 41st. The rest of Windham's Brigade, consisting of the 47th and 49th, were in reserve, together with Warren's brigade of the same division, of which the 30th and 55th were called into action, and suffered severely. Brigadier Shirley was on board ship, but as soon as he heard of the assault he resolved to join his brigade, and he accordingly came up to the camp that very morning. Colonel Unett, of the 19th Regiment, was the senior officer in Brigadier Shirley's absence, and on him would have devolved the duty of leading the storming column of the light division, had the latter not returned. Colonel Unett, ignorant of the Brigadier's intention to leave shipboard, had to decide with Colonel Windham, who should take precedence in the attack. They tossed, and Colonel Unett won. He had it in his power to say whether he would go first or follow Colonel

Windham. He looked at the shilling, turned it over, and said, "My choice is made; I'll be the first man into the Redan." But fate willed it otherwise, and he was struck down badly wounded ere yet he reached the abattis although he was not leading the column. Scarcely had the men left the fifth parallel when the guns on the flank of the Redan opened on them as they moved up rapidly to the salient, in which there were of course no cannon, as the nature of such a work does not permit of their being placed in that particular position. In a few seconds Brigadier Shirley was temporarily blinded by the dust and the earth knocked into his eyes by a shot. He was obliged to retire, and his place was taken by Lieutenant-colonel Bunbury, of the 23d Regiment, who was next in rank to Colonel Unett, already struck down and carried to the rear. Brigadier Van Straubenzee received a contusion on the face, and was also forced to leave the field. Colonel Handcock fell mortally wounded in the head by a bullet, and never spoke again. Captain Hammond fell dead. Major Welsford was killed on the spot. Captain Grove was severely wounded. Many officers and men were hit and fell; and of the commanders of parties, only acting Brigadier-general Windham, Captain Fyers, Captain Lewes, and Captain Maude got, untouched, into the Redan, and escaped scatheless from the volleys of grape and rifle balls which swept the flanks of the work towards the salient.

It was a few minutes after twelve when our men left the fifth parallel. The musketry commenced at once, and in less than five minutes, during which the troops had to pass over about thirty yards from the nearest approach to the parapet of the Redan, they had lost a large proportion of their officers, and were deprived of the aid of their leaders, with the exceptions I have stated. The riflemen advanced admirably, but, from their position, they could not do much to reduce the fire of the guns on the flanks and below the reëntering angles. The bravery and coolness of that experienced, deserving, and much-neglected officer, Captain Fyers, were never more brilliantly displayed, or urgently called for. As they came nearer the enemy's fire became less fatal. They crossed the abattis without difficulty; it was torn to pieces and destroyed by our shot, and the men stepped over and through it with ease. The light division made straight for the salient and projecting angle of the Redan, and came to the ditch, which is here about fifteen feet deep. The party detailed for the purpose placed the ladders, but they were found to be too short. However, had there been enough of them, that would not have mattered much, but some had been left behind in the hands of the dead

or wounded men, and others had been broken, so that if one
can credit the statements made by those who were present,
there were not more than six or seven ladders at the salient.
The men, led by their officers, leaped into the ditch and scrambled up the other side, whence they got up the parapet almost
without opposition, for the few Russians who were in front ran
back and got behind their traverses and breastworks as soon
as they saw our men on the top, and opened fire upon them.
To show what different impressions the same object can make
on different people, let me remark that one officer of rank told
me the Russians in the Redan did not exceed 150 men when
he got into it, and that the men could have carried the breastwork with the greatest ease if they had only made a rush for
it, and he expressed an opinion that they had no field pieces
inside the breastwork. A regimental officer, on the other hand
positively assured me that when he got on top of the parapet
of the salient he saw, about one hundred yards in advance of
him, a breastwork with gaps in it, through which were run the
muzzles of field pieces, and that in the rear of it were compact masses of Russian infantry, the front rank kneeling with
fixed bayonets as if prepared to receive a charge of cavalry,
while the two rear ranks over them kept up a sharp and destructive fire on our men. The only way to reconcile these
discrepancies is to suppose that the first spoke of the earliest
stage of the assault, that the latter referred to a later period
when the Russians may have opened the embrasures in the
breastwork, and had been reinforced by the fugitives from the
Malakoff, and by the troops behind the barracks in its rear.
Lamentable as it no doubt is, and incredible almost to those
who know how the British soldier generally behaves before
the enemy, the men, when they got on the parapet, were seized
by some strange infatuation, and began firing, instead of following their officers, who now began to fall fast as they rushed
on in front and tried to stimulate their soldiers by their example. Notwithstanding the popular prejudice to the contrary,
most men stand fire much better than closing with an enemy.
It is difficult enough sometimes to get cavalry to charge if
they can find any decent excuse to lay by their swords and
take to pistol and carbine, with which they are content to pop
away for ever, but when cover of any kind is near at hand, a
trench-bred infantry-man finds the charm of the cartridge quite
irresistible. The small party of the 90th, much diminished,
went on gallantly towards the breastwork, but they were too
weak to force it, and they had to retire and get behind the
traverses, where men of different regiments had already con-
gregated, and were keeping up a brisk fire on the Russians,

whose heads were just visible above the breastwork. Simultaneously with the head of the storming party of the Light Division, Colonel Windham had got inside the Redan on their right, below the salient on the proper left face of the Redan; but, in spite of all his exertions, could do little more than the gallant officers of the 90th and 97th, and of the supporting regiments.

As the Light Division rushed out in the front they were swept by the guns of the Barrack Battery and by several pieces on the proper right of the Redan, loaded heavily with grape, which caused them considerable loss ere they reached the salient or apex of the work at which they were to assault. The storming columns of the second division issuing out of the fifth parallel rushed up immediately after the light division, but when they came up close to the apex, Brigadier Windham very judiciously brought them by a slight detour on the right flank of the light division, so as to come a little down on the slope of the proper left face of the Redan. The first embrasure to which they came was in flames, but, moving on to the next, the men leaped into the ditch, and with the aid of ladders and each other's hands, scrambled up on the other side, climbed the parapet, or poured in through the embrasure, which was undefended. Colonel Windham was the first or one of the first men in on this side, and with him entered Daniel Mahoney, a great grenadier of the 41st, Killeany and Cornellis of the same regiment. As Mahoney entered with a cheer, he was shot through the head by a Russian rifleman, and fell dead across Colonel Windham, and at the same moment Killeany and Cornellis were both wounded. The latter claims the reward of £5 offered by Colonel Herbert to the first man of his division who entered the Redan. Running parallel to the faces of the Redan there is an inner parapet intended to shield the gunners at the embrasures from the effects of any shell which might fall into the body of the work, and strike them down if this high bank were not there to protect them from the splinters. Several cuts in the rear of the embrasures permitted the men to retire in case of need inside; very strong and high traverses ran along the sides of the work itself to afford them additional shelter. At the base of the Redan, before the reëntering angles, is a breastwork, or, rather, a parapet with an irregular curve, up to a man's neck, which runs in front of the body of the place. As our men entered through the embrasures, the few Russians who were between the salient and this breastwork retreated behind the latter, and got from the traverses to its protection. From it they poured in a quick fire on the parapet of the salient, which was crowded by the men of the Light

Division, and on the gaps through the inner parapet of the Redan; and our men, with an infatuation which all officers deplore, but can not always remedy on such occasions, began to return the fire of the enemy without advancing or crossing behind the traverses, loaded and fired as quickly as they could, but did little execution, as the Russians were well covered by the breastwork. There were also groups of Russian riflemen behind the lower traverses near the base of the Redan, who kept up a galling fire on our men. As the alarm of an assault was spread, the enemy came rushing up from the barracks in rear of the Redan, and increased the force and intensity of their fire, while our soldiers dropped fast, and encouraged the Russians by their immobility and the weakness of their fusilade, from which the enemy were well protected. In vain the officers, by voice and act, by example and daring, tried to urge our soldiers on. They had an impression that the Redan was all mined, and that if they advanced they would all be blown up; but many of them acted as became the men of Alma and Inkermann, and, rushing to the front, were swept down by the enemy's fire. The officers fell on all sides, singled out for the enemy's fire by their courage. The men of the different regiments became mingled together in inextricable confusion. The 19th men did not care for the orders of the officers of the 88th, nor did the soldiers of the 23d heed the commands of an officer who did not belong to their regiment. The officers could not find their men—the men had lost sight of their own officers. All the brigadiers save Colonel Windham were wounded or rendered unfit for the guidance of the attack. That gallant officer did all that man could do to form his men for the attack, and lead them against the enemy. Proceeding from traverse to traverse, he coaxed the men to come out, and succeeded several times in forming a few of them, but they melted away as fast as he laid hold of them, and either fell in their little ranks or retired to cover to keep up their fusilade. Many of them crowded to lower parts of the inner parapet and kept up a smart fire on the enemy, but nothing would induce them to come out into the open space and charge the breastwork. This was all going on at the proper left face of the Redan, while nearly the same scene was being repeated at the salient. Every moment our men were diminishing in numbers, while the Russians came up in swarms from the town, and rushed down from the Malakoff, which had now been occupied by the French. Thrice did Colonel Windham send officers to Sir W. Codrington, who was in the fifth parallel, begging of him to send up supports in some order of formation; but all these three officers were wounded as they passed from the ditch of the Redan

to the rear, and the colonel's own aid-de-camp, Lieutenant
Swire, of the 17th, a gallant young officer, was hit dangerously
in the hip, as he went on his perilous errand. Supports were,
indeed, sent up, but they came up in disorder from the fire to
which they were exposed on their way, and arrived in driblets
only to increase the confusion and the carnage. Finding that
he could not collect any men on the left face, Colonel Windham passed through one of the cuts of the inner parapet and
walked over to the right face, at the distance of thirty yards
from the Russian breastwork, to which he moved in a parallel
line, exposed to a close fire, but, wonderful to say, without
being touched. When he got behind the inner parapet at the
right face, he found the same state of things as that which existed at the left. The men were behind the traverses, firing
away at the Russians, or blazing at them from the broken parts
of the front; and the soldiers, who came down from the salient
in front, only got behind these works for cover while they
loaded and fired at the enemy. The Colonel got some riflemen
and a few men of the 88th together; but no sooner had he
brought them out than they were killed, wounded, or dispersed
by a concentrated fire. The officers, with the noblest devotion,
aided Colonel Windham, and became the special marks of the
enemy's riflemen. The narrow neck of the salient was too
close to allow of any kind of formation, and the more the men
crowded into it the more they got out of order, and the more
they suffered from the enemy's fire. This miserable work
lasted for an hour. The Russians were now in dense masses
behind the breastwork, and Colonel Windham walked back
again across the open space to the left to make one more attempt to retrieve the day. The men on the parapet of the
salient, who were firing at the Russians, sent their shot at him,
and the latter, who were pouring volley after volley on all
points of the head of the work, likewise directed their muskets
against him, but he passed through this cross fire in safety,
and got within the inner parapet on the left, where the men
were becoming thinner and thinner. A Russian officer now
stepped over the breastwork, and tore down a gabion with his
own hands ; it was to make room for a field-piece. Colonel
Windham exclaimed to several soldiers who were firing over
the parapet, "Well, as you are so fond of firing, why don't
you shoot that Russian?" They fired a volley and missed him,
and soon afterwards the field-piece began to play on the head
of the salient with grape. Colonel Windham saw there was no
time to be lost. He had sent three officers for reïnforcements,
and above all, for men in formation, and he now resolved to go
to General Codrington himself. Seeing Captain Crealock, of

the 90th, near to him, busy in encouraging his men, and exerting himself with great courage and energy to get them into order, he said: "I must go to the general for supports. Now mind, let it be known, in case I am killed, why I went away." He crossed the parapet and ditch, and succeeded in gaining the fifth parallel, through a storm of grape and rifle bullets, in safety. Sir William Codrington asked him if he thought he really could do any thing with such supports as he could afford, and said he might take the Royals, who were then in the parallel. "Let the officers come out in front—let us advance in order, and if the men keep their formation the Redan is ours," was the Colonel's reply; but he spoke too late, for at that very moment our men were seen leaping down into the ditch, or running down the parapet of the salient, and through the embrasures out of the work into the ditch, while the Russians followed them with the bayonet, and with heavy musketry, and even threw stones and grapeshot at them as they lay in the ditch. The fact was, that the Russians having accumulated several thousands of men behind the breastwork, and seeing our men all scattered up and confused behind the inner parapet of the traverse, crossed the breastwork, through which several field-pieces were now playing with grape on the inner face of the Redan, and charged our broken groups with the bayonet, at the same time that the rear ranks, getting on the breastwork, poured a heavy hail of bullets on them over the heads of the advancing column. The struggle that took place was short, desperate, and bloody. Our soldiers, taken at every disadvantage, met the enemy with the bayonet too, and isolated combats took place in which the brave fellows who stood their ground had to defend themselves against three or four adversaries at once. In this melee the officers, armed only with their swords, had little chance; nor had those who carried pistols much opportunity in using them in such a rapid contest. They fell like heroes, and many a gallant soldier with them. The bodies of English and Russians, locked in an embrace which death could not relax, but had rather cemented all the closer, lay next day inside the Redan as evidences of the terrible animosity of the struggle. But the solid weight of the advancing mass, urged on, and fed each moment from the rear by company after company and battalion after battalion, prevailed at last against the isolated and disjointed band, who had abandoned the protection of unanimity and courage, and had lost the advantage of discipline and obedience. As though some giant rock had advanced into the sea and forced back the waters that buffeted it, so did the Russian columns press down against the spray of soldiery which fretted their edge with fire and steel, and contended in vain against their weight. The struggling band was forced back by the enemy, who moved on, crushing friend and foe beneath their solid tramp; and bleeding, panting, and exhausted, our men lay in heaps in the ditch beneath the parapet, sheltered themselves behind stones and in bomb-craters in the slope of the work, or endeavored to pass back again to our advanced parallel and sap, and had to run the gauntlet of a tremendous fire. Many of them lost their lives, or were seriously wounded in this attempt. The scene in the ditch was appalling, although some of the officers have assured me that they and the men were laughing at the precipitation with which many brave and gallant fellows did not hesitate to plunge headlong upon the mass of bayonets, muskets, and sprawling soldiers. The ladders were all knocked down or broken, so that it was difficult for the men to get up at the other side, and the dead, the dying, the wounded, and the sound were all lying in heaps together. The Russians came out of the embrasures, plied them with stones, grapeshot, and the bayonet, but were soon forced to retire by the fire of our batteries and riflemen, and under cover of this fire many of our men escaped to the approaches. In some instances the enemy persisted in remaining outside in order to plunder the bodies of those who were lying on the slope of the parapet, and paid the penalty of their rashness in being stretched beside their foes; but others came forth on a holier errand, and actually brought water to our wounded.

General Pelissier observed the failure of our attack from the rear of the Malakoff, and sent over to General Simpson to ask if he intended to make another attack. The English Commander-in-Chief replied that he did not then feel in a condition to do so. All this time the Guards and Highlanders, the third and fourth divisions, and most of the reserves, were untouched. They could, indeed, have furnished ample materials for another assault; but the subsequent movements of the Russians render it extremely doubtful whether the glory of carrying the Redan, and of redeeming the credit of our arms would not have been dearly purchased by the effusion of more valuable blood. As soon as we abandoned the assault, the firing almost ceased along our front, but in the rear of the Malakoff there was a fierce contest going on between masses of Russians, now released from the Redan, or drawn from the town, and the French, inside the work; and the fight for the Little Redan, on the proper left of the Malakoff, was raging furiously. Clouds of smoke and dust covered the scene, but the rattle of musketry was incessant, and betokened the severe nature of the struggle below. Through the breaks in the smoke there could be seen now and

then a tricolor, surmounted by an eagle, fluttering bravely over
the inner parapet of the Malakoff. The storm of battle rolled
fiercely round it, and beat against it; but it was sustained by
strong arms and stout hearts, and all the assaults of the enemy
were directed in vain against it. We could see, too, our noble
allies swarming over into the Malakoff from their splendid approaches to it from the Mamelon, or rushing with swift steps
towards the right, where the Russians, continually reïnforced,
sought in vain to beat back their foes and to regain the key of
their position.

Our attack lasted about an hour and three-quarters, as well
as I could make out, and in that time we lost more men than
at Inkermann, where the fighting lasted for seven hours. At
1.48 P.M., which was about the time we retired, there was an
explosion either of a tumbril or of a fougasse between the Mame-
lòn and the Malakoff, to the right, which seemed to blow up
several Frenchmen, and soon afterwards the artillery of the
Imperial Guard swept across from the rear towards the Little
Redan, and gave us an indication that our allies had gained a
position from which they could operate against the enemy with
their field-pieces. From the opening of the attack the French
batteries over Careening Bay had not ceased to thunder against
the Russian fleet, which lay silently at anchor below, and there
was a lively cannonade between them and the Inkermann batteries till the evening, which was interrupted now and then by
the intervention of the Redout Victoria, the English Redoubt,
and the late Selinghinsk and Volhynia Redoubts, which engaged the Russian batteries over the last end of the harbor.
At one o'clock wounded men began to crawl up from the batteries to the camp; they could tell us little or nothing. "Were
we in the Redan?" "Oh! yes; but a lot of them was killed,
and the Russians were mighty strong." Some were cheery,
others desponding; all seemed proud of their wounds. Half
an hour more, and the number of wounded increased; they
came up by twos and threes, and what I had observed before
as a bad sign—the number of stragglers accompanying them,
under the pretense of rendering assistance, became greater
also. Then the ambulances and the cacolets (for mule litters)
came in sight along the Woronzoff road, filled with wounded.
Every ten minutes added to their numbers, and we could see
that every effort was made to hurry them down to the front as
soon as they were ready for a fresh load. The litter-bearers
now added to the length of the melancholy train. The temporary hospitals in front were full, and the surgeons were beginning to get anxious about accommodation for the wounded.
It may here be observed, that on the occasion of the 18th

of June, some of these temporary hospitals, which are intended to afford immediate aid in cases requiring operations on the spot, were under fire, and a shell burst in the very tent in which Dr. Paynter and his assistants were operating, the ground around it being continually torn up by round shot. On this occasion more care was taken in determining the sites of the tents. Another bad sign was, that the enemy never ceased throwing up shell to the front, many of which burst high in the air over our heads, while the pieces flew with a most unpleasant whir around us. These shells were intended for our reserves; and, although the fuses did not burn long enough for such a range, and they all burst at a considerable elevation, they caused some little injury and annoyance to the troops in the rear, and hit some of our men.

The old soldiers behaved admirably, and stood by their officers to the last; nor was there any lack of courage among the young lads just joined, but they were wanting in discipline, and in confidence in their officers. No one can doubt that the assault by the third and fourth divisions would have been quite successful had it been necessary. General Simpson remained in the Greenhill Battery till six o'clock, at which hour General Pelissier sent to inform him that the Malakoff was quite safe, and to ask him what the English intended to do with respect to the Redan. General Simpson had by this time arrived at the determination of attacking it the following morning at five o'clock, with the third and fourth divisions.

This Redan has cost us more lives than the capture of Badajoz, not to speak of those who have fallen in the trenches and approaches to it; and, although the enemy evacuated it, we can scarcely claim the credit of having caused them such loss that they retired owing to their dread of a renewed assault. On the contrary, we must, in fairness, admit that the Russians maintained their grip of the place till the French were fairly established in the Malakoff, and the key of the position was torn from their grasp. They might, indeed, have remained in the place longer than they did, as the French were scarcely in a condition to molest them from the Malakoff with artillery, and could not be permitted to interfere with our attack had they been able to send reïnforcements to us; but the Russian general is a man of too much genius and experience as a soldier to lose men in defending an untenable position, and his retreat was effected with masterly skill and with perfect ease in the face of a victorious enemy. Covering his rear by the flames of the burning city, and by tremendous explosions, which spoke in tones of portentous warning to those who might have wished to cut off his retreat, he led his battalions in narrow files across a deep arm of the sea, commanded by our guns and in the face of a most powerful fleet, paraded them in our sight as they crossed, and carried off all his most useful stores and munitions of war. He left us few trophies and many bitter memories. He sank his ships and blew up his forts without molestation, save some paltry efforts to break down the bridge by cannon shot, or to shell the troops as they marched over. His steamers towed his boats across at their leisure; and when every man was across, and not till then, the Russians began to dislocate and float off the portions of their bridge and to pull it over to the north side.

THE STORMING OF THE MALAKOFF.

MARSHAL PELISSIER'S DISPATCHES.

HEAD-QUARTERS AT SEBASTOPOL, SEPT. 11.—Me le Maréchal: I shall have the honor to send you by the next courier a detailed report on the attack which has placed Sebastopol in our power. To-day I can only give you a rapid sketch of the principal achievements of this great event of the war.

Since the 16th of August, the day of the battle of the Tchernaya, and notwithstanding repeated warnings of a new and more formidable attack by the enemy against the positions which we occupy on this river, every preparation was made to deliver a decisive assault against Sebastopol itself. The artil· ¹ :ry of the right attack commenced on the 17th August a well-sustained fire against the Malakoff, the Little Redan, the neighboring defenses, and the roads, in order to permit our engineers to establish defenses close to the place, from which the troops might be able instantly to throw themselves upon the *enceinte*. Our engineers nesides prepared materials for escalade, and on the 5th of September all our batteries of the left opened a very violent fire against the town. The English on their side kept up a hot cannonade against the Great Redan and its redoubt, which they were to attack.

All being ready, I resolved, in concert with General Simpson, to give the assault on the 8th of September, at the hour of noon.

General M'Mahon's division was to carry the works of the Malakoff; General Dulac's division was to attack the Little Redan; and in the centre the division of General La Motterouge was to march against the curtain connecting these two extreme points. Besides these troops, I had given to General Bosquet General Mellinet's division of the Guards, to support the first three divisions. Thus far for the right.

In the centre the English were to attack the Great Redan, escalading it at its salient.

On the left the 1st corps, to which General de la Marmora had wished to join a Sardinian brigade, having at its head General Levaillant's division, was to penetrate into the interior of the town by the Central Bastion, and afterwards turn the Flagstaff Bastion in order to establish a lodgment there likewise. General de Salles had instructions not to pursue his attack further than circumstances might render it advisable.

Further, the fleets of Admirals Lyons and Bruat were to operate a powerful diversion by firing against the Quarantine, the Roadstead, and the sea-front of the fortress; but the state of the sea, agitated by a violent north-west wind, was such that neither the line-of-battle ships nor the frigates were able to quit their anchorage. The English and French mortar-boats, however, were able to go into action. Their fire was of remarkable excellence, and they rendered us great assistance. At noon exactly, the divisions of Generals M'Mahon, La Motterouge, and Dulac, electrified by their chiefs, sprang to the Malakoff, the Curtain, and the Little Redan of the Careenage. After unexampled difficulties, and a most exciting foot-to-foot combat, General M'Mahon's division succeeded in effecting a lodgment in the anterior part of the Malakoff. The enemy showered down a storm of projectiles of all kinds upon our brave troops. The Redan of the Careenage, especially battered by the *maison en croix* and the steamers, it was necessary to evacuate after its occupation; but the division of General La Motterouge made its ground good on one part of the Curtain, and that of General M'Mahon gained ground in the Malakoff, where General Bosquet sent continually the reserves which I sent forward to him. The other attacks were subordinated to that of the Malakoff, that being the capital point of the defenses of the whole place.

Standing in the Brancion Redoubt (on the Mamelon) I considered that the Malakoff was safely in our power, and I gave the signal which had been agreed upon with General Simpson.

The English immediately advanced bravely against the salient of the Great Redan. They were able to effect a lodgment in it, and struggled a considerable time to maintain their position, but, crushed by the Russian reserves, which advanced incessantly, and by a violent fire of artillery, they were forced to return into their parallel.

At the same moment General de Salles had directed an attack against the Central Bastion. The Levaillant Division had begun to establish itself in it, as well as in the right Lunette; a tremendous fire of grape was succeeded by the arrival

of Russian reïnforcements so considerable in number that our
troops, already decimated by the fire of the enemy, and whose
chiefs had been disabled, were compelled to fall back on the
place whence they had sallied.

Convinced that the taking of the Malakoff would be decisive
of success, I prevented the renewal of any attacks on other
points, which, by compelling the hostile army to remain on all
its points, had already attained their main object. I then
directed my sole attention to the retaining possession of the
Malakoff, which General M'Mahon had been previously enabled
completely to obtain. Besides, a great and critical moment
was impending.

General Bosquet had just been struck by the bursting of a
shell, and his command I gave to General Dulac. A powder
magazine near the Malakoff exploded at this moment, from
which contingency I anticipated the most serious results.

The Russians, hoping to profit by this accident, immediately
advanced in dense masses, and, disposed in three columns,
simultaneously attacked the centre, the left, and the right of
the Malakoff. But measures of defense had already been taken
in the interior of the fortress; for which purpose General
M'Mahon opposed to the enemy bodies of undaunted troops,
whom nothing could intimidate; and after the most desperate
efforts the Russians were compelled to make a precipitate
retreat. From that moment the discomfited enemy appears to
have renounced all idea of further attack. The Malakoff was
ours, and no effort of the enemy could wrest it from us. It
was half-past four o'clock.

Measures were immediately taken for enabling us to repulse
the enemy, in case he should attempt against us a nocturnal
attack. But we were soon released from our uncertainty. As
soon as it became night, fires burst forth on every side, mines
exploded, magazines of gunpowder exploded in the air. The
sight of Sebastopol in flames, which the whole army contemplated, was one of the most awe-inspiring and sinister pictures
that the history of wars can have presented. The enemy was
making a complete evacuation; it was effected during the night
by means of a bridge constructed between the two shores of
the roadstead, and under cover of the successive explosions that
prevented me from approaching and harassing him. On the
morning of the 9th the whole southern side of the town was
freed and in our power.

Deign to accept, Monsieur le Maréchal, the expression of my
respectful devotion.—The General in Chief.   PELISSIER.

Head-Quarters, Sebastopol, Sept. 14.

M. LE MARECHAL: 1 have the honor to address to your Excellency, as I promised in my dispatch of the 11th, my report on the taking of Sebastopol by assault.

The moment of this assault seemed to have arrived. On the left our engineers had some time before carried their works within from 30 to 40 metres of the Flagstaff and Central Bastions. On the right, our approaches, pushed forward very actively under the protection of the sustained artillery fire which had been opened since the 17th, were only 25 metres distant from the salient of the Malakoff and the Lesser Redan. The artillery had finished nearly 100 batteries, which were in a perfect state, completely provisioned, and having in all 350 cannons in our left attacks and 250 in our right. The English on eithir side, although stopped by difficulties of the ground, had rarived at about two hundred metres from the Great Redan, and they had about 200 guns in their batteries. The Russians, improving the time, raised on the Malakoff side a second enceinte, which it was important not to allow them to finish. Finally, the army of relief had just been completely defeated on the 16th, on the Tchernaya. There it had experienced considerable losses, and it was not probable that it would return to relieve the place, and attack our positions, which we had rendered stronger, and in which we were prepared to repulse all the efforts of the enemy.

It was then agreed between General Simpson and myself that we should deliver a decisive attack. The generals commanding the artillery and engineers of both armies were unanimously of opinion that this should be our next measure. The 8th of September was the day fixed for the purpose.

As I have already had the honor to point out to your Excellency, the proper course was to attack the enemy in the principal points of his vast enceinte, so that he might not be able to direct all his reserves against one single attack; and to make him uneasy respecting the town, from which the bridge started whereby he was to retreat. On the left, General de Salles, with the 1st corps, reïnforced by a Sardinian brigade, the assistance of which had been offered to me by General de la Marmora, was to attack the town. In the centre the English were to seize the Great Redan; and, lastly, on our right, General Bosquet, was to attack the Malakoff and the Little Redan, the salient points of the enceinte of Karabelnaia.

The following arrangements had been made for each of these attacks. On the left, General Levaillant's division, (2d of the 1st corps, Brigade Couston; 9th Battalion of the Chasseurs à pied, Commander Rogié; 21st of the line, Lieut.-Colonel Villeret; 42d of the line, Lieut.-Colonel de Mallet. Brigade Trochu: 46th of the line, Lieut.-Colonel Le Banneur; 80th of the line, Colonel Laterrade,) which was charged with the duty of attacking the Central Bastion and its lunettes, was placed in the most advanced parallels. On its right was the division of General d'Autemarre (Brigade Niol: 5th Battalion of Chasseurs à pied, Commander Garnier; 19th of the line, Colonel Guinard; 26th of the line, Colonel de Sorbiers. Brigade Breton: 39th of the line, Colonel Comignan; 74th of the line Colonel Guyot de Lespart,) which was to penetrate in the track of Levaillant's Division, and seize the gorge of the Flagstaff Bastion, and the batteries which had been raised there. The Sardinian Brigade of General Cialdini, stationed at the side of General d'Autemarre's Division, was to attack the right flank of the same bastion. Finally, General Bouat's Division (4th of the 1st Corps, General Lefevre; 10th Chasseurs à pied, Commander Guiomard; 18th of the line, Colonel Dantin; 79th of the line, Colonel Grenier. 2d Brigade: General Roquette; 14th of the line, Colonel de Negrier; 43d of the line, Colonel Broutta,) and General Paté's Division (3d of the 1st Corps, General Beuret's Brigade: 6th Battalion of Chasseurs à pied, Commander Fermier de la Prévotais; 28th of the line, Col. Lartigues; 98th of the line, Col. Conseil-Dumesnil. General Bazaine's Brigade: 1st regiment of the Foreign Legion, Lieut.-Col. Marteriot de Cordoue; 2d Regiment of the Foreign Legion, Col. de Chabrieres) formed the reserve of Levaillant's division. Besides these, and in order to be prepared on this side for any eventualities which might arise, I had ordered the 30th and 35th regiments of the line from Kamiesch, and placed them under the orders of General de Salles, who had posted them on the extreme left; thus strongly securing the possession of our lines on this side. Before Karabelnaia, as I have already said, our attack was to be made in three directions—at the left on the Malakoff and its redoubt; at the right, on the Lesser Redan; and in the centre on the curtain which unites these two works. Evidently the Malakoff system of works was the most important point. Its capture must necessarily entail the ruin of the defenses of the place in succession, and I had added to the troops of General Bosquet all the infantry of the Imperial Guard.

The left attack on the Malakoff was confided to General M'Mahon, (1st Division of the 2d Corps,) 1st Brigade, Col. De caen; 1st Zouaves, Colonel Colineau; and 7th of the line, Col. Decaen; 2d Brigade, Gen. Vinoy; 1st Battalion of Chasseurs a pied, Commandant Gambier; 20th of the line, Colonel Orianne; 27th of the line, Colonel Adam, who had in reserve the

brigade Wimpfeen; 3d of Zouaves, Colonel Polhès; 50th of
the line, Lieutenant-Colonel Nicolas; and the Tirailleurs Alge-
riens, Colonel Rose, detached from Camou's Division, and the
two battalions of the Zouaves of the Guard, under Colonel
Janinn.

The attack on the right of the Redan was confided to Gen-
eral Dulac, (Brigade Saint Pol;) 17th Chasseurs à pied, commandant de Férrussac; 57th of the line, Colonel Dupuis; 85th,
Colonel Javel; 2d Brigade, General Bisson; 10th of the line,
Commandant de Lacontrie; 61st of the line, Colonel de Taxis,
having in reserve the Brigade Marolles; 15th of the line, Col.
Guerin; 96th of the line, Colonel Malherbe, of the Division
d'Aurelles, and the Battalion of Chasseurs à pied of Gard,
Commandant Cornulier de Luciniéere. Finally General de
Motterouge (Brigade du General Bourbeki. 4th Chasseurs à
pied, Commandant Clinchant; 86th of the line, Colonel de Ber-
thier; 100th of the line, Col. Mathieu; 2d Brigade, Colonel
Picard; 91st of the line, Colonel Picard; 94th of the line, Col.
Kergdern) commanded the attack in the centre at the Curtain,
having in reserve the Voltigeurs, Colonel Montéra et Douay,
and the Grenadiers of the Guard, Colonels Blanchard and Dal-
ton, under the direct orders of General Millinet, having under
him Brigadier-Generals Pontevés and De Failly.

With reference to the situation of these troops, our trenches
have been divided into three portions, each of which was to
contain in its advanced part nearly the whole of the attacking
division; and the reserves were to be placed some in the old
trenches, which were well adapted to hold them, and others in
the Karabelnaia and Careenage ravines.

It was of the first importance, in order to deceive the enemy,
that the assembling of all these troops should take place without observation, and for this purpose all the lines of communication leading to our advanced places d'armes had been examined
with great care, and wherever they permitted the enemy to see
our men, the protecting crests were raised so as to give sufficient covering.

At the left attacks, as well as at those of the right, detachments of engineers and of artillery, furnished with tools, had
been appointed to proceed at the head of each column of attack. The Sappers were to be ready with the auxiliaries of the
advanced guard of each attack, to throw bridges, in the use of
which they had been exercised, and the materials for which
had been placed forward in the first line. The gunners were
to be furnished with hammers, and all kinds of tools proper to
spike or unspike guns as the case might be, and to turn against
the enemy those which should be conquered. Moreover, in

the first battalions of each attack, a certain number of men were to be furnished with handy tools, such as they could carry in their waist-belts, and fit to open passages, fill up ditches, to turn traverses, and, in a word, to accomplish those important works which require to be executed on the instant.

Moreover, reserves of field artillery had been prepared, so as to be able to come up rapidly and take part in the action. At the left attacks a field battery was to be placed in a quarry, near the *enceinte*, with its horses attached. Two other batteries, of the First Division, were to be held ready at the Clocheton. Finally, a fourth battery was to be in waiting at the left extremity of the Lazaret.

At the right attack a reserve of 24 field guns was to be placed, 12 in the old Lancaster battery and 12 in the Victoria redoubt. Working parties were posted in points indicated, ready at the opportune moment to prepare the way for the artillery.

In order to be ready for every event, the 1st Division of Aurelle's Brigade was posted so as to be able, with the aid of the batteries and redoubts existing in that direction, to repulse any attempt which the enemy might make on the counterforts of Inkermann.

On the side of our lines General Herbillon had orders to occupy the positions of the Tchernaya with his infantry, cavalry, and artillery, to act at a moment's notice. I had besides ordered General Forton's Brigade of Cuirassiers to be near him. General de la Marmora had been previously informed of these arrangements.

General d'Alonville had orders to retire in the night of the 7th from the valley of Baidar, and take a position of concentration, near the bridge of Kreutzen, which would be advantageous in case of any attempt made by the army of relief.

General Simpson and I had by common consent fixed the hour of attack at 12 o'clock. The hour chosen was in many respects advantageous. It gave us a better chance of suddenly surprising the enemy, and in case the Russian army of relief had been inclined to make a desperate attempt to succor the place, it would have been impossible for it to make a vigorous movement against our lines before the end of the day. In any case, whatever the result of the attack, we should have until the morning to advise upon it.

On the morning of the 8th the artillery of our left attacks, which from daybreak on the 5th had kept up violent fire, continued to crush the enemy with its projectiles. At the right attack our batteries also fired rapidly, but kept up the system which they had adopted several days before, in expectation of that which might take place.

Towards eight o'clock the engineers threw upon the Central Bastion two mines of projection, each charged with a hundred kilogrammes of powder, and at the same time they exploded before our approaches on the front of the Malakoff three mining chambers charged in all with 1500 kilogrammes of powder, in order to destroy the lower galleries of the Russian miners.

As the possession of the Malakoff works must decide the day, the other attacks were subordinated to it, and it was agreed with General Simpson that the English should not attack the Great Redan until I should have given a signal that we were sure of the Malakoff. In the same way General de Salles was not to attack with his troops until a moment which I was to indicate to him by another signal.

A little before noon all the troops were in readiness, and in perfect order on the points indicated, and the other arrangements had been punctually executed. General de Salles was ready; General Bosquet was at the fighting-post which he had chosen in the 6th parallel; and I, with Generals Thiry of the Artillery, Niel of the Engineers, and Martimprey, the chief of my staff, was at the Brancion redoubt, which I had chosen for my head-quarters.

All our watches had been regulated. At noon precisely all our batteries ceased to thunder, in order that they might be adjusted to a longer range, so as to reach the reserves of the enemy. At the word of their chiefs, the divisions of Generals M'Mahon, Dulac, and De la Motterouge, left the trenches. The drums and the clarions beat and sounded the charge, and to the cry of "Vive l'Empereur!" a thousand times repeated along the whole line, our intrepid soldiers precipitated themselves upon the enemy's defenses. It was a solemn moment. The first brigade of M'Mahon's division, the 1st regiment of Zouaves leading, followed by the 7th of the line, and having the 4th Chasseurs à pied on its left, sprang to the left face and the salient of the Malakoff work. The breadth and depth of the ditch, the height and steepness of the slope, rendered the ascent extremely difficult to our men; but finally they gained the parapet, manned with Russians, who, in default of muskets, picked up whatever came to hand—mattocks, stones, or rammers—and used them as weapons. Then took place a hand-to-hand struggle—one of those exciting combats in which nothing but the intrepidity of our soldiers and their chiefs can give them the victory. They immediately sprang into the work; they drove back the Russians who continued to resist, and, in

a few seconds afterwards, the flag of France was finally planted
on the Malakoff.

At the right and centre, with that same impetuous dash
which had overthrown so many obstacles and forced the enemy
to fly, the divisions Dulac and De la Motterouge, led by their
chiefs, had seized the Little Redan at the Careening Bay, and
also the Curtain, forcing their way even as far as the second
enceinte that was being constructed. Everywhere we were in
possession of the works attacked. But this first and brilliant
success had near cost us very dear. Struck by a large splinter
from a bomb on his right side, General Bosquet was compelled
to quit the field of battle. I confided the command to General
Dulac, who was admirably seconded by General de Liniers,
chief of the staff of the 2d corps.

The engineers who accompanied the storming columns were
already at work; they filled up the ditches, opened passages,
and threw across bridges. The second brigade of General de
M'Mahon advanced rapidly to reïnforce the troops in the Malakoff. I gave the signal agreed upon with General Simpson for
the attack on the Great Redan, and shortly after for the attack
on the town.

The English had 200 metres to cross under a terrible fire of
grape. This space was soon strewed with dead; nevertheless,
this did not stop the march of the storming column, which advanced towards the capital of the work. It descended into the
ditch, which is nearly five metres deep, and, despite all the
efforts of the Russians, it scaled the escarpe, and carried the
salient of the Redan. There, after the first brunt of the engagement, which cost the Russians dear, the English soldiers
found in front of them only a vast open space, crossed by the
balls of the enemy, who kept himself close behind some distant
traverses. Those who came up hardly replaced those who had
been disabled. It was not until they had sustained for nearly
two hours this unequal contest that the English decided on
evacuating the Redan. They did so with so firm an aspect
that the enemy did not dare follow.

In the mean time, on the left, at the appointed signal, the
columns of Levaillant's division, commanded by Generals
Couston and Trochu, dashed headlong against the left flank of
the Central Bastion and the left lunette. In spite of a shower
of balls and projectiles, and after a very sharp contest, the spirit
and vigor of these brave troops triumphed at first over the
enemy's resistance, and, notwithstanding the accumulated difficulties in their front, they forced their way into the two works.
But the enemy, having fallen back on his successive traverses,

kept his ground everywhere. A murderous fire of musketry was opened from every ridge. Guns unmasked for the first time, and field-pieces, brought up to several points, vomited grape and decimated our men. Generals Couston and Trochu, who had just been wounded, were obliged to give up their command. Generals Rivet and Breton were killed; several mine-chambers, fired by the enemy, produced a moment of hesitation. At length an attack in their turn by numerous Russian columns compelled our troops to abandon the works they had carried, and to retire into our advanced *places d'armes*.

Our batteries on this part of the attacks, skillfully conducted by General Lebœuf, aided so devotedly and intelligently, as on all occasions, by Rear-Admiral Rigault de Genouilly, changed the direction of their fire while increasing its intensity, and compelled the enemy to take shelter behind the parapets. General de Salles, causing d'Autemarre's division to advance, was preparing during this time a second and formidable attack; but as we had secured the possession of the Malakoff, I sent word to him not to let it advance.

Our possession of this work, however, was energetically disputed.

By means of the batteries from the *maison en croix*, of the guns of his steamers, of field guns brought to favorable points, and of the batteries on the north side of the roadstead, the enemy deluged us with grape, and with projectiles of every kind, and committed great ravages in our ranks. The powder magazine of the Russian Postern Battery had just exploded, thereby increasing our loss, and causing the eagle of the 91st to disappear for a moment. A great many superior officers and others were either wounded or killed. The Generals de Saint Pol and de Marolles died gloriously, and Generals Mellinet, de Pontèves, and Bourbaki, had been wounded at the head of their troops. Three times the division of Dulac and De la Motterouge seized the Redan and the Curtain, and three times they were obliged to fall back before a terrible fire of artillery and the dense masses arrayed in front of them. Nevertheless the two field batteries of reserve from the Lancaster battery descended at a trot, crossed the trenches, and boldly stationed themselves within half-range. They succeeded in driving away the enemy's columns and the steamers. A part of these two divisions, supported in this heroic struggle by the troops of the Guard, who on this day covered themselves with glory, made good their footing in the entire left of the Curtain, from which the enemy could not drive them. During the renewed combats of the right and the centre, the Russians redoubled their efforts to reconquer the Malakoff. This work, which is a sort of earthen

citadel of 350 metres in length and 150 metres in width, armed
with 62 guns of different calibre, crowns a mamelon which
commands the whole interior of the Karabelnaia quarter, takes
in reverse the Redan which was attacked by the English, is
only 1200 metres from the south harbor, and threatens not
merely the only anchorage now remaining for the ships, but
the only means of retreat open to the Russians, namely, the
bridge thrown across the roadstead from one bank to the other.

Thus during the first hours of the strife of the two armies,
the Russians constantly renewed their attempts; but General
M'Mahon, in resisting these incessant attacks, was assisted successively by Vinoy's brigade of his division, by the Zouaves of
the Guard, General Wimpffen's reserve, and a part of the Voltigeurs of the Guard; in all directions he resisted the enemy,
who were everywhere repulsed. The Russians, however, made
a last and desperate attempt. Formed in deep column, they
thrice assailed the breast of the work, and thrice they were compelled to retire with enormous loss before the solidity of our
troops.

After this last struggle, which ended about five in the evening, the enemy appeared resolved to abandon the spot, and only
his batteries continued until night to send us some projectiles,
which no longer did us much harm.

The detachments of the engineers and artillery, who during
the combat were gallantly fighting or actively engaged in their
special work, quickly set about carrying out the works that
were pressing in the interior of the fort under the direction of
their officers.

According to my orders, Generals Thiry and Niel instructed
Generals Beuret and Frossard, commanding the artillery and
engineers of the 2d corps, to take all necessary steps for establishing ourselves firmly in the Malakoff, and on that part of
the curtain which was in our power, so that we might, in case
of need, resist a night attack of the enemy, and be in a position
to drive him the next day from the Little Redan of the Careening Bay, the Maison en Croix, and all this portion of his defenses.

These arrangements became, however, unnecessary. The
enemy, hopeless of retaking the Malakoff, took an important
resolution—he evacuated the town.

Towards the close of the day I had a suspicion of this, for I
had seen long lines of troops and baggage defile along the
bridge and reach the north bank, and the conflagrations which
arose in every direction soon removed all doubt. I should have
liked to push forward, gain the bridge, and cut off the enemy's
retreat; but the besieged was at every moment blowing up one

or other of his defenses, his powder magazines, and his establishments. These explosions would have destroyed us in detail, and so they rendered the idea impracticable. We remained in position until the day should arise upon this scene of desolation.

The sun in rising lighted up this work of destruction, which was very much greater than we had been able to imagine. The last Russian vessels anchored the evening before in the roadstead were sunken; the bridge was disconnected; the enemy had only reserved his steamers, which carried off the last fugitives and some infatuated Russians who were still walking amongst the fires in this unhappy city. But presently these men, as well as the steamers, were driven to seek refuge in the indentations of the bank north of the roadstead.

Thus terminated this memorable siege, during which the army of relief has been twice defeated in order of battle, and the offensive and defensive means of which have attained to colossal proportions. The besieging army had, at its various attacks, 800 guns in battery, which have fired more than 1,600,000 times; and our approaches, excavated in the course of 336 days, in rocky ground, and presenting an extent of more than 80 kilometres (20 leagues), have been executed under the constant fire of the place, and disturbed by incessant combats day and night.

The day of September 8, on which the allied armies proved themselves superior to an army almost equal in number, not invested, entrenched behind formidable defenses, provided with more than 1100 guns, protected by the guns of the fleet, and of the batteries north of the roadstead, and still disposing of immense resources, will remain an example of what may be expected from an army, brave, disciplined, and inured to war.

Our losses on this day were five generals killed, four wounded, and six contused; 24 superior officers killed, 20 wounded, and two missing; 116 subaltern officers killed, 224 wounded, eight missing; 1489 sous-officers and soldiers killed, 4259 wounded, and 1400 missing—total 7551.

As you see, Monsieur le Maréchal, these losses are numerous; many of them are deeply to be regretted, but yet they are less than I had reason to fear.

Every one, Monsieur le Maréchal, from the general to the soldier, has gloriously done his duty, and the army, of which the Emperor may be proud, has deserved well of the country. I shall have many rewards to claim, and many names to make known to your excellency. That will be a task that would be out of place here.

It had been arranged that the fleets of Admirals Lyons and

Bruat should come and bring their broadsides to bear at the entrance of the Sebastopol roadstead, so as to effect a powerful diversion.   But it blew a heavy gale from the northeast, which, while it annoyed us very much on land, rendered the sea exceedingly rough, and prevented the ships from leaving their moorings. The English and French bomb-ketches were, nevertheless, able to act, and they fired most successfully into the roadstead, the town, and the various maritime forts.   As at all times, the sailors who had landed and the ship-gunners, were the worthy rivals of the land artillery, and distinguished themselves by the vigor and precision of their fire.

The English army conducted itself with its habitual intrepidity.   It prepared a second attack, which, doubtless, would have triumphed over the unexpected obstacles which had met their first; but the possession of the Malakoff properly led to the countermanding of this second attack.

The Sardinian brigade of General Cialdini, which General de la Marmora had placed at my disposition to reïnforce the first corps, bore the terrible fire which cut up our trenches with the firmness of veteran troops.   The Piedmontese burned with desire to come to blows with the enemy; but the attack on the Flagstaff Bastion having been postponed, it was impossible to satisfy the ardor of these brave troops.   As at all times, our wounded, and even those of the enemy, have been the objects of most zealous, intelligent, and complete care.   We owe to the good organization of all our hospital services, and to the devotedness of those to whom they are committed, the satisfaction of being able to save a great number of the wounded.

Accept, etc.,   PELISSIER.

PRINCE GORTSCHAKOFF'S ACCOUNT OF THE CAPTURE OF SEBASTOPOL.

Head-quarters, Heights of Inkermann, in the vicinity of Sebastopol, August 20, (Sept. 12,)
Taking advantage of the superiority of their fire at short range, the enemy, after the concentrated action of their artil·lery during thirty days—which cost our garrison from 500 to 1000 men per day—commenced that terrible bombardment (*bombardement d'enfer*) from their innumerable engines of war, and of a calibre hitherto unknown, which destroyed our defenses, which had been repaired at night with great labor and at great loss, under the incessant fire of the enemy—the principal work, the Korniloff Redoubt, on the Malakoff Hill (the key of Sebastopol, as a point dominating the whole town) having experienced considerable and irreparable damage.

To continue, under these circumstances, the defense of the south side, would have been to expose our troops, daily, to useless butchery ; and their preservation is, to-day, more than ever necessary to the Emperor of Russia.

For these reasons, with sorrow in my heart, but with a full conviction, I resolved to evacuate Sebastopol, and take over the troops to the north side by the bridge constructed beforehand over the bay, and by boats.

Meantime, the enemy, beholding, on the 27th of August, (8th of Sept.,) at 10.30, the half-ruined works before them and the Korniloff redoubt, with its ditches filled up, resolved upon a desperate assault, first on Bastions No. 2 (Korniloff) and No. 3 (Redan) and, after three hours, upon Bastion No. 5, and the Belkin Schwartz redoubts.

Of these six attacks, five were gloriously repulsed. Some of the points of attack, like that on Bastion No. 2, on which the enemy had succeeded in bringing guns by flying bridges, having at various times been taken and retaken, remained finally ours. But the Korniloff redoubt, more damaged than the others by the bombardment, was taken by the French, who brought more than 30,000 men against it, and could not be retaken after the great losses we had suffered at the commencement of this combat ; for it would have been necessary to ascend, in the midst of the ruins, a very steep incline, and then cross a narrow ridge above a deep ditch of the rear face occupied by the French. Such an undertaking might have prevented us achieving the proposed object, and would have cost us, without the slightest doubt, incalculable losses.

The attempt was the more needless, as for reasons already mentioned I had resolved to evacuate the place. Therefore, as the success of the enemy was confined to the sole capture of the Korniloff redoubt, I ordered that no attack should be made on that redoubt, but to remain in front of it, to oppose any continuation of the enemy's attack on the town itself, an order which was executed despite all the efforts of the French to get beyond the gorge of the redoubt.

At dusk the troops were ordered to retire according to the arrangements previously made.

The examples of bravery you gave during that day, valiant comrades, aroused such a feeling of esteem in the enemy, that despite the knowledge they must have had of our retreat by the explosion of our mines, which our troops exploded one after the other as they gradually retreated, they not only did not pursue us in columns, but even ceased firing with their artillery, which they might have continued with impunity.

Valiant comrades, it is painful, it is hard to leave Sebastopol

in the enemy's hands. But remember the sacrifice we made
upon the altar of our country in 1812. Moscow was surely as
valuable as Sebastopol—we abandoned it after the immortal
battle of Borodino. The defense of Sebastopol during 349
days is superior to Borodino, and when the enemy entered
Moscow in that great year of 1812, they only found heaps of
stones and ashes. Likewise it is not Sebastopol which we have
left to them, but the burning ruins of the town which we ourselves set fire to, having maintained the honor of the defense in
such a manner that our great-grandchildren may recall the remembrance thereof with pride to all posterity.

Sebastopol kept us chained to its walls; with its fall we
acquire freedom of movement, and a new war commences, a
war in the open field, that most congenial to the Russian soldier. Let us prove to the Emperor, let us prove to Russia,
that we are still imbued with the spirit which animated our
ancestors in our memorable and patriotic struggle. Wherever
the enemy may show himself we will present our breasts to
him, and defend our native land as we defended it in 1812.

Valiant warriors of the land and sea forces!—In the name of
the Emperor I thank you for the unexampled courage, firmness, and constancy you have displayed during the siege of
Sebastopol.

[Here follow the names of the officers who most distinguished
themselves.]

In thus expressing the gratitude your worthy commanders
are entitled to, who are still living, let us also honor, comrades,
those who have fallen honorably for our faith and for our
country on the ramparts of Sebastopol.

Let us remember the immortal names of Nachimoff, Korniloff,
and Istomine, and let us address prayers to the Most High that
he will grant them peace, and eternalize their memory as an
example to the future generations of the Russians.

DESCRIPTION OF SEBASTOPOL AFTER ITS ABAN-
DONMENT BY THE RUSSIANS.

The wonder of all visitors to the ruins of Sebastopol is
divided; they are astonished at the strength of the works, and
that they were ever taken; they are amazed that men could
have defended them so long with such ruin around them.
These feelings are apparently in opposition to each other, but
a glance at the place could explain the apparent contradiction.
Their enormous bomb-proofs, large and numerous as they were,

could not hold the requisite force to resist a general concerted attack made all along the line with rapidity, and without previous warning. On the other hand, the strength of the works themselves is prodigious. But it is evident that the Russian has been enabled to sustain the most tremendous bombardment ever known, and an eleven months' siege, that he was rendered capable of repulsing one general assault, and that a subsequent attack upon him at four points was only successful at one, which fortunately happened to be the key of his position; and the inference is, that his engineers were of consummate ability, and furnished him with artificial strength that made him equal to our best efforts. It is sufficient to say that of the three or four points attacked, the Little Redan and the Malakoff on the right, and the Bastion Central and the reëntering angle of the Flagstaff Work on the left, but one was carried, and that was a closed work. The Great Redan, the Little Redan, and the line of defense on the left, were not taken, although the attack was resolute, and the contest obstinate and bloody for both assailants and defenders. It is certain that the Russian knew his weakness, and was too good a strategist to defend a position of which we held the key. Sebastobol in flames, his ships sunk, told the story next morning, and some ten thousand French and English soldiers were its commentators. The tremendous explosions, which shook the very ground like so many earthquakes, failed to disturb many of the wearied soldiers.

All was ready on the part of the English for a renewed assault on the Redan, but the Russians having kept up a brisk fire from the rifle pits and embrasures to the last moment, and having adopted the same plan along their lines, abandoned it. as is supposed, about twelve o'clock, and the silence having attracted the attention of the Allies, some volunteers crept up and looked through an embrasure, and found the place deserted by all save the dead and dying. Soon afterwards, wandering fires gleamed through the streets and outskirts of the town; point after point became alight; the flames shone out of the windows of the houses; rows of mansions caught and burned up, and, ere daybreak, the town of Sebastopol, that fine and stately mistress of the Euxine, was on fire from the sea to the Dockyard Creek. Fort Alexander was blown up with a stupendous crash that made the very earth reel, early in the night. At sunrise four large explosions on the left followed in quick succession, and announced the destruction of the Quarantine Forts and the magazines of the batteries of the Central Bastion and Flagstaff Fort. In a moment afterwards the proper left of the Redan was the scene of a very heavy explosion, which must have destroyed a number of wounded

men on both sides. Fortunately the soldiers who had entered
it early in the night were withdrawn. The Flagstaff and Garden batteries blew up, one after another, at 4.45. At 5.30
there were two of the largest and grandest explosions on the
left that ever shook the earth—most probably from Fort Alexander and the Grand Magazine. The rush of black smoke, of
gray and white vapor, of masses of stone, beams of timber,
and masonry, into the air, was appalling, and then followed
the roar of a great bombardment; it was a magazine of shells
blown up into the air, and exploding like some gigantic pyro-
technic display in the sky—the effect of the innumerable flashes
of fire twittering high up in the column of dark smoke over the
town, and then changing rapidly into as many balls of white
smoke like little clouds. All this time the Russians were marching with sullen tramp across the bridge, and boats were busy
carrying off materiél from the town, or bearing men to the south
side, to complete the work of destruction and renew the fires of
hidden mines, or light up untouched houses. Of the fleet, all that
remained visible were the eight steamers and the masts of the
sunken line of battle ships. As soon as it was dawn, the French
began to steal from their trenches into the burning town, undis-
mayed by the flames, by the terrors of these explosions, by the
fire of a lurking enemy, or by the fire of their own guns, which
kept on slowly discharging cannon-shot and grape into the suburbs at regular intervals, possibly with the object of deterring
stragglers from risking their lives. But red breeches and blue
breeches, kepi and Zouave fez, could soon be distinguished in
amid the flames, and moving from house to house. Ere 5
o'clock there were numbers of men coming back with plunder,
such as it was, and Russian relics were offered for sale in the
camp before the Russian battalions had marched out of the city.
The sailors too, were not behindhand in looking for "loot,"
and Jack could be seen staggering under chairs, tables, and
lumbering old pictures, through every street, and making his
way back to the trenches with vast accumulations of worthless-
ness. Several men lost their lives by explosions on this and
the following day. At 7 ten several detonations of shells and
powder magazines took place in the town, behind the Redan and
also on the left of the Dockyard Creek. At 7.12 immense
clouds of black smoke rose from behind Fort Paul, probably
from a steamer which was burning in the dockyard. The Russian columns, which had been defiling in a continuous stream
across the bridge, now became broken into small bodies, or went
over in intermittent masses unscathed by the shot and shell
which plunged into the water close beside them. At 6 45 the
last dense column marched past, and soon afterwards the bridge

was pulled asunder, and the pieces were all floated across to the north side at 8.7. The boats did not cease to pull backward and forward all the time, and the steamers were exceedingly busy long after the garrison moved. At nine there were many explosions in the town amid the burning ruins, and the battlements of Fort Nicholas appeared in flames. Still there was no explosion there, nor in Fort Paul. As the rush from camp now became very great, and every one sought to visit the Malakoff and the Redan, which were filled with dead and dying men, a line of English cavalry was posted across the front from their extreme left to the French right. They were stationed in all the ravines and roads to the town and trenches, with orders to keep back all persons except the generals and staff, and officers and men on duty.

The ambulances never ceased, now moving heavily and slowly with their burdens, again rattling at a trot to the front for a fresh cargo, and the ground between the trenches and the camp was studded with cacolets or mule litters. Already the funeral parties had commenced their labors. The Russians all this time were swarming on the north side, and took the liveliest interest in the progress of the explosions and conflagrations. They took up ground in their old camps, and swarmed all over the face of the hills behind their northern forts. Their steamers cast anchor, or were moored close to the shore among the creeks, on the north side, near Fort Catharine. By degrees the generals, French and English, and the staff officers, edged down upon the town; but Fort Paul had not yet gone up, and Fort Nicholas was burning, and engineers declared the place would be unsafe for 48 hours. Moving down, however, a small party managed to get out among the French works between the Mamelon and Malakoff. The ground is here literally paved with shot and shell, and the surface is deeply honeycombed by the explosion of the bombs at every square yard.

There were many ghastly sights—Russians who had died, or were dying as they lay, brought so far towards the hospitals from the fatal Malakoff. Passing through a maze of trenches, of gabionades, and of zig-zags and parallels, by which the French had worked their sure and deadly way close to the heart of the Russian defense, and treading gently among the heaps of dead, where the ground bears full tokens of the bloody fray, we come at last to the head of the French sap. It is barely ten yards from that to the base of the huge sloping mound of earth which rises full twenty feet in height above the level, and shows in every direction the grinning muzzles of its guns. The tri-color waves placidly from its highest point, and already the French are busy constructing a

semaphore on the top. Step briskly out of the sap—avoid
those poor mangled braves who are lying all around, and come
on. There is a deep ditch at your feet, some 20 or 22 feet deep,
and 10 feet broad. See, here is the place where the French
crossed—here is the bridge of planks, and here they swarmed
in upon the unsuspecting defenders of the Malakoff. They had
not ten yards to go. The English had 200, and were then out
of breath. Were not planks better than scaling ladders? See
how easily the French crossed. You observe on your right
hand, as you issue from the head of the French trench, a line
of gabions on the ground running up to this bridge. That is a
flying sap, which the French made the instant they got out of
the trench into the Malakoff, so that they were enabled to pour
a continuous stream of men into the works, with comparative
safety from the flank fire of the enemy. In the same way
they at once dug a trench across the work inside, to see if there
were any galvanic wires to fire mines. Mount the parapet and
descend—of what amazing thickness are those embrasures!
From the level of the ground inside to the top of the parapet
can not be less than 18 feet. There are eight rows of gabions
piled one above the other, and as each row recedes towards the
top it leaves in the ledge below an excellent banquette for the
defenders. Inside the sight is too horrible to dwell upon.
The French are carrying away their own and the Russian
wounded, and there are five distinct piles of dead formed to
clear the way. The ground is marked by pools of blood, and
the smell is already noisome; swarms of flies settle on dead
and dying; broken muskets, torn clothes, caps, shakos, swords,
bayonets, bags of bread, canteens, and haversacks are lying in
indescribable wreck all over the place, mingled with heaps of
shot, of grape, bits of shell, cartridges, case and canister, loose
powder, official papers, and cooking tins. The traverses are so
high and deep that it is impossible almost to get a view of the
whole of the Malakoff from any one spot, and there is a high
mound of earth in the middle of the work, either intended as a
kind of shell-proof, or the remains of the old White Tower. The
guns, which to the number of 60 were found in the work, are all
ship's guns, and mounted on ship's carriages, and worked in
the same way as ship's guns. There are a few old-fashioned,
oddly-shaped mortars. Look around the work, and you will
see that the strength of the Russian was his weakness—he fell
into his own bomb-proofs. In the parapet of the work may be
observed several entrances—very narrow outside, but descending and enlarging downwards, and opening into rooms some
four or five feet high and eight or ten square. These are only
lighted from the outside by day, and must have been pitch

dark at night, unless the men were allowed lanterns. Here the garrison retired when exposed to a heavy bombardment. The odor of these narrow chambers is villainous, and the air reeks with blood and abominations unutterable. There are several of these places, and they might set defiance to the heaviest mortars in the world : over the roof is a layer of ship's masts, cut in junks and deposited carefully; then there is over them a solid layer of earth, and above that a layer of gabions, and above that a pile of earth again. In one of these dungeons, which is excavated in the solid rock, and was probably underneath the old White Tower, the officer commanding seems to have lived. It must have been a dreary residence. The floor and the entrance was littered a foot deep with reports, returns. and perhaps dispatches assuring the Czar that the place had sustained no damage. The garrison were in these narrow chambers enjoying their siesta, which they invariably take at twelve o'clock, when the French burst in on them like a torrent, and, as it were, drowned them in their holes. The Malakoff is a closed work ; it is only open at the rear to the town, and the French having once got in, threw open a passage to their own rear, and closed up the front and the lateral communications with the curtains leading to the Great Redan and to the Little Redan. Thus they were enabled to pour in their supports, in order and without loss, in a continued stream, and to resist the efforts of the Russians, which were desperate and repeated, to re-take the place. They brought up their field guns at once, and swept the Russian reserves and supports, while Strange's battery from the Quarries carried death through their ranks in every quarter of the Karabelnaia. With the Malakoff the Russians lost Sebastopol. The ditch outside towards the north was yet full of French and Russians piled over each other in horrid confusion. On the right, towards the Little Redan, the ground was literally strewn with bodies as thick as they could lie, and in the ditch they were piled over each other. Here the French, victorious in the Malakoff, met with a heavy loss and a series of severe repulses. The Russians lay inside the works in heaps, like carcases in a butcher's cart, and the wounds, the blood—the sight exceeded all I had hitherto witnessed. Descending from the Malakoff we come upon a suburb of ruined houses open to the sea ; it is filled with dead. The Russians have crept away into holes and corners of every house to die like poisoned rats ; artillery horses, with their entrails torn open by shot, are stretched all over the space at the back of the Malakoff, marking the place where the Russians moved up their last column to retake it, under the cover of a heavy field battery. Every house, the church, some public buildings, sentry boxes, all alike are broken and riddled by cannon and mortar. Turning to the left, we proceed by a very tall snow-white wall of great length to the dockyard gateway. This wall is pierced and broken through and through with cannon. Inside are the docks, which naval men say, are unequalled in the world. Gates and store sides are splintered and pierced by shot. There are the stately dockyard buildings on the right, which used to look so clean, and white, and spruce. Parts of them are knocked to atoms, and hang together in such shreds and patches that it is only wonderful they cohere. The soft white stones, of which they and the walls are made, are readily knocked to pieces by a cannon shot. Fort Paul is untouched. There it stands, as if frowning defiance at its impending fate, right before us, and warning voices bid all people to retire, and even the most benevolent retreat from the hospital, which is in one of these buildings, where they are tending the miserable wounded.

HORRORS OF THE HOSPITAL AT SEBASTOPOL.

Of all the pictures of the horrors of war which have ever been presented to the world, the hospital of Sebastopol presents the most horrible, heart-rending, and revolting. It can not be described, and the imagination of a Fuseli could not conceive any thing at all like unto it. How the poor human body can be mutilated and yet hold its soul within, when every limb is shattered, and every vein and artery is pouring out the life stream, one might study here at every step, and at the same time wonder how little will kill! The building used as an hospital is one of the noble piles inside the dock-yard wall, and is situate in the centre of the row at right angles to the line of the Redan. The whole row was peculiarly exposed to the action of shot and shell bounding over the Redan, and to the missiles directed at the Barrack Battery, and it bears in sides, roofs, windows, and doors, frequent and destructive proofs of the severity of the cannonade. Entering one of these doors I beheld such a sight as few men, thank God, have ever witnessed! In a long low room supported by square pillars, arched at the top, and dimly lighted through shattered and unglazed window frames, lay the wounded Russians. The wounded, did I say? No, but the dead, the rotten and festering corpses of the soldiers who were left to die in their extreme agony, untended, uncared for, packed as close as they could be stowed, some on the floor, others on wretched tressels and bedsteads, or pallets of straw, sopped and saturated with blood, which oozed and trickled through upon the floor, mingled with the droppings of corruption. With the roar of exploding fortresses in their ears, with shells and shot forcing through the roof and sides of the rooms in which they lay, with the crackling and hissing of fire around them, those poor fellows, who had served the Czar but too well, were consigned to their terrible fate. Many might have been saved by ordinary care. Many lay, yet alive, with maggots crawling about in their wounds. Many nearly mad by the scenes around them, or seeking escape from it in their extremest agony, had rolled away under the beds, and glared out on the heart-stricken spectators, oh! with such looks. Many with legs and arms broken and twisted, the jagged splinters sticking through the raw flesh, implored aid, water, food, or pity, or, deprived of speech by the approach of death, or by dreadful injuries on the head or trunk, pointed to the lethal spot. Many seemed bent alone on making their peace with Heaven. The attitudes of some were so hideously fantastic as to appal and root one to the ground by a sort of dreadful fascination. Could that bloody mass of clothing and white bones ever have been a human being, or that burnt black mass of flesh have ever had a human soul? It was fearful to think what the answer must be. The bodies of numbers of men were swollen and bloated to an incredible degree, and the features distended to a gigantic size, with eyes protruding fron the sockets, and the blackened tongue lolling out of the mouth, compressed tightly by the teeth which had set upon it in the death-rattle, made one shudder and reel round. In the midst of one of these " chambers of horrors"—for there were many of them—we found some dead and some living English soldiers, and among them poor Captain Vaughan, of the 90th, who has since succumbed to his wounds. I confess it was impossible for me to stand the sight, which horrified our most experienced surgeons—the deadly clammy stench, the smell of the gangrened wounds, of corrupt blood, of rotting flesh, were intolerable and odious beyond endurance. But what must the wounded felt who were obliged to endure all this, and who passed away without a hand to give them a cup of water, or a voice to say one kindly word to them? Most of these men were wounded on Saturday—many perhaps on the Friday before—indeed, it is impossible to say how long they might have been there.

The Great Redan was next visited. Such a scene of wreck and ruin! All the houses behind it a mass of broken stones —a clock turret, with a shot right through the clock—a pagoda in ruins—another clock tower with all the clock destroyed save the dial, with the words " Barwise, London," thereon—cook-

11

houses, where human blood was running among the utensils: in one place a shell had lodged in the boiler and blown it and its contents, and probably its inhabitants, to pieces. Everywhere wreck and destruction. This evidently was a *beau quartier* once. The oldest inhabitant could not recognize it now. Climbing up to the Redan, which was fearfully encumbered with the dead, we witnessed the scene of the desperate attack and defense, which cost both sides so much blood The ditch outside made one sick—it was piled up with English dead, some of them scorched and blackened by the explosion, and others lacerated beyond recognition. The quantity of broken gabions and gun carriages here was extraordinary—the ground was covered with them. The bomb-proofs were the same as in the Malakoff, and in one of them a music book was found, with a woman's name in it, and a Canary bird and vase of flowers were outside the entrance.

RUSSIAN SHIPS DESTROYED AT SEBASTOPOL.

The following is a statement of the Russian fleet at Sebastopol previous to the invasion of the Crimea, by the allies. It consisted of the following ships :

Ships of the Line.—Twelve Apostles, 120; Paris, 120; Three Saints, 120; Grand Duke Constantine, 120 ; Vladimir, 120; Sviotoslaw, 84; Rostislaw, 84; Selaphœl, 84; Three Hierarchies, 84; Tro-Sviatitalia, 84; Varna, 84; Gabriel, 84; Empress Maria, 84; Tschesme, 80.

Frigates.—Cagul, 60; Koulefgi, 60 ; Cavarna, 60 ; Medea, 60.

Corvettes and Brigs.—Calypso, 18; Pylade, 18 ; Ptolemy, 20; Theseus, 20; Eneas, 20.

Smaller Vessels. — The Nearch, Streilla, Orlanda, Drolik, Ziabiaka, Lastorga, Smaglaga, 11 transports and 64 gunboats.

Steamers, 12—6 large, and 6 small. Among the first are the Vladimir, Bessarabia, and Gromnostetz, which were remarkable for their power and the range of their guns.

In all, 108 sail, mounting 2200 guns.

THE BOOTY FOUND IN SEBASTOPOL.

The joint commission appointed to report on the booty found in Sebastopol, and to determine its mode of distribution, has completed its labors. The report was signed by the Commissioners on the 1st inst. 3800 cannon of large and small calibre, 6 steam-engines, 18,000 or 19,000 balls, bomb-shells, anchors, chains, rigging of all kinds, etc., have been found. The Commission has decided that all the booty shall be divided between France and England. But it has been agreed at the same time that, after having valued the different articles according to their weight, the distribution should take place in proportion to the number of men in each army; and that if on this calculation England should have a right to only one fourth of the whole, she would restore to France the value of the additional amount she may have received, at the rate of 10c. per kilogramme, the price of old iron. There is no mention of the Turks in the report. As to the Sardinians, it is necessary to say that, being included in the English army, they have a claim to a portion of the amount assigned to the latter. The following arrangements have been made with regard to the town: That portion of the city comprised within the Quarantine, Fort Nicholas, the Military Harbor, and the Flagstaff Battery, shall be the exclusive property of the French. The English shall have for their part, the Karabelnaia suburbs, at the same time the French will be free to erect hospitals there, and to use Careening-bay, the docks, etc.

THE CZAR IN THE CRIMEA.

SEPTEMBER 10TH.—The Czar Alexander quitted Russia for the Crimea, for the purpose of inspiring by his presence the sinking energies of his army. His arrival at Nicolaieff was greeted with demonstrations of great joy by the soldiers and inhabitants, who now, for the first time, felt confidence in the ultimate success of their cause.

Nicolaieff possesses twelve dock yards, six for ships of the line and six for smaller vessels; also immense arsenals, and almost exhaustless materials for ship building. It employs 600 workmen in ordinary times, and 12,000 on occasions of emergency.

On the 29th, the allied fleet appeared off the port, and opened its guns upon the town. At the entreaty of his officers and suit, the Czar retired some miles into the interior; but his brother, the Grand Duke of Constantine, could not be prevailed upon to leave the scene of conflict. After a bombardment of five hours, which was gallantly returned by the allied fleet, drew off, having accomplished but little else than the destruction of an inconsiderable number of comparatively valueless buildings. Shortly after the bombardment, the Czar left Nicolaieff for Elisabetgrad, a small fortified town about 160 miles north of that important port. The momentous fall of Kinburn, a few weeks later, materially affecting the face of affairs in the campaign, the Czar, accompanied by his brother and suit, hastily returned to St. Petersburg.

CAPTURE OF A RUSSIAN FLOTILLA.

SEPTEMBER 18TH.—The English frigate Dragon, while cruising off Haddigarne, opposite the Islands of Narken, unexpectedly fell in with and captured a flotilla of Russian merchantmen, consisting of seventeen vessels of different rigs and sizes, which have been sent to England as prizes.

DESTRUCTION OF MERCHANT SHIPPING AT OLD SALIS.

On SEPTEMBER 25TH, a couple of large steam-frigates, under the British flag, arrived off the mouth of the river Salis, about 50 miles higher up the coast, and cast anchor within gun-shot of the town of Old Salis. A boat was immediately lowered, which, manned by an officer and seven sailors, proceeded to sound and reconnoitre the mouth of the river and the channel. On having accomplished this, they gave a signal to the ships, when four more boats, containing four officers and fifty-four men, pushed off and joined the first boat. These five boats then pulled in toward the shore, the foremost of them displaying a white flag in her bows, which was answered by a similar one hoisted on the flagstaff on the shore, in the hope of thereby saving the ten timber vessels lying at anchor about a verst up the river, without their masts and rigging. Whilst the lastly-arrived four boats lay on their oars, the first one approached the landing-place, and the English officer in command inquired of Herr Von Behaghel, the principal proprietor and inhabitant of Old Salis, whether the vessels lying in the river belonged to the government or were private property? This gentleman replied that they belonged to him and his people, upon which the lieutenant expressed his regret, but his positve orders were to destroy them and all others they might find along the coast. Representations and entreaties were of no avail; the sailors set fire to all the vessels, after which they returned to the frigate. As soon as the latter were out of sight, attempts were made by the inhabitants of Old Salis to extinguish the flames and save some of the burning vessels, but without much success, as only two were partially saved, whilst the remaining eight were burned to the water's edge and totally destroyed.

THE BOMBARDMENT OF THE FORTS AT DUNAMUNDE.

SEPTEMBER 27TH.—Early on the morning of this date, the inhabitants of Riga were suddenly aroused from their slum-bers by a severe and heavy cannonade. During the night eight British men-of-war—four line-of-battle ships, a frigate, and three corvettes—had approached the coast unperceived, and at daybreak opened their fire upon the batteries at Dunamunde, the mouth of the Duna. The bombardment was kept up for nearly three hours, without, however, inflicting much damage on the batteries, except dismounting a few guns, after which the hostile squadron stood off to the westward, and took up a position opposite the colony of Bullen, situated at the mouth of one of the channels of the Duna. Here they opened a heavy fire on the batteries, which was but feebly answered by the Russian artillerymen. This second bombardment lasted for two hours, and the damage done was considerably more important than at Dunamunde. About noon the ships drew off altogether, and disappeared in a northerly direction.

THE CAVALRY AFFAIR NEAR EUPATORIA.

SEPTEMBER 29TH. — As had been agreed pon between Ahmet Mushir Pasha and General d'Allonville, three columns left Eupatoria on the 29th, at 3 o'clock in the morning, to march against the Russians. The first column, directed to the south-east, went to take up a position at the extremity of the isthmus, towards Saki. It had only a few squadrons be-fore it, and these it easily kept in check, assisted as it was by two gun-boats. The second commanded by the Mushir in person, passing through Orar Atchin and Teiech, advanced on Djollchak, destroying on its march all the enemy's stores. The third, at the head of which was General d'Allonville, consisted of twelve squadrons of his division, of Armand's battery (horse-artillery), with 200 irregular horse and six Egyptian battalions. This column crossed one of the arms of Lake Sasik, and marched through Chiban on Djollchak, the joint rendezvous, where the two other columns arrived at about ten o'clock in the forenoon. The two latter columns had driven before them some Russian squadrons, which had fallen back successively on their reserves.

General d'Allonville was having the horses baited, when he observed a move on the part of the Russians, who, with eighteen squadrons, several sotnias of Cossacks, and same artillery, were endeavoring to turn the General's right by advancing between him and the lake. General d'Allonville, whom the Mushir caused to be supported in the rear by two regiments of Turkish cavalry and the six Egyptian battallions, immediately proceeded towards the end of the lake, in order to surround the enemy. The promptitude of this movement enabled the 4th Hussars, to charge the enemy with drawn sabres, while the 6th and 7th Dragoons dashed at the Russian Uhlans, and drove them into headlong flight, harrassing them for more than two leagues. As the Russians kept their ground at no one point, and were flying in all directions, Gen. d'Allonville caused his squadrons to halt, picking up before retiring, all that remained on the field of battle.

In this action the French captured 6 guns, 12 ammunition chests with their teams, 169 prisoners, and 250 horses. The losses in killed and wounded were—Russians 50 ; French 35.

THE CONQUEST OF KARS BY THE RUSSIANS.

SEPTEMBER 29TH.—The Russians, under General Mouravieff, the Commander-in-chief of the Russian forces in Asia Minor, invested Kars, the stronghold of the Turks, and made preparations to carry it by escalade. Kars was defended by Gen. Williams, who, with 16,000 English and Turks, determined to give the enemy a warm reception. The Russians advanced to the assault in full force, at 8 a. m., but were met by a sudden slaughterous fire from the parapets and embrasures in the walls surrounding the city that threw them into confusion and compelled them to fall back. Again, however, they pushed forward, and again they were driven off. Mouravieff now changed his plan of attack, and concluded, by a single bold effort, to force his way into the city. He concentrated his troops around the main entrance, in the face of a galling fire from the besieged, and while his troops picked off the heads that peered above the parapets, his cannon thundered furiously at the gate, which for a time endured the assault but finally suddenly gave way, when, as if they had only been waiting for such an event, the Turks and English unexpectedly rushed out in a steady compact mass, to the number of 15,000, and, hastily forming into columns, fiercely charged the besiegers. For a few minutes, the Russians were in confusion ; but the skill coolness and steady courage of Mouravieff were equal to the emergency. Hurriedly giving his orders, he dashed forward, at full gallop, in the face of the enemy, calling, with a ringing shout, on his men to follow. The example of their General was electric. With a wild nuzzah, the Russians bore down as one man, to meet the advancing Turks. The two armies met with a staggering shock, but recovered, and were soon as a turbulent mutinous host, in which all the fiercest elements in man's nature were aroused and seething. The combat was close, furious and slaughterous. Turks and Russians, English and Mingrelian, locked in savage embrace, fell in blood heaps—the field was strewed with the dying and the dead, and still the battle raged. By a happy combination of incidents at this juncture, the opposing Generals each succeeded in sparating or calling off his troops, and in disposing them for more effective work. Mouravieff recaptured his guns, and opened them with tremendous effect upon the Turks, who however, under the masterly guidance of their brave leader, General Williams, could neither be decoyed nor driven from their position near the gate. Meanwhile, the embrasures in the walls, poured forth upon the left flank of the Russians a raking fire which swept them down in hundreds. Calling at length to his men from the walls and city, and making his dispositions to conform to his plan, General Williams rushed forward, with the determination to bring the action to a close by risking all upon a single charge. The experiment was successful. The Russians, whose thinned ranks rendered them unable to sustain themselves against a force thrice that of their own, turned, and were soon in full flight, leaving behind them four thousand killed and wounded, three hundred prisoners, and a great quantity of stores. The action from the beginning to the close, lasted seven hours and a half, and was one of the fiercest in modern history.

But though whipped, Mouravieff was not inclined to consider himself defeated. He gave his troops a few days rest, sent off for reinforcements, and then returned to Kars, which he surrounded, and, sitting down, calmly determined to starve the city into submission. Hearing that Omar Pasha was advancing with a force of thirty thousand men, he issued a proclamation calling the entire population of Imeretia, Guriel and Mingrelia, to rise and wage a war of extermination against the enemies of the Cross. This appeal was not without its effect. Every where, throughout the Caucasus, the inhabitants flew to arms. On learning this fact, Omar Pasha broke up his march, and retreated, leaving Kars to its fate. Meanwhile, Mouraveiff continued the siege. The Turks made several sorties, but were driven back. At length in the city, affairs began to assume a serious aspect. Shut in from communication with the surrounding country, there was but one prospect before the inhabitants—famine. All hopes of help from Omar Pasha became meagre, and finally vanished. Weeks passed away, and the provisions were all consumed. The people had now no resources except in their horses ; these disappeared, then their dogs, then their cats. Men, women and children became delirious with hunger. Still, Gen. Williams would not surrender. At length the famine which was tearing the vitals of the inhabitants reached his own table. There was no merit in longer holding out. He capitulated, and Kars was in the hands of the Russians. As the latter entered the city, they were struck with pity at the pale, ghastly, emaciated appearance of their late foes, who were drawn up in lines, in the great square, to receive them. The Turks could scarcely stand erect. Here and there one fell to the earth from exhaustion. They were like lines of dying men. The Russians were moved to compassion. They broke from the ranks, and rushing forward offered them their canteens. Mouravieff's dispatch, announcing the final conquest of Kars, thrilled the court at St. Petersburg with joy, and the allied powers with indignation. 16,000 prisoners, 12 standards, 130 cannon, and 30,000 muskets fell into the hands of the victors.

CAPTURE OF RUSSIAN VESSELS.

OCTOBER 2D.—The French corvette d'Assas and the English steamers Tartar and Harrier, captured 11 Russian vessels, anchored at Biornabord, in the gulf of Bothnia, of an aggregate burden of 2,500 tons.

DESIRE FOR PEACE.

OCTOBER 10TH.—Paris, London and St. Petersburg, are anxious for a return of peace. Active negotiations are opened by Austria with the conflicting powers.

THE FALL OF KINBURN.

OCTOBER 14TH.—The allied fleet moved from the roads of Odessa and anchored, at night, off Kinburn, which commands the Bay of Khasan and also the mouths of the rivers Dneiper and Bug. The troops disembarked in the darkness, and encamped on the landside of the fort under General Bozaine ; while the fleet bore up abreast of the fortress which was thus threatened in front and rear. At daylight the Russians discovered the precariousness of their position ; but, nothing daunted, they opened their batteries upon the enemy, whose guns slowly responded. A storm rising about 9 o'clock, impaired the aim of the fleet, which ceased firing and drew off to await a more favorable hour. The day passed off, and on the following morning, the fleet drew up in line abreast of the fort, and commenced a well-directed fire, which was promptly answered by the latter. At the same time the mortars of General Bozaine commenced their deadly discharges. The bombardment was fiercely pressed for four hours and a half, when the fort began to exhibit evidences of weakness. Its embrasures lightened less frequently with the flashes of its guns ; a few ceased altogether : and large gaps were visible in the walls. At length the fire of the fleet met with only an occasional response—the fort was fighting its last blow. Admiral Lyon, of the allied fleet, thinking it right to respect the courage of the brave men at the guns, made a signal to the fleet to cease firing, and hoisting a flag of truce, dispatched a boat ashore with a demand for the capitulation of the fort, which was accepted, and the garrison, numbering one general officer, ten minor officers, and 1,380 men—surrendered themselves prisoners, and were allowed to march out with the honors of war. 174 pieces of cannon, 250,000 projectiles, 120,000 cartridges, and ammunition and supplies of every kind, were the fruits of this well-managed expedition. The Russians, in their despair at the fall of this important fortress, blew up, on the following day, the fort of Otchakoff, and three adjoining batteries, to prevent them from falling into the hands of the enemy. With Kinburn in their possession, the allies have Nicolaieff and Kherson comparatively at their mercy.

PEACE CONFERENCE PROPOSED.

OCTOBER 25TH.—A peace conference is proposed by Austria, and accepted by France and England, who fear, however, that Russia will not accept the only terms on which *they* will treat, viz : for a *lasting* peace.

BOMBARDMENT OF MARIONOPLE.

OCTOBER 31.—The English fleet bombarded Marionople, on the north coast of the sea of Azoff, and captured it after a brief engagement of two hours and forty minutes.

BATTLE OF THE INGOUR.

NOVEMBER 6TH.—The Ingour is one of the principal streams which enter the Black Sea upon its eastern shore, and it is the boundary of Abasia and Mingrelia ; rising in the snowy Caucasus, it winds through the densely-wooded country which extends from the base of the range to the sea, and debouches at Anaklia. Approaching the bank of the river, as if stalking deer, " I was enabled," says a correspondent of a London paper, " to see across the river, and to follow the line of stockades erected among the trees upon the opposite bank, beyond which appeared the heads of great numbers of Russian soldiers and Mingrelian militia. At one point there was an intrenchment, where thirty or forty were grouped together ; at others they were posted at regular distances behind the stockades or amid the thick brushwood. In the afternoon a dropping shot or two informed us that we had been perceived by the enemy, and a company of Rifles was marched down for a little Minie practice. On the 3d November desultory fire of this sort was pretty brisk, and the utmost caution was required in reconnoitering. The bed of the river at this point averages about 200 yards in breadth ; but there is very little water in it at present, and large stony islands intersect it in every direction. In the course of the afternoon Omar Pasha arrived and inspected the position himself. He rode over the ground, and ordered two batteries to be constructed to command the passage of the river, and which should at the same time enfilade a great portion of the opposite bank. These were constructed with the greatest success. Although right under the enemy, the working parties were not discovered before dawn, when the batteries were almost completed, and only one man was killed by the fire which was then opened upon them. The strength of the Russians was estimated at about 10,000, of which half were regular troops, the remainder Mingrelian militia. In many places the opposite bank was flat, and nowhere do the banks seem to exceed 100 feet in height.

The energy with which Omar Pasha pushed forward operations resulted in the utter defeat of the Russians and the successful passage of the Ingour, after a short but bloody battle. In the morning the order came for the troops to get under arms immediately, and at 11 o'clock, a. m. we crossed one branch of the river, about two miles lower down, without opposition. We now found ourselves upon an island five or six miles long and about two miles broad, across which the troops marched. Three battalions of Rifles, under Colonel

Ballard, were sent forward to line the woods, through which we advanced by a narrow path. About one o'clock we reached a large field of Indian corn, and heard the Rifles hotly engaged with the enemy in a thick wood in our front. The Russians were soon driven from this across the river, and opened a tremendous fire from behind a battery upon the wood, of which the Rifles had now taken possession. Meantime, as the leading column of the Turkish army showed itself upon the plain, a battery consisting of five guns opened upon them, which was speedily replied to by our artillery. A path was formed under cover of a steep bank, under which the infantry advanced to the support of the Rifles in the wood, who had been sustaining and replying in the most determined manner to the tremendous fire which the enemy had been concentrating upon them. While this was the position of affairs opposite the battery, Omar Pasha detached Osman Pasha with six battalions to a ford which had been discovered about a mile and a half down the river. Here they found themselves warmly received by the enemy, drawn up in force upon the opposite bank. Notwithstanding the velocity of the current and the depth of the water, the Turkish troops after firing a volley, dashed across the river in the face of a cruel fire, and in splendid style drove the Russians into the woods behind at the point of the bayonet. At almost the same moment Colonel Simmonds, at the head of two battalions of infantry and three companies of Rifles, crossed the river in front of the fort, and assaulted it under a murderous fire. Here his aid-de-camp, Captain Dymock, was killed while gallantly charging at the head of his battalion, while a Russian column which attacked them in flank was promptly met by the column under Colonel Simmonds, at the point of the bayonet and completely routed. This decided the day. The Russians evacuated the battery in the utmost confusion, leaving five guns and ammunition wagons in our hands, besides about fifty prisoners. The ground was strewn with killed and wounded ; their loss must have been very great, though so many escaped into the woods to die that it is difficult to form any just estimate. Upwards of 300 have already been found, among which were the bodies of eight officers and two colonels. I counted twenty-two horses lying dead in one heap. Our own loss amounts to 400 killed and wounded, of which about one hundred were killed. The Rifles alone lost twenty-six men killed and seventy-five wounded. The English officers concerned in this affair all behaved most gallantly ; of the five attached to the army, three had horses shot under them, and one was killed. There

can be no doubt that this victory will exercise a most important influence upon the population of Mingrelia. Of the
force which was opposed to us a very correct estimate cannot be formed, but from the accounts we have received it
cannot have been far short of ten thousand, of which four
thousand were Mingrelians and the rest regular troops. The
Russian army is now in full retreat.

NEW BRITISH COMMANDER-IN-CHIEF.

NOVEMBER 12TH.—General Simpson has retired, and the
supreme command of the British forces has been assumed by
General Sir William Codrington. The change was received
by the general officers with much dissatisfaction.

A SHARP BUT UNIMPORTANT ACTION.

DECEMBER 8TH.—Twenty-six hundred Russians attacked a
large body of the allies at Baga, Orkousta, Skrada,—three villages on the eastern extremity of the valley of Baiden—but
after an hour of sharp fighting, were compelled to beat a
rapid retreat, leaving thirty prisoners and sixty killed and
wounded.

DEFEAT OF ANGLO-TURKISH CAVALRY.

DECEMBER 16TH.—Two sotnias of Cossacks attacked and
defeated a strong squadron of Gen. Vivian's Anglo-Turkish
cavalry, near Kertch, capturing the commanding officer.

PROSPECT OF PEACE.

JANUARY 3RD.—The Emperor of France is satisfied that
peace is at hand, and gives orders to his minister of war to
cease the conscription.

England is not so confident, and having ready a fresh, en-
larged and well equipped fleet, holds herself in readiness for
whatever may be the result of the peace conference.

JANUARY 19TH—The Czar Alexander transmits to his diplomatic agents the following circular, in which it will be seen
that he accepts the pacific proposals of the Emperor of
Austria.

" Public opinion in Europe has been strongly excited by the

intelligence that propositions of peace concerted between the Allied Powers and Austria had been transmitted to St. Petersburg through the intervention of the Cabinet of Vienna.

" Already the Imperial Cabinet, upon its side, had made a step in the path of conciliation, by pointing out, in a despatch bearing date the 11th (23rd) of December, published in all the foreign journals, the sacrifices which it was prepared to make, with a view to the restoration of peace.

" This twofold proceeding proved the existence on either side of a desire to profit by the compulsory cessation imposed by the rigor of the season on the military operations, in order to respond to the unanimous wishes which were everywhere manifested in favor of a speedy peace.

" In the despatch cited above, the Imperial Government had taken for basis the four points of guarantee admitted by the conferences at Vienna, and had proposed, with regard to the third point—which had alone led to the rupture of the conferences,—a solution which differed rather in form than in substance from the one put forward at that epoch by the Allied Powers.

" The propositions transmitted to-day by the Austrian government, speak of the same fundamental proposition— that is to say, the neutralization of the Black Sea by a direct treaty between Russia and the porte, to regulate by common agreement the number of ships of war which each of the adjacent powers reserves the right of maintaining for the security of its coast. They only differ appreciably from those contained in the despatch of the 11th (23rd) of December by the proposal for rectyfying the frontier between Moldavia and Bessarabia, in exchange for the places on the Russian territory in the actual occupation of the enemy.

" This is not the place to inquire if these propositions unite the conditions necessary for insuring the repose of the East and the security of Europe, rather than those of the Russian Government. It is sufficient here to establish the point, that at last an agreement has been actually arrived at on many of the fundamental bases of peace.

" Due regard being had to this agreement, to the wishes manifested by the whole of Europe, and to the existence of a coalition the tendency of which was every day to assume larger proportions, and considering the sacrifices which a protraction of the war imposes upon Russia, the Imperial Government has deemed it its duty not to delay by accessory discussions a work, the success of which would respond to its heartfelt wishes.

" It has, in consequence, just given its adhesion to the propositions transmitted by the Austrian Government as a project of preliminaries for negotiations for peace.

" By the energy of its attitude in the face of a formidable coalition, Russia has given a measure of the sacrifices which she is prepared to make to defend her honor and dignity ; by this act of moderation, the Imperial Government gives at the same time a new proof of its sincere desire to arrest the effusion of blood, to conclude a struggle so grevious to civilization and humanity, and to restore to Russia and to Europe the blessings of peace.

" It has a right to expect that the opinion of all civilized nations will appreciate the act."

CONCLUSION OF PEACE.

At the Peace Conference, in Paris, it was decided, in effect :

1. That the Black Sea, so long controlled by Russia, should in future be thrown open to all nations ;

2. That Russia should give up her long-claimed right to the control of the mouth of the Danube, and not interfere with the navigation of that river in future ;

3. That Russia should give up one-half of Bessarabia ;

4. That Russia should not re-fortify Sebastopol, Nicolaieff, or the Aland Isles ;

5. That Russia should relinquish her claim to protect the Greeks in Turkey ;

6. That Russia should restore to Turkey all the territory and fortresses in Asia conquered by Mauravieff.

The Sultan of Turkey claimed an indemnity from Russia for his expenses in the war, but it was not granted. Lord Palmerston designed to put forward a similar claim ; but on learning that Napoleon would not consent to such a proceeding, he refrained from presenting it.

As the treaty leaves many important points untouched, it is viewed in Europe and in the United States as vague and unsatisfactory, and only a prelude to something yet to come. This impression is strengthened by the discovery of the friendly relations that have suddenly arisen between the French Emperor and the Czar—a fact which fills all lovers of peace with deep uneasiness.

THE TREATY OF PEACE.

ARTICLE I. From the day of exchange of ratifications of the treaty, there shall be peace and friendship between his Majesty the Emperor of the French, her Majesty the Queen of the United Kingdom of Great Britain and Ireland, his Majesty the King of Sardinia, his Majesty the Sultan, of the one part, and his Majesty the Emperor of all the Russias, of the other part, as well as between their heirs and successors, their respective States, and subjects in perpetuity.

ART. II. Peace being happily established between their aforesaid Majesties, the territories conquered, or occupied by their armies, during the war, shall be reciprocally evacuated. Special arrangements shall regulate the mode of evacuation, which shall be effected as soon as possible.

ART. III. His Majesty the Emperor of all the Russias engages to restore to his Majesty the Sultan the town and citadel of Kars, as well as all the other parts of the Ottoman territory of which the Russian troops are in possession.

ART. IV. Their Majesties the Emperor of the French, the Queen of the United Kingdom of Great Britain and Ireland, the King of Sardinia, and the Sultan, engage to restore to his Majesty the Emperor of all the Russias the towns and ports of Sevastopol, Balaklava, Kamiesch, Eupatoria, and Kertch.

ART. V. Their Majesties the Queen of the United Kingdom of Great Britain and Ireland, the Emperor of the French, the Emperor of all the Russias, the King of Sardinia, and the Sultan, grant a full and entire amnesty to those of their subjects who may have been compromised by any participation whatsoever in the events of the war in favor of the cause of the enemy. It is expressly understood that such amnesty shall extend to the subjects of each of the belligerent parties, who may have continued, during the war, to be employed in the service of one of the other belligerents.

ART. VI. Prisoners of war shall be immediately given up, on either side.

ART. VII. Her Majesty the Queen of the United Kingdom of Great Britain and Ireland, his Majesty the Emperor of Austria, his Majesty the Emperor of the French, his Majesty the King of Prussia, his Majesty the Emperor of all the Russias, and his Majesty the King of Sardinia, declare the Sublime Porte admitted to participate in the advantages of the public law and system of Europe. Their Majesties engage, each one on his part, to respect the independence and the territorial integrity of the Ottoman Empire ; guarantee in common the strict observance of that engagement; and will, in consequence, consider any act tending to its violation as a question of general interest.

ART. VIII. If there should arise between the Sublime Porte and one or more of the other signing powers any misunderstanding which might endanger the maintenance of their relations, the Sublime Porte, and each of such powers, before having recourse to the use of force, shall afford the other contracting parties the opportunity of preventing such an extremity by means of their mediation.

ART. IX. His Majesty the Sultan, in his constant anxiety for the well-being of his subjects, having granted a firman, which, in ameliorating their lot, without distinction of religion or race, proves his generous intentions toward the Christian population of his empire, and desiring to give a further proof of his sentiments, in this regard, has resolved to communicate to the contracting powers the said firman, spontaneously emanating from his sovereign will. The contracting powers acknowledge the great value of this communication. It is quite understood that the fact of this communication cannot, in any case, give to the said powers a right to interfere, either collectively or separately, in the relations of his Majesty the Sultan with his subjects, or in the internal administration of his empire.

ART. X. The Convention of July 13, 1841, which maintains the old regulation of the Ottoman empire, relative to the closing of the Straits of the Bosphorus and Dardanelles, has been revised by common accord. The act concluded with this view, and conformably to that principle, between the high contracting parties, is and remains annexed to the present treaty, and shall have the same force and value as if it had formed an integral part of it.

Art. XI. The Black Sea is neutralized. Open to the mercantile marine of all nations, its waters and ports are formally and in perpetuity interdicted to flags of war, whether belonging to the bordering Powers or to any other Power, save and except the exceptions mentioned in Articles XIV. and XIX. of the present treaty.

Art. XII. Freed from all impediments, trade in the ports and waters of the Black Sea shall only be subjected to regulations of health, customs and police, conceived in a spirit favorable to the development of commercial transactions. In order to give every desirable security to the commercial and maritime interests of all nations, Russia and the Sublime Porte will admit Consuls in ports situated on the coast of the Black Sea, conformably to the principles of international law.

Art. XIII. The Black Sea being neutralized, according to the terms of Article XI., the maintenance or establishment on its coasts of military-maritime arsenals becomes as unnecessary as without object. In consequence his Majesty the Emperor of all the Russias and his Majesty the Sultan engage neither to construct nor to preserve any military-maritime arsenal upon that coast.

Art. XIV. Their Majesties the Emperor of all the Russias and the Sultan having concluded a Convention for the purpose of determining the force and number of light vessels necessary for the service of their coasts, which they reserve to themselves the right of keeping up in the Black Sea, this Convention is annexed to the present Treaty, and shall have the same force and value as if it had formed an integral part of it. The Convention can neither be annulled or modified without the assent of the Powers parties to the present Treaty.

Art. XV. The Act of the Congress of Vienna having established the principles destined to regulate the navigation of the river which separate or traverse several States, the contracting Powers stipulate between themselves that for the future these principles shall be also applicable to the Danube and to its embouchures. They declare that this disposition constitutes henceforth a part of the public law of Europe, and they take it (the disposition) under their guaranty. The navigation of the Danube cannot be subjected to any hinderance or dues which shall not be expressly provided for by the stipulations contained in the following articles. In consequence no toll shall be taken that may be based solely upon the fact of the navigation of the river, nor any duty upon merchandise which may be on board vessels. The police and quarantine regulations to be established for the security of the States separated, or traversed by this river, shall be conceived in such a manner as to favor the circulation of vessels as much as possible. Save these regulations, no obstacle whatever shall be placed in the way of the free navigation.

Art. XVI. With the object of realizing the dispositions of the preceding article, a Commission, in which France, Austria, Great Britain, Prussia, Russia, Sardinia, and Turkey, shall each be represented by a delegate, shall be charged to design and cause to be executed the necessary works from Isatcha downward, in order to clear the mouths of the Danube, as well as the neighboring parts of the sea, from the sands and other obstacles which obstruct them, so as to put that part of the river, and the said parts of the sea, in the best possible state of navigability. To cover the expenses of these works, as well as of the establishments having for their object to assure and facilitate the navigation of the mouths of the Danube, fixed duties, at a proper rate, to be settled by the Commission by a majority of votes, may be levied, on the express conditions that in this respect, as in all others, the flags of all nations shall be treated on a footing of perfect equality.

Art. XVII. A Commission shall be appointed, composed of delegates of Austria, Bavaria, the Sublime Porte, and Wurtemburg, (one for each of these Powers,) to which Commission, the Commission of the three Danubian Principalities, whose nomination shall have been approved by the Porte, shall be joined. This Commission, which shall be permanent, will first draw up the regulations of navigation and of fluvial police ; secondly, remove the obstacles, of whatever nature they may be, which as yet prevent the application of the dispositions of the Treaty of Vienna to the Danube ; thirdly, give orders for and cause to be executed the necessary works throughout the whole course of the river ; and fourthly, after the dissolution of the European Commission, see to the maintenance of the navigability of the mouths of the Danube, and the neighboring parts of the Sea.

ART. XVIII. It is understood that the European Commission will have fulfilled its task, and that the Bordering Commission will have terminated the works designated in the preceding article under the numbers 1 and 2, within the space of two years. The Powers, parties to this treaty, assembled in conference and informed of these facts, will, after having taken note of them, pronounce the dissolution of the European Commission, and thenceforth the permanent Bordering Commission shall enjoy the same powers as those with which the European Commission will have been invested up to that time.

ART. XIX. In order to assure the execution of the regulations which shall have been settled by common accord, in accordance with the principles hereinbefore enunciated, each of the contracting Powers shall have the right to station two light-vessels at the mouths of the Danube.

ART. XX. In exchange for the towns, ports and territories enumerated in Article IV. of the present treaty, and in order the better to assure the liberty of the navigation of the Danube, his Majesty the Emperor of all the Russias consents to the rectification of his frontier in Bessarabia. The new frontier will start from the Black Sea at one kilometre to the east of Lake Bourna Sola, will perpendicularly rejoin the Akerman road, follow this road as far as the Valley of Trajan, pass to the south of Belgrade, reascend along the river Yalpuck as far as Saratiska, and will terminate at Kakamori, on the Pruth. Above this point the old frontier between the two empires will undergo no modification. Delegates of the contracting Powers will settle, in its details, the boundary line of the new frontier.

ART. XXI. The territory ceded by Russia shall be annexed to the Principality of Moldavia, under the suzerainty of the Sublime Porte. The inhabitants of this territory will enjoy the rights and privileges assured to the Principalities, and during the space of three years they shall be permitted to remove their domicils elsewhere, freely disposing of their property.

ART. XXII. The Principalities of Wallachia and Moldavia will continue to enjoy, under the suzerainty of the Porte and under the guaranty of the contracting Powers, the privileges and immunities of which they are in possession. No exclusive protection shall be exercised over them by any one of the guaranteeing Powers. There shall be no private right of interference in their internal affairs.

ART. XXIII. The Sublime Porte engages to preserve to the aforesaid Principalities an independent and national administration, as well as full liberty of worship, legislation, commerce, and navigation. The laws and statutes now in force shall be revised. To establish a complete accord as to this revision, a special Commission, with regard to the composition of which the high contracting parties will come to an understanding, will assemble without delay at Bucharest, together with a Commission of the Sublime Porte. The task of this Commission will be to inquire into the actual state and condition of the Principalities, and to propose the basis of their future organization.

ART. XXIV. His Majesty the Sultan promises to convoke immediately in each of the provinces a Divan, *ad hoc*, composed in such a manner as to constitute the most exact representation of the interests of all classes of society. These Divans are to give expression to the wishes of the population relative to the definitive organization of the Principalities. An instruction of the Congress will regulate the relations of the Commission with these Divans.

ART. XXV. Taking into consideration the opinion expressed by the two Divans, the Commission will, without delay, transmit the result of its own labors to the present seat of the Conferences. The final understanding with the Suzerain Power will be recorded in a Convention concluded at Paris between the high contracting parties, and a hattischeriff conformable to the stipulations of the Convention will definitively constitute the organization of these provinces—placed thenceforth under the collective guaranty of all the powers parties to the treaty.

ART. XXVI. It is agreed that there shall be in the Principalities an armed national force, organized with the object of maintaining the security of the interior, and assuring that of the frontiers. No impediment is to be placed in the way of such extraordinary measures of defence as, in accordance with the Sublime Porte, the Principalities may be under the necessity of taking to repulse any foreign aggression.

ART. XXVII. If the internal tranquillity of the Principalities should be menaced or compromised, the Sublime Porte will come to an understanding with the other contracting Powers, as to the measures to be taken to maintain or re-establish legal order. No armed intervention can take place without a previous accord with these Powers.

ART. XXVIII. The Principality of Servia will continue to be dependent upon the Sublime Porte, conformably to the Imperial Hatts, which fix and determine its rights and immunities, placed henceforth under the collective guaranty of the contracting Powers. In consequence, the said Principality will preserve its independent and national administration, as well as full liberty of worship, legislation, commerce. and navigation.

ART. XXIX. The right of garrison of the Sublime Porte, such as is stipulated for by anterior regulations, is maintained. No armed intervention is to take place in Servia without a previous accord between all the contracting Powers.

ART. XXX. His Majesty the Emperor of all the Russias and his Majesty the Sultan keep in its integrity the state of their possessions in Asia, such as it existed legally before the rupture. In order to prevent any local contest, the boundary of the frontier will be verified, and, if need be, rectified, but so that no territorial prejudice shall result to either of the two parties from any such rectification. With this view a mixed Commission, composed of two Russian Commissioners, two Ottoman Commissioners, one French Commis sioner, and one English Commissioner, shall be sent to the locality immediately after the re-establishment of diplomatic relations between the Court of Russia and the Sublime Porte. The labors of this Commission are to be terminated within the space of eight months, dating from the exchange of the ratifications of the present treaty.

ART. XXXI. The territories occupied during the war by the troops of their Majesties the Emperor of the French, the Emperor of Austria, the Queen of the United Kingdom of Great Britain and Ireland, and the King of Sardinia, under the terms of the Conventions signed at Constantinople on March 12, 1854, between France, Great Britain, and the Sublime Porte, the 14th of June of the same year between Austria and the Sublime Porte, and the 15th March, 1855, between Sardinia and the Sublime Porte, shall be evacuated as soon as possible after the ratification of the present treaty. The time within which the evacuation is to be effected and the means of execution will be the subject of a Convention between the Sublime Porte and the powers whose troops occupy the territories.

ART. XXXII. Until the treaties or conventions which existed before the war between the belligerent Powers shall have been renewed or replaced by new acts, the commerce of importation and exportation shall go on reciprocally upon the footing of the rules in force before the war, and their subjects shall in all other respects be respectively treated upon the footing of the most favored nation.

ART. XXXIII. The Convention concluded this day between their Majesties the Emperor of the French, the Queen of the United Kingdom of Great Britain and Ireland of the one part, and his Majesty the Emperor of all the Russias of the other part, relative to the Aland Isles, is and remains annexed to the present treaty, and shall have the same force and value as if it had made part of it.

ART. XXXIV. The present treaty shall be ratified, and the ratifications shall be exchanged in Paris, within the space of four weeks, or sooner, if possible. In faith of which the respective Plenipotentiaries have signed it and have hereto affixed the seal of their arms.

In witness whereof the respective Plenipotentiaries have signed the same, and have affixed thereto the seal of their arms.

Done at Paris, the 30th day of the month of March, in the year 1856.

CLARENDON.
COWLEY.
BUOL-SCHAUENSTEIN.
HUBNER.
A. WALEWSKI.
BOURQUENEY.
MANTEUFFEL.
C. M. D'HATZFELDT.
ORLOFF.
BRUNNOW.
C. CAVOUR.
DE VILLAMARINA.
AALI.
MEHEMMED DJEMIL.

ADDITIONAL AND TRANSITORY ARTICLES.

The stipulations of the Convention respecting the Straits, signed this day, shall not be applicable to the vessels of war employed by the belligerent Powers for the evacuation by sea of the territories occupied by their armies, but the said stipulations shall resume their entire effect as soon as the evacuation shall be terminated.

Done at Paris, the 30th day of the month of March, in the year 1856.

[Here follow the signatures.]

CONVENTIONS

ANNEXED TO THE PRECEDING TREATY.

I.—Convention between her Majesty, the Emperor of Austria, the Emperor of the French, the King of Prussia, the Emperor of Russia, and the King of Sardinia, on the one part, and the Sultan on the other part, respecting the Straits of the Dardanelles and of the Bosphorus.

(Signed at Paris, March 30, 1856. Ratification exchanged at Paris, April 27, 1856.)

IN THE NAME OF ALMIGHTY GOD.

ARTICLE I. His Majesty the Sultan, on the one part, declares that he is firmly resolved to maintain for the future the principle invariably established as the ancient rule of his empire, and in virtue of which it has at all times been prohibited for the ships of war of foreign Powers to enter the Straits of the Dardanelles and of the Bosphorus, and that, so long as the Porte is at peace, his Majesty will admit no foreign ship of war into the said Straits.

And their Majesties the Queen of the United Kingdom of Great Britain and Ireland, the Emperor of Austria, the Emperor of the French, the King of Prussia, the Emperor of all the Russias, and the King of Sardinia, on the other part, engage to respect this determination of the Sultan, and to conform themselves to the principle above declared.

ART. II. The Sultan reserves to himself, as in past times, to deliver firmans of passage for light vessels under flag of war, which shall be employed, as is usual, in the service of the missions of foreign Powers.

ART III. The same exception applies to the light vessels under flag of war, which each of the contracting Powers is authorized to station at the mouths of the Danube, in order to secure the execution of the regulations relative to the liberty of that river, and the number of which is not to exceed two for each Power.

ART. IV. The present convention, annexed to the general treaty signed at Paris this day, shall be ratified, and the ratifications shall be exchanged in the space of four weeks, or sooner, if possible.

In witness whereof, the respective Plenipotentiaries have signed the same, and have affixed thereto the seal of their arms.

Done at Paris, the 30th day of the month of March, in the year 1856.

[Here follow the signatures.]

2.—Convention between the Emperor of Russia and the Sultan, limiting their naval force in the Black Sea.

(Signed at Paris, March 30. Ratifications exchanged at Paris, April 27, 1856.)

IN THE NAME OF ALMIGHTY GOD.

ARTICLE I. The high contracting parties mutually engage not to have in the Black Sea any other vessel of war than those of which the number, the force and the dimensions are hereinafter stipulated.

ART. II. The high contracting parties reserve to themselves each to maintain in that sea six steam vessels, of fifty metres in length at the line of floatation, of a tonnage of 800 tons at the maximum, and four light steam or sailing vessels, of a tonnage which shall not exceed 200 tons each.

ART. III. The present convention, annexed to the general treaty signed at Paris this day, shall be ratified, and the ratifications shall be exchanged in the space of four weeks, or sooner, if possible.

In witness whereof the respective Plenipotentiaries have signed the same, and have affixed thereto the seal of their arms.

Done at Paris, the 13th day of the month of March, in the year 1856.

ORLOFF.
BRUNNOW.
AALI.
MEHEMMED DJEMIL.

3.—Convention between her Majesty, the Emperor of the French, and the Emperor of Russia, respecting the Åland Islands.

(Signed at Paris, March 30, 1856. Ratifications exchanged at Paris, April 27, 1856.)

IN THE NAME OF ALMIGHTY GOD.

ARTICLE I. His Majesty the Emperor of all the Russias, in order to respond to the desire which has been expressed to him by their Majesties the Queen of the United Kingdom of Great Britain and Ireland, and the Emperor of the French, declares that the Åland Islands shall not be fortified, and that no military or naval establishment shall be maintained or created there.

ART. II. The present convention, annexed to the general treaty signed at Paris this day, shall be ratified, and the ratifications shall be exchanged in the space of four weeks, or sooner, if possible.

In witness whereof the respective Plenipotentiaries have signed the same and have affixed thereto the seal of their arms.

Done at Paris, the 30th day of the month of March, in the year 1856.

CLARENDON.
COWLEY.
A. WALEWSKI.
BOURQUENEY.
ORLOFF.
BRUNNOW.

MARITIME LAW.

DECLARATION respecting maritime law, signed by the Plenipotentiaries of Great Britain, Austria, France, Prussia, Russia, Sardinia and Turkey, assembled in Congress at Paris, April 16, 1856 :

The Plenipotentiaries who signed the treaty of Paris, of the 30th of March, 1856, assembled in conference—

Considering—

That maritime law, in time of war, has long been the subject of deplorable disputes ;

That the uncertainty of the law and of the duties in such a matter, gives rise to differences of opinion between neutrals and belligerents which may occasion serious difficulties, and even conflicts ;

That it is consequently advantageous to establish a uniform doctrine on so important a point ;

That the Plenipotentiaries assembled in Congress at Paris cannot better respond to the intentions by which their governments are animated, than by seeking to introduce into international relations fixed principles in this respect :

The above-mentioned Plenipotentiaries, being duly authorized, resolved to concert among themselves as to the means of attaining this object ; and having come to an agreement, have adopted the following solemn declaration :

1. Privateering is, and remains, abolished.

2. The neutral flag covers enemy's goods, with the exception of contraband of war.

3. Neutral goods, with the exception of contraband of war, are not liable to capture under enemy's flag.

4. Blockades, in order to be binding, must be effective—that is to say, maintained by a force sufficient really to prevent access to the coast of the enemy.

The Governments of the undersigned Plenipotentiaries engage to bring the present declaration to the knowledge of the States which have not taken part in the Congress of Paris, and to invite them to accede to it.

Convinced that the maxims which they now proclaim cannot but be received with gratitude by the whole world, the undersigned Plenipotentiaries doubt not that the efforts of their Governments to obtain the general adoption thereof will be crowned with full success.

The present declaration is not and shall not be binding, except between those Powers who have acceded, or shall accede, to it.

Done at Paris, the 16th of April, 1856.

[Here follow the signatures.]

MILITARY TERMS.

ABBATIS. A species of entrenchment, affording an excellent and ready addition to the defense of a post, being simply trees felled and laid with their branches so interwoven as to present a thick row of pointed stakes towards the enemy.

ALARM POST. The place appointed for every regiment or detachment to assemble, in case of a sudden alarm.

APPROACHES. The first, second, and third parallels, trenches, saps, mines, etc., by which the besiegers approach a fortified place.

APRON. A piece of thin or sheet-lead used to cover the vent of a cannon.

BARBET BATTERIES. Platforms elevated behind a parapet or breast-work, to enable the guns mounted on them to have a free range over the surrounding country.

BARRICADE. To barricade is to block up every avenue to a post by which the enemy might have access. This is performed by means of abbatis, breast-works, wagons, etc.; and small ditches may be occasionally dug across the road, leaving a narrow retiring-path for the sentries posted in front.

BASTION. The leading principle in the construction of a bastion is, that every part of it should be defended by the flanking fire of some other part of the works. It is composed of a large mass of earth excavated from the ditch, and revêted towards the country with masonry.

BIVOUAC. From *bis*, "double," and the German *wache*, "a guard." An army is said to bivouac, when it does not encamp at night.

BREACH. An opening or gap effected in any part of the works of a fortified place by the fire of the enemy's artillery.

BREAST-WORK. A parapet thrown up as high as the breasts of the troops defending it.

CAPONIERE. In fortification, is a passage from the body of the place to an outwork; it is usually sunk below the surface of the ground, and is called single or double, according as it is provided with a parapet on one or both sides.

CASEMATE. A chamber made within the ramparts of a fortification, to contain a number of guns, embrasures being out for them through the revêtement.

CHAIN-SHOT. Two balls connected by a chain, principally used in destroying the rigging of ships.

MILITARY TERMS.

CHAMBER OF A MORTAR. A cavity at the bottom of the bore to receive the charge.

COVER. In military operations, cover expresses security or protection. In the field, it implies that the files are placed exactly in rear of each other.

COUNTERSCARP. The outer boundary of the ditch, which in permanent fortifications should be revêted with masonry, in order that the slope may be as steep as possible.

COUNTERSIGN. A particular word or number which is exchanged between guards, and intrusted to those employed on duty in camp or garrison.

DEBOUCHE. The outlet of a wood or narrow pass.

DEBRIS. A French term for the wreck or remains of an army which has been routed.

DEFILE. A narrow passage or road, in marching through which the troops can present only a small front.

DEMI-BASTION. That which has one face and one flank cut off by the capital. The heads of horn and crown works are terminated by demi-bastions.

DITCH. An excavation or trench made round the works of a fortification, from whence the earth necessary for the construction of the rampart and parapet is raised.

ECHELLON. From the French word echelon. A formation in the field exercise of the army, in which the divisions of a regiment are placed in a situation resembling the steps of a ladder, a circumstance which has caused the movement to be thus designated.

EMBRASURE. An embrasure is an opening cut through the parapet, in order to enable the artillery to command a certain extent of the surrounding country.

ENCEINTE. The rampart inclosing the body of the place, composed of the bastions and curtains, and surrounded by the main ditch, is called the enceinte.

ENFILADE. To sweep the whole length of any work or line of troops by a fire from a battery placed on the prolongation of that side.

EPAULEMENT. An elevation of earth, thrown up to cover troops from the fire of the enemy; it is composed of filled gabions or fascines filled with earth.

ESCALADE. The attack of a fortress, by scaling the walls.

ESCARP. The side of the ditch next the rampart. In permanent fortification it is usually faced with bricks, supported by counter-forts, and surmounted by an edging of stone, called the cordon or tablette. This wall of masonry is called the revêtement.

FASCINES. A species of long cylindrical fagots, made of brushwood or small branches of trees, and bear different names according to their length and the purpose for which they are intended. The larger kind are called saucissons.

FILE. A line of soldiers drawn up behind one another. As a general term, a file means two soldiers, the front and rear rank men. Every soldier of infantry covers a space of 21 inches.

FLECHE OR REDAN. The most simple species of field-works, and being quickly and easily constructed, they are frequently used in the field. They usually consist of two faces, forming a salient angle towards some object—thus ∧.

FUSE. The tube which is fixed into a shell, filled with combustible materials, and furnished with a quick match. It is cut to a length proportional to the distance it is to be thrown, in order that it may continue burning during the time the shell is in its range, and afterwards, by setting fire to the powder, cause the shell to explode as soon as it touches the ground.

GABIONS. Cylindrical baskets of various dimensions, without bottoms, and employed in entrenchments or embrasures for guns. The gabions generally used in field-works are three feet high and two feet in diameter. To construct gabions, tie a cord of eleven inches long to two sticks, and having driven one of these into the earth, describe a circle with the other upon the level ground. At proper distances upon the circumference of this circle insert the staves or pickets for the gabions; these should be four feet long, and from one inch to one inch and a half thick. Bind them at top and bottom with a strong wreath of pliant twigs, then proceed to interweave the twigs, passing them alternately inside of one picket and outside the next two, until the work is completed, driving them down from time to time with a mallet. Two men are required to construct a gabion, besides another employed in cutting the wood.

GALLERY. A passage or communication to that part of a mine where the powder is lodged.

GLACIS. The superior slope of the parapet of the covered way, produced in a gentle declivity to the level of the surrounding country.

GORGE. The entrance into a bastion, demilune, or redoubt.

GUIDONS. The silk standards of regiments of dragoons and light dragoons. They are broad at one extreme, and almost pointed at the other.

INTRENCHMENT OR ENTRENCHMENT. As a general term, it denotes a ditch, or trench, with a parapet.

MASK. A battery is said to be masked when its external appearance is such as to mislead and lull the suspicions of a reconnoitring or approaching enemy.

PARAPET. The parapet in permanent fortification is a mass of earth elevated on the edge of the rampart next to the country. It is made about eighteen feet thick, in order that cannon-shot may not penetrate it, and about seven and a half feet high, to screen the troops behind it from the fire of the enemy.

PETARD. An engine made of gun-metal, fixed upon a board, and containing about nine pounds of powder, with a hole at the end opposite to the plank to fill it, into which the vent is screwed; the petard thus prepared is fixed to the gate of a fortress, and being fired bursts it open. Leathern bags containing fifty pounds of powder have recently been ascertained to be more expeditious and successful than petards.

POSTERN. A passage constructed under the rampart, serving as a communication from the town into the ditch.

RAMPART. A broad embankment or mass of earth which surrounds a fortified place, and forms the *enceinte* or chain of main works. On its exterior edge the parapet is placed, beyond which it is bounded by the main ditch, while towards the town it is terminated by the interior slope of the rampart, on which ramps (oblique roads) are made for the easy ascent the troops and artillery.

MILITARY TERMS.

RANK AND FILE. This term denotes corporals as well as privates, as they carry firelocks, and parade in the ranks in the same manner.

RAZED. Works or fortifications are said to be razed when they are totally demolished.

REDOUBTS. Redoubts are frequently used in the field, and as they are generally occupied by a stronger detachment than a redan, they may be safely trusted at a greater distanse from the main body, and are expected to make a proportionate defense, sufficient at any rate to allow time for the arrival of succors from the army. Redoubts are extremely proper for covering an advanced post, for defending a defile or a height, for protecting a retreat or the passage of a river or bridge, for supporting the wings of an army, etc. The figure of a redoubt is commonly square, but a circular redoubt is superior in its defense to that of any polygon.

REVEILLE. The beat of drums at daybreak, after which the sentries cease to challenge.

RICOCHET. An important branch of artillery practice, in which the guns, being loaded with a small charge and pointed at an elevation rarely exceeding ten degrees, the shot is so projected as merely to clear the parapet of the enemy's fortifications, from whence it bounds along the rampart, destroying the carriages of the guns, and causing a great loss of life to the defenders.

RUNNING-FIRE. That in which troops fire rapidly in succession.

SALLY. A sally or sortie is a secret movement of attack made by strong detachments of troops from a besieged place, for the purpose of destroying the enemy's works.

SAND-BAGS. Bags from twelve to fourteen inches wide, and about thirty inches long, filled with earth, for the purpose of repairing breaches and embrasures when damaged by the enemy's fire.

SHELLS, (in French BOMBE.) Hollow iron balls thrown among the enemy from mortars and howitzers. Being filled with powder, and provided with a fuse which sets fire to the contents, the shell explodes, causing great havoc among the enemy's troops.

SPIKE. To spike a cannon is to drive a large nail or iron-spike into the vent, which will render the cannon unserviceable for a time. Many inventions have been suggested for forcing out the nail, but the best remedy is to drill a new vent.

STRATEGY. The science of military command, and of the different means or manner of conducting all the operations of war.

SURPRISE. To fall upon an enemy unexpectedly, to attack him while in camp, or engaged in passing a defile, river, etc.

TETES. Têtes (or Têtes de Pont) are works thrown up for covering the communication across a river.

TRENCHES. Ditches made during a siege, in order that the assailants may approach the works more securely, on which account they are also called the approaches.

TUMBRILS. Covered carts, which are employed to convey ammunition, and the tools for pioneers, miners, etc.

WELLS'

EVERY MAN HIS OWN LAWYER,

AND

United States Form Book.

☞BEING A COMPLETE AND RELIABLE GUIDE,☜

In all matters of Law, and Business Negotiations, for Merchants, Manufaturers,
Mechanics, Inventors, Farmers, Artists, Authors, and all men who
wish to do their own legal business, and thereby save them-
selves needless expense, anxiety and loss of time.

CONTAINING LEGAL FORMS OF

Deeds, Mortgages, Leases, Affidavits, Depositions, Bonds, Orders, Contracts,
Powers of Attorney, Certificates of Citizenship, Agreements, Assignments,
Awards, Declarations, States of Demand, Demands, Letters of
Credit, Arbitration Bonds, Partnership Articles, Resolves, Ad-
ministrator's and Executor's Deeds, and Instructions, Orders, Wills, Codicils, Apprenticeship Indentures, Sub-
missions, Land Jointures, Tenant's and Landlord's
Agreements, Receipts, Pensions, Public
Lands, Land Warrants, Composition
with Creditors, Oaths, Satisfaction
of Mortgages, Preemption
Laws, Patent Laws, giv-
ing full instructions
to Inventors,

ALSO, CONTAINING LIST OF PROPERTY EXEMPT FROM EXECUTION, LIEN LAW,

LAW OF LIMITATIONS, LAW OF CONTRACTS, USURY LAWS,

CONSTITUTION OF THE UNITED STATES,

A COMPLETE SYSTEM OF BOOK KEEPING,

Interest Tables, Gold and Silver Coin Tables,

&c., &c., &c.

12mo,, 300 pages—price $1 00.

☞No labor or expense has been spared, in the preparation of this Book, to
make it every way fully adapted to the wants of every business man in every
State in the Union, and the Publisher has entire confidence in its superiority
over any form book published, as a

☞ BUSINESS MAN'S COMPANION. ☜

*** Energetic and reliable Agents wanted to sell this Work in every State
in the Union.

ADDRESS,

JOHN G. WELLS,

Publishing Agent.

11 BEEKMAN ST., NEW YORK.

WELLS'

NATIONAL HAND-BOOK:

EMBRACING NUMEROUS

INVALUABLE DOCUMENTS

CONNECTED WITH THE

Political History of America.

AMONG WHICH ARE

THE DECLARATION OF INDEPENDENCE,

Constitution of the United States,

WASHINGTON'S FOUR MOST IMPORTANT ADDRESSES,

FUGITIVE SLAVE LAW OF 1850, KANSAS AND NEBRASKA ACT OF 1854, COMPROMISE OF 1820

Population of the United States at Decennial Periods,

FORMATION OF THE ORIGINAL AMERICAN UNION,

Electoral Votes for President and Vice-President,

FROM 1789 TO 1854,

GREAT SEAL OF THE UNITED STATES,

WITH AN ILLUSTRATED HISTORY AND DESCRIPTION,

Seals of the Thirty-One States, with Descriptions and Illustrations.

BIOGRAPHICAL SKETCHES OF THE EX-PRESIDENTS,

WITH PORTRAITS OF EACH,

LIVES AND PORTRAITS OF THE NOMINEES FOR PRESIDENT AND VICE-PRESIDENT,

Platforms of the Three Political Parties,

CONGRESS OF THE UNITED STATES,

&c., &c., &c.

INTERSPERSED WITH

THE INTERESTING INCIDENTS OF EACH ADMINISTRATION.

FIFTY-TWO ILLUSTRATIONS.

NEW YORK:

JOHN G. WELLS, PUBLISHING AGENT, 11 BEEKMAN ST.

1856.